Group Dynamics and Emotional Expression

The study of emotional expressions has a long tradition in psychology. Although research in this domain has extensively studied the social context factors that influence the expresser's facial display, the perceiver was considered passive. This book focuses on more recent developments that show that the perceiver is also subject to the same social rules and norms that guide the expresser's behavior and that knowledge of relevant emotion norms can influence how emotional expressions shown by members of different groups are perceived and interpreted. Factors such as ethnic-group membership, gender, and relative status all influence not only emotional expressions but also the interpretation of emotional expressions shown by members of different groups. Specifically, the research presented asks the question of whether and why the same expressions shown by men or women, members of different ethnic groups, or individuals high and low in status are interpreted differently.

Ursula Hess is Professor of Psychology at the University of Quebec at Montreal. She received her Ph.D. in psychology from Dartmouth College and is a Fellow at the Association for Psychological Science. Her current research is in the area of emotion psychology – in particular, the communication of affect with an emphasis on two main lines of research: psychophysiological measures and the role of social influences in the encoding and decoding of emotional expressions.

Pierre Philippot is Professor of Psychology at the University of Louvain in Belgium. He is also a Master of Research at the Belgium National Science Foundation. He received his Ph.D. in psychology from the University of Louvain. He has published many books and written many articles for international, peer-reviewed scientific journals.

.

STUDIES IN EMOTION AND SOCIAL INTERACTION
Second Series

Series Editors

Keith Oatley
University of Toronto

Antony S. R. Manstead
University of Cambridge

This series is jointly published by Cambridge University Press and the Editions de la Maison des Sciences de l'Homme, as part of the joint publishing agreement established in 1977 between the Fondation de la Maison des Sciences de l'Homme and the Syndics of Cambridge University Press.

Cette publication est publiée en co-édition par Cambridge University Press et les Editions de la Maison des Sciences de l'Homme. Elle s'intègre dans le programme de co-édition établi en 1977 par la Fondation de la Maison des Sciences de l'Homme et les Syndics de Cambridge University Press.

Titles published in the Second Series:

The Psychology of Facial Expression, by
James A. Russell and José Miguel Fernández-Dols

Emotion, the Social Bond, and Human Reality: Part/Whole Analysis, by
Thomas J. Scheff

Intersubjective Communication and Emotion in Early Ontogeny, by
Stein Bråten

The Social Context of Nonverbal Behavior, by
Pierre Philippot, Roberts S. Feldman, and Erik J. Coats

Communicating Emotion: Social, Moral, and Cultural Processes, by
Sally Planalp

Continued on page following Index

Group Dynamics and Emotional Expression

Edited by

Ursula Hess
University of Quebec at Montreal

Pierre Philippot
University of Louvain, Belgium

161101

CAMBRIDGE
UNIVERSITY PRESS

CAMBRIDGE UNIVERSITY PRESS
Cambridge, New York, Melbourne, Madrid, Cape Town, Singapore, São Paulo

Cambridge University Press
32 Avenue of the Americas, New York, NY 10013-2473, USA

www.cambridge.org
Information on this title: www.cambridge.org/9780521842822

First published 2007

Printed in the United States of America

A catalog record for this publication is available from the British Library.

Library of Congress Cataloging in Publication Data

Group dynamics and emotional expression / edited by Ursula Hess, Pierre Philippot.
   p. cm. – (Studies in emotion and social interaction)
Includes bibliographical references and index.
ISBN-13: 978-0-521-84282-2 (hardback)
ISBN-10: 0-521-84282-4 (hardback)
1. Emotions. 2. Social groups. I. Hess, Ursula. II. Philippot, Pierre, 1960– III. Title.
BF531.G77 2007
305.01 – dc22   2006019239

ISBN   978-0-521-84282-2 hardback

Contents

Contributors

Reginald B. Adams, Jr.
The Pennsylvania State University

Patrick Bourgeois
University of Quebec at Montreal

John F. Dovidio
University of Connecticut

Hillary Anger Elfenbein
University of California, Berkeley

Michelle Hebl
Rice University

Ursula Hess
University of Quebec at Montreal

Robert E. Kleck
Dartmouth College

David Matsumoto
San Francisco State University

Pierre Philippot
University of Louvain

Jennifer Richeson
Northwestern University

J. Nicole Shelton
Princeton University

Stephanie A. Shields
The Pennsylvania State University

Kristi Lewis Tyran
Western Washington University

Leah R. Warner
The Pennsylvania State University

Yanélia Yabar
University of Canterbury, New Zealand

Introduction: The Tale I Read on Your Face Depends on Who I Believe You Are

Introducing How Social Factors Might Influence the Decoder's Interpretation of Facial Expression

Pierre Philippot and Ursula Hess

Authors' Note

The writing of this chapter has been facilitated by grants from the "Fonds National de la Recherche Scientifique de Belgique" 8.4510.99 and 8.4510.03 and by a grant ARC 96/01-198 from the University of Louvain to the first author, and by a grant from the "Fonds de Formation des Chercheurs et l'Aide la Recherche" to the second author. Correspondence regarding this chapter should be addressed to Pierre Philippot, who is at Faculté de Psychologie, Université de Louvain, place du Cardinal Mercier, 10, B-1348 Louvain-la-Neuve, Belgique. Electronic mail may be sent via Internet to Pierre.Philippot@psp.ucl.ac.be.

Introduction

More than three decades ago, the study of emotional facial expression saw a spectacular development (Ekman & Friesen, 1971; Izard, 1972). To date, this impetus does not seem to have lessened. From the beginning, research on emotional facial expression has been grounded in a Neo-Darwinian theoretical framework (Tomkins, 1980). In this framework, facial expressions are considered as innate signals that have evolved phylogenetically to fulfil important adaptive functions. In a social species such as ours, effective coordination among conspecifics is vital. By conveying information about individuals' inner state and behavioral intent, facial expression plays an important role in social coordination.

1

From this perspective, a wealth of research has demonstrated that, indeed, emotional facial expressions were decoded at a clearly much better than chance level, within and among many cultures (Kupperbusch, Matsumoto, Kooken, Loewinger, Uchida, et al., 1999). This observation supported the notion that emotional facial expressions are foremost an innate signal. However, there is also evidence that this innate signal can be modulated by social conventions: so-called display rules (Matsumoto, 1998). Through social and cultural shaping, people learn how to suppress, minimize, maximize, or alter their facial displays to convey socially prescribed emotional attitudes.

Looking back at these three decades of research on nonverbal communication, a striking feature emerges: Most of it has focused on the decoder's performance. That is, this research has been primarily devoted to establishing whether emotional facial expressions are accurately decoded and to identifying decoder characteristics that are predictive of a better decoding performance. Little attention has been devoted to those characteristics of the encoder (i.e., the expressing individual) that might influence how their facial expression is attended to and interpreted. In fact, this lack of interest for encoder characteristics is congruent with the Neo-Darwinian perspective that dominates the field: If emotional facial expressions are indeed strong innate signals and act as unconditioned stimuli (Öhman, 1999), they result from automatic processes that leave little room for variation. Thus, there are few reasons to investigate how individual differences or personal characteristics might modulate such an automatic and biologically determined behavior.

However, the recent interest of social cognition for emotion in general, and facial expression in particular, has somewhat challenged the notion that encoder characteristics are of little interest for the study of nonverbal facial communication. Indeed, it is now established that emotion plays a critical role in the formation, activation and maintenance of attitudes and stereotypes (Fiske, 1998; Hugenberg & Bodenhausen, 2004). Moreover, stereotypes also include emotional information. For instance, some emotions, like anger, might be stereotypically attributed to members of an outgroup whose stereotype is connotated by aggressivity (Philippot & Yabar, 2005). Also, more refined emotions are preferentially attributed to ingroup members, whereas more basic emotions are overly attributed to outgroup members (Paladino, Leyens, R. Rodriguez, A. Rodriguez, Gaunt, & Demoulin, 2002).

This social-cognitive perspective thus suggests that the activation of stereotypes must result in congruent biases in the interpretation of outgroup versus ingroup members' facial expressions of emotion. For instance, the facial expression of an individual from a group that is stereotyped as violent and aggressive might be perceived as more angry than the same facial expression displayed by an individual from a group that is not stereotyped as violent or aggressive.

The question raised is thus whether the interpretation of a given facial expression might be modulated by the a priori or stereotype that the decoder holds regarding the encoder. This formulation of the question makes it obvious that a crucial aspect of the understanding of emotional nonverbal communication rests in the *interaction* between the sender/encoder and the receiver/decoder. From this perspective, a nonverbal message such as a facial expression can be understood only if one considers the relationship that links the sender/encoder and the receiver/decoder and the (stereotyped) representations they hold for each other.

Is this question trivial? Evidently, we think that it is not. Our conviction is based on several considerations. At the theoretical level, the Neo-Darwinian perspective that still prevails in the field states that emotional facial expressions are powerful innate signals – which leaves little room for modulating their interpretation once they are emitted. This suggests that a display of anger is interpreted as conveying anger and threat no matter what representation the decoder might have of the encoder. In contrast, the social-cognitive perspective presented previously postulates that the interpretation of any individual information is biased by the stereotype that is attached to that individual. Facial expression decoding would not be an exception to this general rule. Hence, these two theoretical perspectives offer contrasting predictions: The Neo-Darwinian perspective implies that facial expression decoding should be minimally affected by the group membership of the sender, whereas the social-cognitive perspective predicts the opposite.

At the empirical level, one needs to recognize that in everyday life, full-blown facial expressions are by far the exception rather than the rule (except perhaps in Hollywood sit-coms). Rather, what is observed in natural settings are most often weak and transient facial expressions. Furthermore, facial expressions are not necessarily expressed in the canonic form established by emotion researchers (e.g., Ekman, Sorenson, & Friesen, 1969). Indeed, facial expressions can be expressed partially or they can be the result of blends that convey different emotions at the same time (Ekman & O'Sullivan, 1991). Thus, in real life, facial expressions rarely occur in the form of the clear, prototypical signals such as the stimuli originally constructed by Ekman et al. (1969) – even though these extreme stimuli are the ones most often used in emotion expression research. Rather, facial expression is often weak, elusive or blended, resulting in a signal that might often be ambiguous. This ambiguity itself suggests that significant interpretive work is needed, which opens the possibility for all kinds of interpretive biases, such as those underlain by the representations that the sender/encoder and the receiver/decoder hold for each other.

In sum, there are good theoretical as well as empirical reasons to investigate whether the interpretation of facial expressions of emotion might be modulated by the characteristics that the decoder attributes to the encoder. Still, this field of research is just emerging and few directly relevant data have been collected. In this volume, we aim to present the recent theoretical and empirical developments that recognize that the perceiver is also subject to the same social rules and norms that guide the expressors' behavior. In turn, this knowledge of relevant emotion norms can influence how emotional expressions shown by members of different groups are perceived. Factors such as ethnic group membership, gender and relative status all influence not only emotional expressions but also the interpretation of emotional expressions shown by members of different groups. Specifically, the research presented here addresses the questions of whether and why the same expressions shown by men or women, members of different ethnic groups, or individuals high and low in status are interpreted differently. Possible mechanisms addressed include the physical characteristics of the face (e.g., morphological face difference between races or genders), its interaction with social rules and norms, the biasing impact of beliefs and expectations regarding members of different groups, and the impact of matches versus mismatches of expressor and decoder groups.

This book consists of eight chapters. It is introduced by a general chapter by John Dovidio and colleagues discussing social-group influences on the interpretation of emotions and their implications for everyday life. In the next section, two chapters focus on the interpretation of facial expressions of emotion shown by men and women (Leah Warner and Stephanie Shields; Ursula Hess and colleagues). Then, two chapters consider the influence of the ethnic-group membership of the expressor on emotion communication. One chapter (Hillary Elfenbein) focuses on biases in the decoding of emotional expressions, the other (Pierre Philippot and colleagues) on the influence of social- and ethnic-group membership on reactions to facial expressions, specifically in terms of facial morphology and mimicry. Another chapter (Kristi Lewis Tyran) focuses on the influence of relative status on the interpretation of emotional expressions and the attribution of behavioral intentions to the expressor. These chapters are complemented by a chapter (David Matsumoto) that presents relevant methodological concerns particular to this area of research. Finally, a summary and integration chapter (Hess and Philippot) concludes the book.

The goal of the book is to underline the importance of understanding emotion communication in its social context. This perspective implies that the very channels that transmit the emotion signal – voice, face, posture – all also transmit information about the social context of the expressors, their sex, their age, their race and even their socioeconomic status. Thus, social context is literally embodied in the emotion signal, therefore making it impossible to consider emotion signals in social isolation.

References

Ekman, P., & Friesen, W. V. (1971). Constants across cultures in the face and emotion. *Journal of Personality and Social Psychology, 17*, 124–129.

Ekman, P., & O'Sullivan, M. (1991). Facial expression: Methods, means, and moues. In R. S. Feldman & B. Rimé (Eds.), *Fundamentals of nonverbal behavior* (pp. 163–199). New York: Cambridge University Press.

Ekman, P., Sorenson, E. R., & Friesen, W. V. (1969). Pan-cultural elements in facial displays of emotions. *Science, 164*, 86–88.

Fiske, S. T. (1998). Stereotyping, prejudice and discrimination. In D. T. Gilbert, S. T. Fiske, & G. Lindsey (Eds.), *The handbook of social psychology (4th ed.), 2*, 357–411. New York: McGraw-Hill.

Hugenberg, K., & Bodenhausen, G. V. (2004). Ambiguity in social categorization: The role of prejudice and facial affect in race. *Psychological Science, 15*, 342–345.

Izard, C. E. (1972). *Patterns of emotion*. New York: Academic Press.

Kupperbusch, C., Matsumoto, D., Kooken, K., Loewinger, S., Uchida, H., Wilson-Cohn, C., & Yrizarry, N. (1999). Cultural influences on nonverbal expressions of emotion. In P. Philippot, R. S. Feldman, & E. J. Coats (Eds.), *The social context of nonverbal behavior* (pp. 17–44). New York: Cambridge University Press.

Matsumoto, D. (1990). Cultural similarities and differences in display rules. *Motivation & Emotion, 14*, 195–214.

Öhman, A. (1999). Distinguishing unconscious from conscious emotional processes: Methodological consideration and theoretical implications. In T. Dalgleish & M. J. Power (Eds.), *Handbook of cognition and emotion* (pp. 765–782). Chichester, England: John Wiley & Sons.

Paladino, M., Leyens, J., Rodriguez, R., Rodriguez, A., Gaunt, R., & Demoulin, S. (2002). Differential association of uniquely and non uniquely human emotions with the ingroup and outgroup. *Group Processes and Intergroup Relations, 5*, 105–117.

Philippot, P., & Yabar, Y. (2005). Stereotyping and action tendencies attribution. *European Journal of Experimental Social Psychology, 35*, 517–536.

Tomkins, S. S. (1980). Affect as amplification: Some modification in theory. In R. Plutchik & H. Kellerman (Eds.), *Theories of emotion* (pp. 141–164). New York: Academic Press.

1. Implications of Ingroup-Outgroup Membership for Interpersonal Perceptions

Faces and Emotion

Jennifer Richeson, John F. Dovidio, J. Nicole Shelton, and Michelle Hebl

Authors' Note

Correspondence concerning this article should be addressed to Jennifer A. Richeson, Department of Psychology, Northwestern University, 2029 Sheridan Road, Evanston, IL 60208. E-mail: jriches@northwestern.edu.

Introduction

Nonverbal behavior is a critical component of social interaction. People rely on nonverbal aspects of behavior during interactions to assess how their interaction partners are feeling and how to respond to them (Feldman, Philippot, & Custrini, 1991). One aspect of nonverbal behavior that can be influential in shaping the dynamics of interpersonal interaction is the communication of emotion. Indeed, the ability to accurately decode the emotional states of others from nonverbal facial and vocal cues has been found to predict social competence (e.g., Feldman et al., 1991; Glanville & Nowicki, 2002).

Recent research suggests that cultural-group membership may play an important role in the accurate communication (i.e., encoding and decoding) of emotion (Elfenbein & Ambady, 2002a, 2002b). Building on this work, we propose that the psychological processes associated with social categorization and social identity produce systematic biases in the recognition of emotion from facial expressions across members of different groups. Thus, the present chapter examines emotional facial expression and communication in an intergroup context. To provide a general conceptual foundation for the relevance of group membership to the communication of emotion, we begin by briefly reviewing how group membership fundamentally affects the way people think about, feel about, and act toward others. We then examine research that directly studies how group membership affects the communication of emotion in the face and how members of different groups, defined by majority and minority status, may be differentially successful at recognizing and interpreting the emotions displayed by outgroup members. We then consider the systematic nature of emotion recognition accuracy and inaccuracy through an examination of potential mechanisms that might contribute to differences in emotion recognition between members of different groups. Finally, we conclude with a conceptual analysis of how the study of facial expression complements previous research on intergroup bias and offers potentially unique theoretical and practical insights into understanding intergroup communication, miscommunication, and relations.

Psychological Impact of Group Membership

Group membership and identity have a profound influence on social perception, affect, cognition, and behavior. People spontaneously categorize others as members of social groups, and they fundamentally distinguish those who are members of their own group from those who are members of other groups (Tajfel & Turner, 1979; Turner, Hogg, Oakes, Reicher, & Wetherell, 1987). Perceptually, when people or objects are categorized into groups, actual differences between members of the same category tend to be minimized and often ignored in making decisions or forming impressions, whereas between-group differences tend to become exaggerated (Tajfel & Turner, 1979). Members of other groups are generally perceived to be more similar to one another than are members of one's own group (Mullen & Hu, 1989). Paralleling these effects, at a basic perceptual level, people have more difficulty recognizing outgroup members than ingroup members, more frequently confusing outgroup members with one another (Meissner & Brigham, 2001). Cognitively, people retain more information in a more detailed fashion for ingroup members than for outgroup members (Park & Rothbart, 1982). Emotionally, people spontaneously experience more positive affect toward members of the ingroup than toward members of the outgroup (Otten & Moskowitz, 2000). And, behaviorally, people are more pro-social toward ingroup than outgroup members (Dovidio, Kawakami, Johnson, Johnson, & Howard, 1997). In part as a consequence of these biases, people have more frequent interaction with members of their own group than other groups (Brigham, 2005). Greater contact and more frequent interaction produce greater perceptual and cognitive differentiation (Linville, Fischer, & Salovey, 1989) and present more opportunities to develop and refine the ability to interpret accurately the behaviors of others.

Taken together, the greater perceptual sensitivity, cognitive elaboration, affective reactions, and behavioral orientations that people have with ingroup than with outgroup members implicate group membership as an important factor for the communication of emotion. Specifically, these processes converge to suggest that people will show greater sensitivity and accuracy in judging the emotional expressions of ingroup than outgroup members.

A second critical element of group membership – one that also is relevant to the communication of emotion – involves the hierarchical organization of groups. In part as a consequence of the factors associated with group categorization, groups tend to relate to one another hierarchically. In fact, Sidanius and Pratto (1999) argue that this type of social dominance is a universal organizing principle in human societies. Differences in group status, in turn, influence the perceptual, cognitive, affective, and behavioral responses of group members in systematic ways. In general, people who have high social status have more freedom of movement and thus may be more open in intergroup encounters than low-status individuals. Conversely, low-status people tend to be inhibited in their actions, particularly in encounters with high-status people (see Ellyson & Dovidio, 1985). In addition, low-status people monitor the specific behaviors and reactions of their interaction partners more closely than do high-status interactants, who are more likely to rely on stereotypes based on the partner's group membership. Keltner, Gruenfeld, and Anderson (2003) argue that high power and status are associated with a general approach orientation, whereas low power and status are related to inhibition.

These processes also have direct implications for the communication of facial expressions. First, because high-status individuals are less inhibited in their behaviors than low-status individuals, members of high-status groups may be more expressive than members of low-status groups, particularly in intergroup encounters. Consistent with this, individual status exerts a strong influence on nonverbal behavior between people. In a meta-analytic review of the literature, Hall, Coats, and Smith LeBeau (2005) found that people who have higher status or social power show greater facial expressiveness than those with low status or power. Also, members of low-status groups, such as stigmatized groups, tend to be more inhibited than members of high-status (i.e., nonstigmatized) groups in their emotional expressiveness (Frable, Blackstone, & Scherbaum, 1990). Second, because low-status individuals monitor the actions of high-status individuals particularly closely, members of low-status groups may be more accurate at decoding the facial expressions of others, particularly in intergroup situations, than high-status people (Henley, 1977; LaFrance & Henley, 1994).

In sum, social categorization initiates a range of perceptual, cognitive, and affective processes that produce more differentiated impressions of ingroup than outgroup members, which suggests that people should be more accurate at judging the emotional expressions of ingroup than outgroup members. Moreover, the closer and more frequent interaction among ingroup than outgroup members produces greater familiarity and experience that further contribute to increased accuracy in interpreting the expressions and behaviors of ingroup compared to outgroup members. However, group status may moderate this effect, such that increased accuracy in recognizing emotions from facial expressions for ingroup versus outgroup members might be more pronounced among members of low-status than high-status groups. In the next section, guided by this framework, we briefly review the literature on group differences in emotion recognition.

Group Differences in Emotion Recognition

In general, people are quite adept at recognizing the emotions displayed in the faces of members of different groups, nations, and cultures (Ekman, 1972; Izard, 1971). Largely based on these findings, emotional facial displays have been thought of as largely universal (Ekman, 1994). Despite the evidence in favor of universality, however, there is also accompanying evidence revealing cultural variations in recognizing expressions of emotion. In an effort to understand and organize the emotion recognition literature, Elfenbein and Ambady (2002a) conducted a meta-analysis of studies bearing on both the universality and cultural specificity of emotion recognition. Although they found overwhelming evidence to support the universality hypothesis – that is, participants were consistently able to detect the emotions displayed in the faces of outgroup members at better than chance levels – they also found evidence suggestive of cultural specificity. That is, they found that individuals were better able to decode the emotions expressed by individuals sharing their own cultural background than those expressed by individuals from a different cultural background (Elfenbein & Ambady, 2002b). The ingroup advantage was observed in studies using a variety of experimental methods, for both positive and negative emotions, and in different nonverbal channels of communication, including both facial expressions and tone of voice (but see Matsumoto, 2002, for a critique).

One clear deviation from the ingroup advantage, however, was among members of minority groups. Specifically, the ingroup advantage was considerably smaller and sometimes nonexistent for studies in which members of minority groups were judging the emotions of members of majority groups from the same nation. For example, Nowicki, Glanville, and Demertzis (1998) found that white college students were better able to decode emotion in the faces of other white targets (i.e., posers) than emotion in the faces of black targets, but black college students were equally able to decode emotion in the faces of white and black targets. Similarly, Collins and Nowicki (2001) found that black and white children were equally accurate at decoding the emotions of white targets. However, the overall pattern of accuracy in recognition of emotional facial expression is consistent with our expectations. We consider potential mediators and moderators of this effect in the next section.

Moderators and Mediators of the Ingroup Advantage

As outlined earlier, social categorization and identity arouse a range of perceptual and cognitive biases, with systematic social consequences, that can operate independently or in concert to produce intergroup differences in the accurate recognition and interpretation of emotional facial expressions. We first consider two explanations for the ingroup advantage that relate to social interaction within and between groups: familiarity and cultural differences. Then, we consider three additional explanations for the ingroup advantage that relate to general intergroup psychological processes identified previously: attention, bias, and power.

Familiarity

Elfenbein and Ambady (2002a) proposed that cultural familiarity is an important moderator of the ingroup advantage effect. Specifically, their meta-analysis revealed that the ingroup advantage was smaller for groups with greater exposure to one another. For instance, cross-cultural accuracy was greater for groups living in the same country than for groups living across national borders. Furthermore, differential familiarity explained the tendency for members of minority groups to reveal less of an ingroup advantage than members of majority groups and sometimes even to reveal an outgroup advantage (Elfenbein & Ambady, 2002a, 2002b). Because of the sheer differences in number, members of minority groups have more opportunities to interact with members of majority groups than the reverse.

Consistent with this interpretation, Elfenbein and Ambady (2003) found that accuracy in decoding the emotional expression of European American models in photographs was greatest among European Americans, followed in order by Chinese Americans, Chinese nationals living in the United States, and Chinese citizens living in China. Chinese citizens in China were most accurate at judging the emotions of Chinese models. In a second study, Elfenbein and Ambady (2003) fully decoupled cultural familiarity with ingroup membership by testing the accuracy with which Tibetan individuals living in China and African individuals living in the United States could recognize the emotional expressions displayed by Chinese and American models. Consistent with the familiarity argument, the Tibetan participants were both more accurate and faster at recognizing the Chinese compared to the American facial expressions, and the African participants were more accurate and faster with the American compared to the Chinese facial expressions. These findings provide support for the role of familiarity in generating the ingroup advantage for emotion recognition.

Although the evidence for the role of familiarity in the ingroup advantage in emotion recognition is compelling, other processes may also be involved and, in fact, may help explain why greater familiarity reduces group differences in emotion recognition accuracy. For instance, greater familiarity with members of other groups may enhance the ability to recognize and interpret cultural differences in emotion display and decoding rules.

*Cultural Differences: Display Rules, Decoding Rules,
and Nonverbal Accents*

In the emotion recognition literature, several factors have been proposed to explain cultural differences in emotional-face recognition. Ekman argued that although emotions are basic, there are cultural differences in the norms that govern the outward display of emotion (Ekman, 1972).

Accordingly, the emotional displays produced by members of some cultures are more difficult to decode (i.e., the displays are not encoded as clearly) than those of other cultures. In contrast to differences in encoding, Matsumoto (1989, 1992) argued that emotional-expression decoding rules (cf. Buck, 1984) differ as a function of culture. Thus, in some cultures, it is impolite to observe certain emotions (largely negative) in other individuals; consequently, members of these cultures may be less likely to attribute certain emotions to another individual based on their facial displays than members of other cultures.

As mentioned previously, Elfenbein and Ambady (2002a) found that a match between the group membership of the encoder and the decoder resulted in better emotion recognition than a mismatch, also known as the ingroup advantage. One possible explanation for the advantage is that shared cultural-group membership is accompanied by an ingroup understanding and congruence of both display rules and decoding rules. For instance, members of a specific culture may tend to display certain emotions with less intensity because of display rules. They have been socialized in the culture and, therefore, are accustomed to observing the muted form of the expression. However, other members of the same culture may be more likely to recognize the subtle cues associated with these muted expressions than members of a different culture. In other words, a relatively ambiguous, low-intensity angry expression may be perceived and interpreted as a clear display of anger by ingroup members but completely missed or misinterpreted by outgroup members. Furthermore, members of the same culture are more likely to be aware of the specific situations in which display rules tend to affect emotional expression, resulting in more accurate emotion recognition, than that found for outgroup members.

Similarly, a mismatch in decoding rules may make it difficult to accurately interpret emotion across group boundaries. If perceiving anger is relatively shunned in an individual's culture, then he or she may be less likely to accurately detect (or report) anger from the face of an outgroup member. It is also possible, however, that display and decoding rules may work against the ingroup advantage. Cultural norms that limit the expression of certain emotions also tend to limit the interpretation and perception of the same emotions. In other words, display and decoding rules are often linked (Matsumoto, Kasri, & Kooken, 1999). The match between display and decoding rules may lead an individual to suppress their anger but also lead a member of the same culture to ignore and perhaps even misperceive any anger that did form on the expressor's face. Consequently, rather than increasing accuracy, shared cultural display and decoding rules may actually undermine the accuracy with which members of the same group interpret emotional facial displays.

As an alternative to the display and decoding rules explanations for the ingroup advantage of emotion recognition, Marsh, Elfenbein, and Ambady (2003) developed the theory of nonverbal accents. The theory suggests that, like different languages, emotional expressions may also have features that vary across cultures. American, British, and Australian English all have many similarities and are essentially the same language, but they also differ in important ways that serve to differentiate members of the three cultures. Similarly, emotional expressions are predicted to vary in subtle ways. For instance, Marsh et al. (2003) asked a sample of North Americans to categorize the nationality of photographs of nine Japanese nationals and nine Japanese Americans bearing one of five emotional facial expressions (e.g., anger, fear, surprise; or a neutral pose). Participants were able to accurately categorize the targets into national groups at better than chance levels for photographs with either neutral or emotional facial expressions; however, they were more accurate for the emotional rather than the neutral faces. In other words, aspects of the facial expressions themselves sufficiently differentiated the two sets of targets (i.e., American and Japanese), and the North American participants were able to tell which set was American.

This result is even more impressive given that the faces used in the experiment were drawn from a set that had undergone extensive pretesting and found to be equivalent on all dimensions relevant to emotion recognition. In other words, it was thought that potential cultural differences had been removed through the rigorous selection process. One possible explanation for Marsh et al.'s (2003) findings is that differences in facial morphology contributed to the observed effects. Recall that participants in the study were able to detect target nationality at better than chance levels in both the neutral facial displays and the emotional displays. There is some evidence suggesting that facial morphology can contribute to the interpretation – and sometimes misinterpretation – of emotional expressions (Beaupré & Hess, 2005; Hess, Adams, & Kleck, 2004). Furthermore, the fact that the participants in the Marsh et al. (2003) study were significantly better able to detect target nationality in the emotional compared with the neutral faces suggests that slight morphological differences may be accentuated by the expression of emotion.

And, by extension, if there are nonverbal accents in emotional displays, even if they are attributable to differences in facial morphology, then ingroup members are likely to recognize the accents of other members of their culture more than members of a different culture. Consequently, it is likely that ingroup members are better able to decode subtle non-verbal accents and, therefore, emotional displays more generally than outgroup members.

As a whole, this work suggests that cultural differences dictating the expression and decoding of emotion contribute to emotion recognition accuracy. Elfenbein and colleagues (Marsh et al., 2003; Elfenbein & Ambady, 2003) suggest that the match between the cultural group memberships of encoders and decoders allows for optimal recognition accuracy because individuals are more likely to share encoding and decoding rules, as well as subtle differences in expressive style – what they call nonverbal accents. Clearly, familiarity with a culture may also make one more knowledgeable about cultural norms regarding encoding and decoding, as well as nonverbal accents. Thus, people may be better able to decode emotion within group boundaries.

Familiarity with members of other social groups and knowledge of the social rules for displaying and decoding emotion may also exert their effects through general psychological mechanisms. In the remainder of this section, we consider three such intergroup mechanisms: attention, biases, and power.

Attention

The nonverbal-accent theory presents the argument that members of different cultures may express the same emotion in different ways that are subtle but meaningful nonetheless. If this is the case, as suggested in the Marsh et al. (2003) experiment, then attentional processes may piggyback on these subtle differences making outgroup emotion recognition more difficult than ingroup emotion recognition. That is, individuals may not be aware of the subtle differences that shape emotional expression in different cultures and, therefore, fail to attend to important cues associated with the expression of the emotion in the outgroup. For instance, blushing may be a cue to embarrassment in racial groups with paler skin tones but not for groups with darker skin tones. Because of this difference, members of groups with paler skin may not detect that a darker skinned person is embarrassed because blushing is not evident.

Attentional differences of this type have been theorized to underlie facial recognition across group boundaries (Brigham, 2005). Reliance on individuation cues that are effective in one's own culture (e.g., eye color) but less discriminating in a different culture is thought to contribute to individuals' relatively poor ability to remember racial outgroup members relative to racial ingroup members.

In addition to the perceptual role for attention, differences in motivation may implicate attention in the manifestation of the ingroup advantage. As individuals navigate their social worlds, they often behave like "cognitive misers," only processing information that is relevant to their goals or needs (Fiske, Lin, & Neuberg, 1999). People may rely on group memberships to direct attention to strangers, with the default strategy of attempting to individuate ingroup members but only categorizing or perhaps even completely ignoring outgroup members (Sporer, 2001). Outgroup membership may serve as a cue to disregard a stranger, unless there is some other contextual factor that makes the stranger worthy of further consideration and/or individuation (Rodin, 1987). An examination of attentional biases of this type revealed that college students tended to disregard middle-aged strangers with whom they had a brief interaction but not strangers who were closer to their own age (Rodin, 1987). In other words, age served as a cue regarding whether to allocate attention to other individuals.

Additional research suggests that there may be a general tendency to direct attention to ingroup rather than to outgroup members. Specifically, using a dot-probe test of visual attention, Trawalter (2005) found that white participants located a dot more quickly if it was in the same location where a white face had been previously than if it was in the same location where a black face had been. Because white participants allocated more attention to other white faces than they did to black faces, they located the dot faster when it appeared in the white face location (Eberhardt, Goff, Purdie, & Davies, 2004). Thus, participants revealed an ingroup attentional advantage. It is interesting, however, that a subsequent experiment with black participants found no significant bias toward ingroup faces. Perhaps like the ingroup-advantage effect and the cross-race memory effect (Brigham, 2005), low-status minority-group members are less likely to reveal an ingroup attentional bias. Nevertheless, if individuals pay differential levels of attention to ingroup and outgroup members in their environments, then they may also process ingroup and outgroup emotional faces differently and, consequently, acquire differential levels of skill at decoding the emotional expressions of ingroup and outgroup members.

Biases (Ingroup Favoritism, Stereotypes, and Prejudice)

The aforementioned attentional bias for ingroup over outgroup members suggests that basic processes associated with group membership contribute to the ingroup advantage in emotion recognition. One of the most pervasive effects of social categorization is ingroup favoritism (Tajfel & Turner, 1979). When individuals are assigned to a group, even on relatively arbitrary and meaningless grounds, they tend to favor other members of their newly assigned group compared to members of an alternate group (Turner et al., 1987). Ingroup favoritism recently has been found to influence beliefs about the emotional qualities of different groups (e.g., Leyens et al., 2000). For instance, Beaupré and Hess (2003) examined the attributions that European Canadians made regarding the likely emotional facial behavior of European, African, and Asian targets in response to a relatively neutral scenario. After reading the scenario, participants were asked to select from among a sample of target photographs the facial display that best represented the emotion experienced by the protagonist of the scenario. The facial displays were either neutral or varied in smiling intensity, ranging from a miserable smile (i.e., a smile with a frown) to an extremely intense smile (i.e., a strong smile with significant wrinkling around the eyes). Results revealed that participants attributed smiles denoting positive affect more often when the protagonist was identified (by photograph) as an ingroup member compared to when the protagonist was identified as an outgroup member (either African or Asian). In contrast, participants attributed a neutral facial expression to outgroup members more frequently than to ingroup members. In a follow-up study, participants of Asian and African ancestry revealed a similar pattern of ingroup bias.

Beaupré and Hess's (2003) findings suggest that the interpretation of emotional experiences is subject to ingroup favoritism. Individuals seem to be predisposed to perceive ingroup members as smiling and perhaps sociable, even when the context does not necessarily trigger positive affect. Research suggests, however, that smiling behavior may be just the tip of the proverbial iceberg regarding differential emotional attributions for ingroup and outgroup members. Specifically, Leyens et al. (2000) argue that a wide array of emotions is attributed to ingroup but not to outgroup members. In their theory of infrahumanization, Leyens et al. (2000) propose that some emotions are perceived as being uniquely human (e.g., admiration, resentment, love, melancholy), whereas others (e.g., fear, surprise, anger, joy) are perceived as being nonuniquely human because they are experienced by both humans and animals. Furthermore, in an effort to claim superior humanity for members of one's own group, individuals associate uniquely human emotions with the ingroup and nonuniquely human emotions with the outgroup (Paladino et al., 2002); and, they are reluctant to attribute uniquely human emotions to outgroup members (Cortes, Demoulin, P. Rodriguez, A. Rodriguez, & Leyens, 2005).

Although the emotions that Leyens et al. (2000) identify as nonuniquely human are those that are most commonly examined in research on emotion recognition through facial displays (Ekman, Sorenson & Friesen, 1969), this research on infrahumanization suggests that more subtle, complex emotions (i.e., the uniquely human emotions) may likely be misinterpreted across group boundaries. Matsumoto (2002) makes a similar argument, noting that "signal clarity" (i.e., how observable an emotion is) is an important moderator of the ingroup advantage for emotion recognition. Furthermore, Elfenbein and Ambady (2002a, 2002b) note that fear and disgust, two of the more ambiguous emotional displays, are the most poorly universally recognized emotions, but they are also the most susceptible to the ingroup advantage. Taken together, this work suggests that subtleties in emotional expression are likely to exacerbate the ingroup-advantage effect. Indeed, ingroup-favoring biases may capitalize on the subtleties and ambiguity associated with emotional expression that occur naturally in everyday interactions.

In concert with this possibility, cultural stereotypes and biases have their most profound effects and are particularly powerful in ambiguous situations (Bodenhausen & Macrae, 1998). For instance, ambiguous behavior performed by black targets is more likely to be interpreted as hostile or violent than is the same behavior performed by white targets (Devine, 1989; Duncan, 1976; Sagar & Schofield, 1980). Work by Hugenberg and Bodenhausen (2003) suggests that ambiguous emotional behavior is also susceptible to the influence of cultural stereotypes. In their study, white participants were shown movie clips in which a target's facial expression changed from angry to happy (Exp. 1) or from happy to angry (Exp. 2). Consequently, there was a period in each clip in which the facial expression of the target was relatively ambiguous.

Two of the targets were computer-generated faces of black individuals and two were of white individuals. Hugenberg and Bodenhausen (2003) predicted that if the cultural stereotype of blacks as violent influences perceptions of emotional displays, then individuals should be slower to recognize happiness but faster to recognize anger in the faces of black targets. Consistent with this prediction, participants were slower to recognize that black faces had changed from angry to happy and faster to recognize that they had changed from happy to angry, but only if the participants held relatively negative implicit associations about blacks.

In addition to these general cultural stereotypes, there are stereotypes and expectations regarding the expressivity of members of different groups (Kirouac & Hess, 1999). For example, in North America, women are thought to be more emotionally expressive in general, as well as more likely to show expressions of happiness and to smile more than men (Briton & Hall, 1995; Hess et al., 2000). Japanese nationals are thought to be less expressive, particularly when displaying anger, than Europeans and European Americans (Pittam, Gallois, Iwawaki, & Kroonenberg, 1995). These stereotypes and, sometimes, actual group differences (LaFrance, Hecht, & Paluck, 2003) can shape the interpretation of emotional facial displays (Kirouac & Hess, 1999). For example, if a person believes that women are less likely to display (and feel) anger than men, then an angry facial display on a female face may be discounted and rated as less intense than the same display on a male face (Hess, Blairy, & Kleck, 1997). Consequently, as Hugenberg and Bodenhausen (2003) note, "stereotypic expectancies appear to penetrate a fundamental aspect of on-line person perception" (p. 643).

Taken together, the research reviewed in this section suggests that social categorization activates – often without awareness or control – ingroup-favoring orientations and stereotypic associations that can influence ongoing attributions of the emotional facial displays of others. In addition, the general evaluative biases that accompany recognition of different group memberships can produce biased evaluation of the emotional behaviors of both ingroup (Beaupré & Hess, 2003) and outgroup (Hugenberg & Bodenhausen, 2003) members. These prejudices may be blatant or subtle (Gaertner & Dovidio, 1986), and often people who have explicitly nonprejudiced attitudes may still harbor implicit intergroup biases (Dovidio & Gaertner, 2004) that shape, in part, the interpretation of facial displays of emotion.

Power and Status

Although differences in nonverbal accents, attention, ingroup favoritism, and stereotypes may help explain the ingroup advantage for emotion recognition, these factors and processes do not provide much of an account for differences in the magnitude of the ingroup advantage. Recall that Elfenbein and Ambady's (2002a) meta-analytic review demonstrated that the advantage in accuracy for judging the emotion from facial expressions of ingroup relative to outgroup members was weaker for minority than majority group members. Psychological processes linked to status and power, however, may provide some insight. Power and status are relational concepts that often are contextually determined; however, because many societies are rigidly structured according to group hierarchy, group membership is often correlated with relatively stable status arrangements. For example, in the United States, whites have generally had higher status and greater social power than blacks.

As outlined earlier, differences in status can systematically affect recognition of emotion from facial expressions in intergroup contexts. Status influences nonverbal expression and, thus, the opportunity to learn to recognize emotions. Because high-status people express their emotions more openly than low-status people, members of minority groups may find it easier to read majority-group members' emotions than majority-group members can accurately interpret the emotional expressions of minority-group members during intergroup interactions. In addition, because minority-group members have more contact with majority-group members than the reverse (Pettigrew & Tropp, 2000), they have higher levels of intergroup familiarity. Relatedly, because minorities have greater exposure to the dominant culture than majority-group members have to subcultures, minorities may have a better knowledge of the differences in display and decoding rules across the groups. All of these factors can help explain why power and status moderate the difference in accuracy in intragroup and intergroup judgments of emotional facial expressions.

In addition, status also influences the motivation to try to interpret emotions from facial expressions. Because they are relatively low in power, members of minority groups tend to pay more attention to the specific actions and expressions of majority-group members, perceive them in a more individualized way, and rely less on stereotypes and other generalized responses than majority-group members do of minority-group members. That is, because members of the majority groups generally have more control over resources than do minority-group members, minorities may be more motivated to understand the actions and expressions of majorities than majorities are to interpret the expressions of minorities. Research reveals that powerful people and those in high-status positions pay less attention to their subordinates than subordinates do to them (Fiske, 1993), largely due to the asymmetry in outcome dependency. That is, lower status individuals' material outcomes tend to depend more on the emotional reactions and impressions of higher status individuals than the reverse. Consequently, members of minority groups may be more motivated to attend to the facial displays of emotions of majority-group members than majority-group members are to the facial displays of minority-group members.

Furthermore, according to the subordination hypothesis (Henley, 1977; LaFrance & Henley, 1994), chronic stigmatization – which involves perceived status differences and associated prejudice – produces functional adaptations. In particular, members of oppressed groups are hypothesized to be more sensitive and attentive to their social environment. According to this perspective, therefore, members of minority groups tend to reveal less of an ingroup advantage than members of majority groups because they are better decoders of nonverbal behavior, including emotional facial displays. In other words, minority-group members reveal less of an ingroup advantage because they are equally as good as majority-group members at decoding the facial expressions of ingroup members but better than majority-group members at decoding outgroup facial expressions.

Evidence in support of the subordination hypothesis has been found in research observing differences in the accuracy with which whites and blacks decode one another's nonverbal behavior. As mentioned previously, for example, Nowicki et al. (1998) found that white college students decoded the emotional facial expressions of white targets more accurately than those of black targets, but black college students were equally able to decode the emotional facial displays of white and black targets. Furthermore, Halberstadt's (1985) meta-analysis of racial differences revealed that although black children (ages four to eleven) showed equivalent or slightly lower levels of decoding accuracy relative to whites, black college students showed a higher level of accuracy than white college students. According to the subordination hypothesis, in other words, the chronic experience of being a low-status group member resulted in the black college students' superior nonverbal decoding accuracy.

Hall, Halberstadt, and O'Brien (1997) found little evidence for the subordination hypothesis, however, especially as an explanation for gender differences in nonverbal sensitivity. Nevertheless, they too argued that lower status individuals may be more sensitive to the nonverbal displays of their superiors under certain conditions. Specifically, they suggest that because status arrangements often are defined in a relational context, status differences in nonverbal sensitivity are more likely to be revealed within the relevant context rather than as stable trait differences. Furthermore, Hall and Halberstadt (1997) proposed that status is unlikely to explain differences in nonverbal sensitivity but rather the role motivations adopted by the individuals in the context. In accordance with the subordination hypothesis and Fiske's research on power (Fiske, 1993), the more subordinates are concerned about pleasing their superiors and predicting their superiors' reactions, the more they are likely to be attuned to their superiors' nonverbal facial displays. Similarly, superiors who are concerned about nurturing their subordinates and fostering teamwork among them may be sensitive to their subordinates' nonverbal facial displays but not superiors who are interested in maintaining rigid lines of authority.

Taken together, the work on status and power provides partial insight into the ingroup advantage, suggesting that on many occasions, members of low-status groups will decode the emotional expressions of majority-group members better than majority-group members will decode the emotional expressions of minority-group members. As Hall et al. (1997) pointed out, however, situational factors are also likely to influence the accuracy with which emotional facial displays are communicated across group boundaries. Both emotional expression and recognition are critical components of communication and, therefore, highly sensitive to social context. Thus, difficulties with emotion communication across group boundaries may be more apparent and particularly important during interactions between members of different groups. In the next section, we explore how the context of an intergroup interaction may influence the communication of emotion through the face and possibly contribute to the ingroup advantage through the exacerbation of emotion recognition inaccuracy across group boundaries.

Implications for Intergroup Interactions

Like other aspects of nonverbal communication, the communication of emotion through facial expressions may be better understood within the context of a naturally occurring interaction. Interactions between members of different social-identity groups provide a meaningful context in which to examine the expression and interpretation of emotional facial displays. It is striking, however, that little research has attempted to examine the communication of emotion through the face during intergroup interactions. Both accurate and inaccurate interpretations of emotional facial displays could undermine successful encounters between members of different groups. Moreover, reactions to the emotional facial displays of outgroup interaction partners are likely to influence individuals' own experiences during the interaction.

The research that has privileged the study of emotional facial displays within the interaction context considers both the expressive and communicative aspects of emotional faces. For instance, anger constitutes an individual's particular feeling state, but it also serves as a signal to other people what that individual might do (Adams & Kleck, 2005; Frijda & Mesquita, 1994). When someone looks at you with an angry facial expression, you know that he or she does not intend to take a nap. Furthermore, within the context of an interaction, facial behavior can serve a number of functions simultaneously. For instance, a frown displayed by one's interaction partner could signal sadness or irritation, effortful processing of what one is saying, or both. Consequently, it is important to consider the context of the interaction, including the concerns that individuals bring with them to the interaction, to understand the facial displays they exhibit and the ways in which those displays are likely to be interpreted by their interaction partners (Kaiser & Wehrle, 2004).

In an effort to shape and direct research on intergroup interactions, Hebl and Dovidio (2005) developed a model that outlines key elements in the dynamics of communication in an intergroup context. Although not expressly developed to understand the nonverbal communication of emotion between members of different groups, the model can advance understanding of this topic. Building on Patterson's (1982) Sequential Functional Model of Nonverbal Exchange, Hebl and Dovidio (2005) note that people approach each other with preexisting orientations (i.e., antecedent conditions) – such as personal factors, experiential factors, and relational/situational factors – that can influence whether and how they interact. These antecedent conditions trigger pre-interaction variables in the context – such as cognitions (including stereotypes) and affective reactions, levels of arousal, and behavioral propensities to act – that mediate the effect of these preexisting orientations on both verbal and nonverbal behavior during the interaction. During the course of the interaction, individuals determine whether both their own and their partner's levels of involvement match their expectations, which, in turn, influence cognition and affect both during and after the interaction.

The model is helpful because it articulates important aspects of both the interactants and the interaction that are likely to influence the expression and interpretation of emotional facial displays. Consider a dyadic interaction between a white and a black individual. According to the Hebl and Dovidio (2005) model, antecedent factors such as the individuals' racial attitudes, previous experience with interracial contact, and relationship to one another are all likely to impact their emotional communication during the interaction. For instance, negative racial attitudes, especially those held at a relatively unconscious level, predispose white individuals to reveal negative nonverbal behavior during interracial interactions that is often detected by their black interaction partners (Dovidio, Kawakami, & Gaertner, 2002). It is interesting that although unaware of their own communication of negative nonverbal behavior, white individuals with more negative, implicit racial attitudes may be especially likely to detect negative affect in the face of black interaction partners (Hugenberg & Bodenhausen, 2003). Considered in tandem, this work makes it relatively easy to see how emotional communication may contribute to the negative experiences individuals have during interactions across group boundaries.

However, interactions in which both interactants have considerable interracial contact experience may proceed quite differently. Previous contact is associated with more positive racial attitudes (Pettigrew & Tropp, 2000) and should translate into more positive emotional facial displays. Furthermore, greater levels of interracial contact suggest greater familiarity with the nonverbal accents of outgroup members, which, in turn, facilitate the accurate communication of emotion (Elfenbein & Ambady, 2002a, 2003).

Similar to the antecedent factors, many of the pre-interaction mediators identified in the Hebl and Dovidio (2005) model are also likely to shape the communication of emotion. As discussed previously, for instance, stereotypes that individuals hold about one another's groups influence both the expression and interpretation of emotion (e.g., Beaupré & Hess, 2003). The affect that is often triggered in interracial interactions is also important to consider when thinking about emotional communication in the intergroup context. Specifically, intergroup contact is often a source of anxiety, distress, and even threat for some individuals (Stephan & Stephan, 2000). Under these circumstances, accurate communication of emotion may be particularly difficult. When individuals are feeling anxious, their own emotional facial displays are likely to be more difficult to decode, while at the same time they will be more susceptible to misinterpreting neutral or slightly negative facial expressions on the part of their interaction partners (Fox et al., 2000).

Moreover, Leyens, Demoulin, Désert, Vaes, and Philippot (2002) found that apprehension associated with intergroup relations may inhibit the expression of emotions that can convey interest and involvement in intergroup contact. Leyens et al. (2002) asked white students in Belgium to pose emotions for a black or white photographer. In addition, the participants were told that individuals of the same race as the photographer would see the pictures. Participants were asked how effectively they communicated their emotions, and judges evaluated how effectively the emotions were conveyed. Results revealed that participants reported that they were more expressive and conveyed their emotions better for an outgroup audience than for an ingroup audience. According to the judges, however, participants conveyed emotions significantly *less* effectively for the outgroup audience than the ingroup audience. Consistent with other work examining the perception of friendship overtures toward ingroup compared to outgroup members (Vorauer, 2005), this work suggests that individuals tend to overestimate the intensity and clarity of their emotional expression during intergroup interactions. Considered in tandem with the research reviewed previously, this work suggests that the affect most often triggered in interracial contact –that is, anxiety – may be the least likely to facilitate accurate emotion recognition or result in positive interaction experiences.

Motivations and goals are another pre-interaction mediator identified in Hebl and Dovidio's (2005) model that should influence both the expression and interpretation of emotion in the face. Whites' concerns about appearing prejudiced often initiate self-regulatory processes designed to suppress and/or control the expression of negative feelings and thoughts during the interaction (Richeson & Trawalter, 2005). These self-regulatory efforts may result in overly controlled, rigid behavior (Richeson & Shelton, 2003). Blacks, in contrast, are often concerned about being the target of prejudice and stereotypes, and these concerns influence their behavior during interracial interactions. Blacks' concerns about being the target of prejudice, for example, can facilitate overtly positive behavior on their part in the service of fostering a smooth interaction (Shelton, Richeson, & Salvatore, 2005).

In addition, these interpersonal concerns about prejudice may influence individuals' ability to decode their interaction partners' facial expressions. For instance, concerns about being the target of prejudice may make black individuals particularly sensitive to the emotional facial displays of their interaction partners (Frable et al., 1990). By contrast, because they are more likely to be self-focused (Vorauer, Hunter, Main, & Roy, 2000), whites who are concerned about appearing prejudiced may be insensitive to the emotional facial displays of their black interaction partners. Consequently, individuals' motivations stemming from their distinct prejudice concerns may set up a scenario in which whites are less accurate at decoding blacks' emotional facial displays than the accuracy with which blacks are able to decode the facial displays of their white partners – a pattern that mimics the differences in the ingroup advantage for members of majority and minority groups discussed previously.

In contrast, the opposite decoding advantage may emerge. That is, white individuals in the interaction may be able to decode their black partner's emotional facial displays more accurately than their partner can detect their facial displays. To the extent that blacks are concerned about being the target of prejudice, they may display overtly positive behavior that is relatively easy to decode. However, the facial displays associated with effortful self-regulation on the part of whites, particularly as they attempt to avoid appearing prejudice, may be particularly difficult to decode. Consequently, the black interaction partner may find it more difficult to read the emotional displays of the white partner than the white partner finds it to read the emotional displays of the black partner. It is important that although individuals may find it relatively hard or easy to decode one another's emotional displays, these displays may not reveal individuals' true emotional reactions to the interaction. As mentioned before, participants' interaction concerns prompt them to attempt to mask their true feelings. Both participants' attempts to dissociate their own facial expressions of emotion from their emotional experiences may make the interpretation of emotional expressions and experiences during interracial interactions particularly difficult and wrought with miscommunication.

In sum, in this section we attempted to explore the implications of previous research on intergroup relations for the communication of emotion through facial displays in an intergroup context. We employed aspects of Hebl and Dovidio's (2005) model of mixed social interactions to underscore the complexity of emotion recognition across group boundaries. The strength of this approach is the simultaneous consideration of how both interaction participants' attitudes, previous experiences, and concerns might shape both their expression and interpretation of emotion in the face. By exploring emotion recognition in the context of intergroup interactions, researchers will be more likely to capture the true richness, ambiguity, and complexity of emotional facial expression and interpretation across group boundaries. Consequently, we believe that this type of research is crucial to understanding intergroup communication and, ultimately, intergroup relations.

Conclusion

The present chapter explored the recognition of emotional facial displays in an intergroup context. Given that group membership fundamentally affects the way people think about, feel about, and behave with others, we proposed that psychological processes associated with social categorization and social identity are likely also to produce systematic biases in the recognition of emotion across group boundaries. Through a review of the literature on emotion recognition, we examined the ways in which group membership affects the recognition of emotion displayed in the face, and how members of different groups – defined by majority and minority status – may be differentially successful at recognizing and interpreting the emotions displayed by outgroup members. That is, we considered the ways in which processes identified in the intergroup-relations literature contribute to the systematic nature of emotion recognition accuracy and inaccuracy between members of different groups.

At the end of the chapter, we considered how the context of an intergroup dyadic interaction is likely to influence the communication of emotional facial displays. This final analysis revealed the complexity of emotion communication across group boundaries. Specifically, drawing on Hebl and Dovidio's (2005) model, we proposed that in addition to their affective states, individuals' previous experiences, goals, concerns, and attitudes are likely to influence the ways in which they express and interpret facial displays of emotion during intergroup interactions. In sum, the chapter provides a conceptual analysis of how the study of facial expressions complements previous research on intergroup bias and, consequently, argues that examining emotional facial displays in an intergroup context offers potentially unique theoretical insight into both emotion recognition and intergroup relations.

References

Adams, R. B., & Kleck, R. E. (2005). Effects of direct and averted gaze on the perception of facially communicated emotion. *Emotion, 5*, 3–11.

Beaupré, M. G., & Hess, U. (2003). In my mind, we all smile: A case of ingroup favoritism. *Journal of Experimental Social Psychology, 39*, 371–377.

Beaupré, M. G., & Hess, U. (2005). Cross-cultural emotion recognition among Canadian ethnic groups. *Journal of Cross-Cultural Psychology, 36*, 355–370.

Bodenhausen, G. V., & Macrae, C. N. (1998). Stereotype activation and inhibition. In R. S. Wyer, Jr. (Ed.), *Advances in social cognition: Vol XI. Stereotype activation and inhibition* (pp. 1–52). Mahwah, NJ: Erlbaum.

Brigham, J. C. (2005). The role of race and racial prejudice in recognizing other people. Nebraska Symposium on Motivation, 2005: Motivational Aspects of Prejudice and Racism.

Briton, N. J., & Hall, J. A. (1995). Gender-based expectancies and observer judgments of smiling. *Journal of Nonverbal Behavior, 19*, 49–65.

Buck, R. (1984). *The communication of emotion*. New York: Guilford Press.

Collins, M., & Nowicki, S. (2001). African American children's ability to identify emotion in facial expressions and tones of voice of European Americans. *Journal of Genetic Psychology, 162*, 334–346.

Cortes, B. P., Demoulin, S., Rodriguez, R. T., Rodriguez, A. P., & Leyens, J. (2005). Infrahumanization or familiarity? Attribution of uniquely human emotions to the self, the ingroup, and the outgroup. *Personality and Social Psychology Bulletin, 31*, 243–253.

Devine, P. G. (1989). Stereotypes and prejudice: Their automatic and controlled components. *Journal of Personality and Social Psychology, 56*, 5–18.

Dovidio, J. F., Kawakami, K., Johnson, C., Johnson, B., & Howard, A. (1997). On the nature of prejudice: Automatic and controlled process. *Journal of Experimental Social Psychology, 33*, 510–540.

Dovidio, J. F., & Gaertner, S. L. (2004). Aversive racism. In M. P. Zanna (Ed.), *Advances in experimental social psychology, Vol. 36* (pp. 1–52). San Diego, CA: Elsevier Academic Press.

Dovidio, J. F., Kawakami, K., & Gaertner, S. L. (2002). Implicit and explicit prejudice and interracial interaction. *Journal of Personality and Social Psychology, 82*, 62–68.

Duncan, B. L. (1976). Differential social perception and attribution of intergroup violence: Testing the lower limits of stereotyping of blacks. *Journal of Personality and Social Psychology, 34*, 590–598.

Eberhardt, J. L., Goff, P. A., Purdie, V. J., & Davies, P. G. (2004). Seeing black: Race, crime, and visual processing. *Journal of Personality and Social Psychology, 87*, 876–893.

Ekman, P. (1972). Universals and cultural differences in facial expressions of emotion. In J. Cole (Ed.), *Nebraska Symposium on Motivation, 1971* (Vol. 19, pp. 207–282). Lincoln: University of Nebraska Press.

Ekman, P. (1994). Strong evidence for universals in facial expressions: A reply to Russell's mistaken critique. *Psychological Bulletin, 115*, 268–287.

Ekman, P., Sorenson, E. R., & Friesen, W. V. (1969). Pancultural elements in facial displays of emotion. *Science, 164*, 86–88.

Elfenbein, H. A., & Ambady, N. (2002a). On the universality and cultural specificity of emotion recognition: A meta-analysis. *Psychological Bulletin, 128*, 203–235.

Elfenbein, H. A., & Ambady, N. (2002b). Is there an ingroup advantage in emotion recognition? *Psychological Bulletin, 128*, 243–249.

Elfenbein, H. A., & Ambady, N. (2003). When familiarity breeds accuracy: Cultural exposure and facial emotion recognition. *Journal of Personality and Social Psychology, 85*, 276–290.

Ellyson, S. L., & Dovidio, J. F. (1985). Power, dominance, and nonverbal behavior: Basic concepts and issues. In S. L. Ellyson & J. F. Dovidio (Eds.), *Power, dominance, and nonverbal behavior* (pp. 1–27). New York: Springer-Verlag.

Feldman, R., Philippot, P., & Custrini, R. (1991). Social competence and nonverbal behavior. In R. Feldman & B. Rime (Eds.), *Fundamentals of nonverbal behavior* (pp. 329–350). New York: Cambridge University Press.

Fiske, S. T. (1993). Controlling other people: The impact of power on stereotyping. *American Psychologist, 48*, 621–628.

Fiske, S. T., Lin, M., & Neuberg, S. L. (1999). The continuum model: Ten years later. In S. Chaiken & Y. Trope (Eds.), *Dual process theories in social psychology* (pp. 231–254). New York: Guilford.

Fox, E., Lester, V., Russo, R., Bowles, R., Pichler, A., & Dutton, K. (2000). Facial expressions of emotion: Are angry faces detected more efficiently? *Cognition and Emotion, 14*, 61–92.

Frable, D. E. S., Blackstone, T., & Scherbaum, C. (1990). Marginal and mindful deviants in social interactions. *Journal of Personality and Social Psychology, 59*, 140–149.

Frijda, N. H., & Mesquita, B. (1994). The social roles and functions of emotions. In S. Kitayama & H. R. Markus (Eds.), *Emotion and Culture* (pp. 51–87). Washington, DC: American Psychological Association.

Gaertner, S. L., & Dovidio, J. F. (1986). The aversive form of racism. In J. F. Dovidio & S. L. Gaertner (Eds.), *Prejudice, discrimination, and racism* (pp. 61–89). Orlando, FL: Academic Press.

Glanville, D. N., & Nowicki, S. (2002). Facial expression recognition and social competence among African American elementary school children: An examination of ethnic differences. *Journal of Black Psychology, 28*, 318–329.

Halberstadt, A. G. (1985). Race, socioeconomic status, and nonverbal behavior. In A. W. Siegman & S. Feldstein (Eds.), *Multichannel integrations of nonverbal behavior* (pp. 227–266). Hillsdale, NJ: Erlbaum.

Hall, J. A., Coats, E. J., & SmithLeBeau, L. (2005). Nonverbal behavior and the vertical dimension of social relations: A meta-analysis. *Psychological Bulletin, 131,* 898–924.

Hall, J. A., & Halberstadt, A. G. (1997). "Subordination" and sensitivity to nonverbal cues: A study of married working women. *Sex Roles, 31,* 149–165.

Hall, J. A., Halberstadt, A. G., & O'Brien, C. E. (1997). "Subordination" and nonverbal sensitivity: A study and synthesis of findings based on trait measures. *Sex Roles, 37,* 295–317.

Hebl, M. R., & Dovidio, J. F. (2005). Promoting the "social" in the examination of social stigmas. *Personality and Social Psychology Review, 9,* 156–182.

Henley, N. M. (1977). *Body politics: Power, sex, and nonverbal communication.* Englewood Cliffs, NJ: Prentice-Hall.

Hess, U., Adams, R. B., & Kleck, R. E. (2004). Facial appearance, gender, and emotion expression. *Emotion, 4,* 378–388.

Hess, U., Blairy, S., & Kleck, R. E. (1997). The relationship between intensity of emotional facial expressions and observers' decoding. *Journal of Nonverbal Behavior, 21,* 241–257.

Hess, U., Senecal, S., Kirouac, G., Herrera, P., Philippot, P., & Kleck, R. E. (2000). Emotional expressivity in men and women: Stereotypes and self-perceptions. *Cognition and Emotion, 14,* 609–642.

Hugenberg, K., & Bodenhausen, G. V. (2003). Facial prejudice: Implicit prejudice and the perception of facial threat. *Psychological Science, 14,* 640–643.

Izard, C. E. (1971). *The face of emotion.* New York: Appleton-Century-Crofts.

Kaiser, S., & Wehrle, T. (2004). Facial expressions in social interactions: Beyond basic emotions. In D. Canamero & R. Aylett (Eds.), *Advances in consciousness research: Animating expressive characters for social interactions.* Amsterdam: John Benjamins Publishing.

Keltner, D., Gruenfeld, D. H., & Anderson, C. (2003). Power, approach, and inhibition. *Psychological Review, 110,* 265–284.

Kirouac, G., & Hess, U. (1999). Group membership and the decoding of nonverbal behavior. In P. Philippot, R. Feldman, & E. Coats (Eds.), *The social context of nonverbal behavior* (pp. 182–210). New York: Cambridge University Press.

LaFrance, M., Hecht, M. A., & Paluck, E. L. (2003). The contingent smile: A meta-analysis of sex differences in smiling. *Psychological Bulletin, 129,* 305–334.

LaFrance, M., & Henley, N. M. (1994). On oppressing hypotheses: Or differences in nonverbal sensitivity revisited. In H. L. Radtke & H. J. Stam (Eds.), *Power/gender: Social relations theory and practice* (pp. 287–311). London: Sage Publications.

Leyens, J.-P., Demoulin, S., Désert, M., Vaes, J., & Philippot, P. (2002). Expressing emotions and decoding them: Ingroups and outgroups do not share the same advantages. In D. M. Mackie & E. R. Smith (Eds.), *From prejudice to intergroup emotions: Differentiated reactions to social groups* (pp. 139–151). New York: Psychology Press.

Leyens, J.-P., Paladino, P. M., Rodriguez-Torres, R., Vaes, J., Demoulin, S., Rodriguez-Perez, A., & Gaunt, R. (2000). The emotional side of prejudice:

The attribution of secondary emotions to ingroups and outgroups. *Personality and Social Psychology Review, 4,* 186–197.

Linville, P. W., Fischer, G. W., & Salovey, P. (1989). Perceived distributions of the characteristics of ingroup and outgroup members: Empirical evidence and a computer simulation. *Journal of Personality and Social Psychology, 57,* 165–188.

Marsh, A., Elfenbein, H. A., & Ambady, N. (2003). Nonverbal "accents": Cultural differences in facial expressions of emotion. *Psychological Science, 14,* 373–376.

Matsumoto, D. (1989). Cultural influences on the perception of emotion. *Journal of Cross-Cultural Psychology, 20,* 92–105.

Matsumoto, D. (1992). American-Japanese cultural differences in the recognition of universal facial expressions. *Journal of Cross-Cultural Psychology, 23,* 72–84.

Matsumoto, D. (2002). Methodological requirements to test a possible ingroup advantage in judging emotions across cultures: Comment on Elfenbein and Ambady (2002) and evidence. *Psychological Bulletin, 128,* 236–242.

Matsumoto, D., Kasri, F., & Kooken, K. (1999). American-Japanese cultural differences in judgements of expression intensity and subjective experience. *Cognition and Emotion, 13,* 201–218.

Meissner, C. A., & Brigham, J. C. (2001). Thirty years of investigation of the own-race bias in memory for faces: A meta-analytic review. *Psychology, Public Policy and Law: Special Edition on the Other-Race Effect, 7,* 3–35.

Mullen, B., & Hu, L. (1989). Perceptions of ingroup and outgroup variability: A meta-analytic integration. *Basic and Applied Social Psychology, 10,* 233–252.

Nowicki, S., Glanville, D., & Demertzis, A. (1998). A test of the ability to recognize emotion in the facial expressions of African American adults. *Journal of Black Psychology, 24,* 335–350.

Otten, S., & Moskowitz, G. B. (2000). Evidence for implicit evaluative ingroup bias: Affect-biased spontaneous trait inference in a minimal group paradigm. *Journal of Experimental Social Psychology, 36,* 77–89.

Paladino, M., Leyens, J., Rodriguez, R., Rodriguez, A., Gaunt, R., & Demoulin, S. (2002). Differential association of uniquely and nonuniquely human emotions with the ingroup and outgroup. *Group Processes and Intergroup Relations, 5,* 105–117.

Park, B., & Rothbart, M. (1982). Perception of outgroup homogeneity and levels of social categorization: Memory for the subordinate attributes of ingroup and outgroup members. *Journal of Personality and Social Psychology, 42,* 1051–1068.

Patterson, M. L. (1982). A sequential functional model of nonverbal exchange. *Psychological Review, 89,* 231–249.

Pettigrew, T. F., & Tropp, L. R. (2000). Does intergroup contact reduce prejudice? Recent meta-analytic findings. In S. Oskamp (Ed.), *Reducing prejudice and discrimination* (pp. 93–114). Hillsdale, NJ: Erlbaum.

Pittam, J., Gallois, C., Iwawaki, S., & Kroonenberg, P. (1995). Australian and Japanese concepts of expressive behavior. *Journal of Cross-Cultural Psychology, 26,* 451–473.

Richeson, J., & Shelton, J. N. (2003). When prejudice does not pay: Effects of interracial contact on executive function. *Psychological Science, 14*, 287–290.

Richeson, J. A., & Trawalter, S. (2005). Why do interracial interactions impair executive function? A resource depletion account. *Journal of Personality and Social Psychology, 88*, 517–530.

Rodin, M. J. (1987). Who is memorable to whom: A study of cognitive disregard. *Social Cognition, 5*, 144–165.

Sagar, H. A., & Schofield, J. W. (1980). Racial and behavioral cues in black and white children's perceptions of ambiguously aggressive acts. *Journal of Personality and Social Psychology, 39*, 590–598.

Shelton, J. N., Richeson, J. A., & Salvatore, J. (2005). Expecting to be the target of prejudice. Implications for interethnic interactions. *Personality and Social Psychology Bulletin, 31*, 1189–1202.

Sidanius, J., & Pratto, F. (1999). *Social dominance: An intergroup theory of social hierarchy and oppression*. New York: Cambridge University Press.

Sporer, S. L. (2001). Recognizing faces of other ethnic groups: An integration of theories. *Psychology, Public Policy, and Law, 7*, 36–97.

Stephan, W. G., & Stephan, C. W. (2000). An integrated threat theory of prejudice. In S. Oskamp (Ed.), *Reducing prejudice and discrimination: The Claremont Symposium on Applied Psychology* (pp. 23–45). Mahwah, NJ: Erlbaum.

Tajfel, H., & Turner, J. C. (1979). An integrative theory of intergroup conflict. In W. G. Austin & S. Worchel (Eds.), *The social psychology of intergroup relations* (pp. 33–48). Monterey, CA: Brooks/Cole.

Trawalter, S. (2005). *Attention bias to ingroup vs. outgroup members*. Unpublished Masters Thesis. Dartmouth College, Hanover, NH.

Turner, J. C., Hogg, M. A., Oakes, P. J., Reicher, S. D., & Wetherell, M. S. (1987). *Rediscovering the social group: A self-categorization theory*. Oxford, England: Basil Blackwell.

Vorauer, J. D. (2005). *Miscommunications surrounding efforts to reach out across group boundaries*. Manuscript submitted for publication.

Vorauer, J. D., Hunter, A. J., Main, K. J., & Roy, S. A. (2000). Meta-stereotype activation: Evidence from indirect measures for specific evaluative concerns experienced by members of dominant groups in intergroup interaction. *Journal of Personality and Social Psychology, 78*, 690–707.

2. When Two Do the Same, It Might Not Mean the Same

The Perception of Emotional Expressions Shown by Men and Women

Ursula Hess, Reginald B. Adams, Jr., and Robert E. Kleck

> When he appears as a Ghost he had a **countenance** more in sorrow than in anger.
> (Shakespeare, *Hamlet*, I.iii.232)

Authors' Note

Ursula Hess, Department of Psychology, University of Quebec at Montreal. Reginald B. Adams, Jr., Department of Psychology, Tufts University. Robert E. Kleck, Department of Psychological and Brain Sciences, Dartmouth College. Preparation of this manuscript was supported by a grant from the Fonds de Formation des Chercheurs et l'Aide à la Recherche to Ursula Hess and Robert E. Kleck. We would like to thank Pierre Philippot for his helpful comments on a previous draft and Francois Labelle for the creation of the "aliens."

Correspondence concerning this article should be addressed to Ursula Hess, Department of Psychology, University of Quebec at Montreal, CP 8888, Station A, Montreal, QC, H3C 3P8, Canada (hess. ursula@uqam.ca).

Introduction

Humans are very sensitive to faces. Faces attract attention and have an important impact on our perception of a social interaction. Faces inform us about the gender, ethnicity, age, and state of health of our interaction partners and also convey information about their likely intelligence, maturity, dominance, sociability, and many other characteristics. In addition, human faces are able to communicate information about the emotions of others. Thus, faces provide us with important hints

33

regarding the behaviors and intentions that we may expect from our interaction partners.

It is interesting that an important aspect of emotional expressions is that they also provide social information to the decoder. In fact, Darwin already suggested that our facial musculature evolved to communicate social and specifically emotional signals (Darwin, 1872/1965). These emotion displays can signal not only the internal state of the sender (e.g., whether they are happy or sad), but they also provide information regarding the sender's understanding of the situation as well as the sender's behavioral intentions (Hess, Banse, & Kappas, 1995).

Frijda, Kuipers, and ter Shure (1989) define emotions as states of action readiness – that is, "the individual's readiness or unreadiness to engage in interaction with the environment" (Frijda et al., 1989, p. 213). These states have been operationalized with statements such as "I wanted to oppose, to assault; hurt or insult" and "I did not want to oppose, I wanted to yield to someone else's wishes" (Frijda et al., 1989). Thus, states of action readiness describe the behavioral intentions of individuals who experience an emotional state. A person who shows anger signals an intention to (aggressively) approach the offending other, whereas a person who in the same situation shows sadness, signals impuissance, and withdrawal.

This view of emotions implies that observers should be able to reverse-engineer a person's perception of an emotion-eliciting event. For example, the person showing anger should be perceived as feeling more dominant because the person sees themselves as able to address the situation at hand and go against opposition. In contrast, the person showing sadness should be perceived as submitting to the situation because they do not see how it is possible to oppose. The ghost in *Hamlet* seems, therefore, to have given up notions of revenge.

In fact, anger displays, smiling, and fear displays have been shown to be associated with dominance and affiliation. Accordingly, drawing the eyebrows together in anger leads to increased attributions of dominance, whereas smiling leads to increased attributions of affiliation (Hess, Blairy, & Kleck, 2000; Knutson, 1996). At the same time, anger expressions are perceived as threatening (e.g., Aronoff, Woike, & Hyman, 1992), whereas smiles are perceived as warm, friendly, and welcoming (e.g., Hess, Beaupré, & Cheung, 2002). Similarly, it has been argued that fear expressions elicit affiliative reactions in conspecifics (see, e.g., Bauer & Gariépy, 2001; Marsh, Ambady, & Kleck, 2005).

Yet, as mentioned previously, facial morphology is also a source of information that people use to infer dispositions and intentions related to the social motives of dominance or affiliation. For example, a square jaw, high forehead, or heavy eyebrows connote dominance (Keating, Mazur, & Segall, 1981; Senior, Phillips, Barnes, & David, 1999), whereas a rounded face with large eyes – a baby face – connotes approachability or affiliation (e.g., Berry & McArthur, 1985).

These two behavioral dispositions are of central importance for our interactions with others and their accurate perception is of high social utility. In hierarchical primate societies, highly dominant alpha individuals pose a certain threat insofar as they can claim resources (e.g., territory, food) from lower status group members (Menzel, 1973, 1974). Hence, the presence of a dominant other should lead to increased vigilance and preparedness for withdrawal (Coussi-Korbel, 1994). In contrast, affiliation is related to nurturing behaviors and should lead to approach.

Darwin (1872/1965) noted the equivalence between certain emotional behaviors in animals and more enduring morphological appearance characteristics. It is important in the present context that he proposed that piloerection and the utterance of harsh sounds by "angry" animals are "voluntarily" applied to make the animal appear larger and hence a more threatening adversary (see, e.g., pp. 95 and 104). Another example has been described by Bauer and Gariépy (2001), who observed that mice may use freezing – a juvenile behavior – as a signal to facilitate affiliative social interaction with conspecifics and thus increase sociality and communality, which may augment the chances of survival.

This suggests that emotional behavior can serve to mimic or simulate certain morphological traits linked to size or juvenescence that are important for social species. Thus, Marsh, Adams, and Kleck (2005) posit that anger and fear expressions mimic features of mature and baby faces, which in turn are associated with dominance and submissiveness. In line with the previous reasoning, they argue that anger and fear derive their signal value as a dominance cue from this feature overlap. In fact, there is evidence that humans generally tend to confuse morphological with expressive traits. Thus, Malatesta and colleagues (Malatesta, Fiore, & Messina, 1987; Malatesta, Izard, Culver, & Nicolich, 1987) found that older people are often perceived as sad based on facial-appearance cues that are simply due to old age, such as sagging corners of the eyes and mouth. This perception may lead health professionals and others to over-attribute depression to this group.

It is important to note that facial cues of dominance and affiliation are not equally distributed among the population. Rather, a number of aspects of facial appearance that lead to perceptions of dominance and affiliation are highly confounded with gender. Thus, a high forehead, a square jaw, and thicker eyebrows have been linked to perceptions of dominance and are typical for men's faces (Keating, 1985; Keating et al., 1981; Senior et al., 1999; Zebrowitz, 1997), whereas a rounded baby face is both feminine and perceived as more approachable (Berry & Brownlow, 1989) and warm (Berry & McArthur, 1986), central aspects of an affiliative or nurturing orientation.

Similarly, the perceived propensity to show emotions such as anger and happiness is also not equally distributed across the genders. In fact, one of the best documented gender stereotypes regards men's and women's emotionality. Thus, women report smiling more and are considered by others to smile more than men, and men's displays of anger have been reported to be more pervasive and are generally perceived as more acceptable (Brody & Hall, 2000; Fischer, 1993; Hall et al., 2002). Even stronger than observed differences in emotional expressivity between men and women are the stereotypical expectations that individuals hold regarding such differences. These expectations are socialized early and can have dramatic consequences for the perception of emotion in others. For example, even children as young as five years tend to consider a crying baby as "mad" when the baby is purported to be a boy but not when it is purported to be a girl (Haugh, Hoffman, & Cowan, 1980).

Two explanations for this gender stereotype have been previously proposed, one emphasizing status and the other social roles. First, Henley (1977, 1995), as well as LaFrance and Henley (1994), emphasize that women generally have less power or status than men and that smiling in women serves as a social appeasement strategy. However, evidence that low power/status is in fact linked to smiling is rather mixed. Although some authors reported evidence for more smiling by individuals with less power/status (Deutsch, 1990; Dovidio, Brown, Heltman, Ellyson, & Keating, 1988; Nagashima & Schellenberg, 1997), others either did not find such an effect or they found just the opposite: that high power/status individuals smile more (Ding & Jersild, 1932; Halberstadt & Saitta, 1987; Hall, LeBeau, Reinoso, & Thayer, 2001; Hecht & LaFrance, 1998).

Anger displays have also been linked to the notion of power. Averill (1997), for example, made the argument that anger has an "entrance requirement" of power. That is, for an anger display to be *perceived* as legitimate, the expressor has to have the power to address the anger-eliciting event successfully. This view is congruent with appraisal theories of emotion (Frijda, 1986; Scherer, 1999) that include "power potential" as a necessary requirement for anger experiences. This link between expectations regarding anger displays and status/power is also reported by Maybury (1997, cited in Shields, 2000). In this study, anger displays by high-status protagonists were judged as more appropriate, favorable, and situationally motivated than those of low- and medium-status protagonists. Similarly, Lewis (2000) found that male leaders were perceived as more competent when reacting with an angry tone of voice than when reacting with a neutral or sad tone of voice. It is interesting that when the leader was a woman, she was perceived as most competent when reacting with a neutral tone of voice, a finding most likely reflective of the somewhat lower status of women.

Thus, expectations regarding both smiling and the display of anger have been linked to the perceived power or status of the expressor. It is plausible, given these results, that differences in the perception of men's and women's penchant to show happiness or anger are directly related to the differences in power/status that are generally found between men and women.

A second explanation for the stereotypical expectations regarding appropriate emotion displays by men and women focuses on their respective social roles (e.g., Brody & Hall, 2000; Shields, 2000, 2002). Specifically, it is generally assumed that women's nurturing role favors the acquisition of superior interpersonal skills and the ability to communicate nonverbally, whereas men's roles are seen as more agentic and hence may foster more goal-directed displays (Eagly & Steffen, 1984). LaFrance and Hecht (1999, 2000) have combined these two explanations by proposing that higher power individuals simply are given more leeway to show what they feel, whereas low-status/power individuals are more strictly bound by social rules and expectations. That is, they hypothesize that one reason women are expected to smile more and show less anger is because their social roles demand them to be more affiliative and less dominant in general. However, this notion also suggests that for high-dominant women, anger displays should be perceived as appropriate in situations that can be expected to elicit anger because as high-dominant individuals, they are freer to show what they feel. Given that men in general are considered to be more dominant than women, they are also freer than women in general to show anger.

Alternatively, we expect men to show more anger because in general they have more power to redress a situation than do women.

In contrast, a low-dominant woman should be more likely to smile in a variety of circumstances because her social-role requirement is to be affiliative. At the very least, she should not show anger because she does not have the power to redress the situation that elicited the anger. In the same vein, if a man is explicitly described as affiliative, then he too should be expected to smile more than a low-affiliative individual, and a low-affiliative woman should be expected to smile less than a high-affiliative individual.

Reenter Darwin with his notions regarding a possible equivalence (in social-signal value) of facial morphology and expressive behavior, and we have yet another plausible account of perceived gender differences in emotionality. Specifically, from this point of view, the anger expression signals dominance and power as does a high forehead and square jaw, and happiness signals approachability as does a baby face. This leads to the interesting proposition that what has been described as a gender bias is a direct result of certain facial-appearance cues being generally confounded with sex. Thus, differences in perceived emotionality across men and women would be a function of the unequal distribution of facial features across genders. Put another way, in a society where the facial appearance of men and women would not differ, there would be no differential attribution of emotions to genders. This hypothesis was tested via a research program that systematically assessed the link among dominance, gender, and perceived emotionality.

Dominance, Gender, and Perceived Emotionality

As mentioned previously, when asked about the frequency of their expression of different emotions or their expectations regarding the frequency of expression by men and women, respondents attribute higher levels of emotional expressivity to women than to men, with the exception of anger, which is seen as more frequent in men (see, e.g., Fischer, 1993). This pattern is also found when participants are presented with vignettes describing a specific emotion-eliciting event (Hess, Senécal, et al., 2000). In line with these expectations, expressions from a standardized set of expressions – assuring equivalence across genders – were rated as more intense when anger was shown by a male actor and when happiness was shown by a female actor than vice versa (Hess, Blairy, & Kleck, 1997). That is, the stereotypical view that associates anger more strongly with men and happiness more strongly with women biases the perception of these emotions and is not just restricted to simple expectations of behavior. Further, we found the stereotypical expectations regarding men's and women's emotionality to be strongly normative. For example, when presented with a vignette that describes a person who just learned that their car was vandalized, participants rated the person as very likely to be angry – regardless of whether the person was described as a man or a woman (Hess, Adams, & Kleck, 2005). However, whereas a man is then expected to show this anger, a woman is expected to show sadness instead – but not if she is described as highly dominant. In this latter case, showing anger is expected for men and women equally. In a similar vein, men are expected to show less happiness unless they are described as high in affiliation, in which case they are expected to smile even more than women. In sum, the judgment of the appropriateness of showing anger or happiness was heavily dependent on the perceived dominance and affiliation of the protagonist and not just the product of gender category membership per se.

We conducted a study to specifically test the hypothesis that the perceived dominance and affiliation of men and women, which differs between the sexes, mediates the perception of emotionality. For this, three groups of participants were asked to rate a series of individuals – all displaying a neutral facial expression – regarding their likelihood to show anger, contempt, fear, sadness, disgust, happiness, and surprise, respectively. They also rated the stimuli on their level of dominance and affiliation (Hess, Adams, & Kleck, 2005). As predicted, women were perceived as more affiliative, whereas men were perceived as significantly more dominant. Further, the actors' sex was significantly correlated with their perceived disposition to show all emotions. Thus, women were expected to show more fear, sadness, surprise, and happiness, whereas men were expected to show more anger, contempt, and disgust.

This study also showed a strong relationship between perceptions of dominance and affiliation and the perceptions of the likelihood that the individual would show a given emotion. Specifically, after controlling for the influence of actor sex, perceived dominance was significantly positively related to the actors' perceived disposition to show anger, disgust, and contempt, and significantly negatively related to the actors' perceived disposition to show fear and sadness. In contrast, perceived dominance was not related to the disposition to show surprise or happiness. Conversely, and again after controlling for the effect of actor

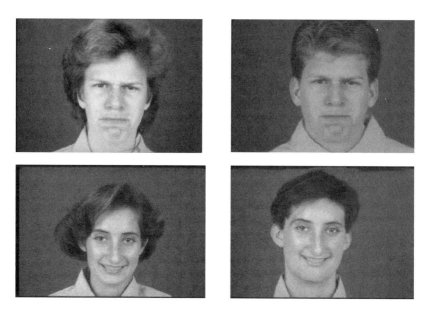

Figure 2.1. Examples for the gender manipulation of faces.

sex, perceived affiliativeness was significantly positively related to the perceived disposition to show happiness, surprise, and fear and significantly negatively related to the perceived disposition to show anger, disgust, and contempt. Mediational analyses showed that the tendency to perceive women as more likely to show happiness, surprise, sadness, and fear was, in fact, mediated by their higher perceived affiliation and lower perceived dominance, respectively. The tendency to perceive men as more prone to show anger, disgust, and contempt was partially mediated by both their higher level of perceived dominance and their lower level of perceived affiliation. That is, if men and women were perceived to be equal on these dimensions, then we would not expect observers to rate their emotionality differently.

To test this expectation experimentally, it is necessary to equate faces regarding the level of dominance and affiliation they convey. If dominance and affiliation exclusively predict emotionality, any gender differences in perceived emotionality should disappear. To equate men's and women's faces with regard to the level of dominance and affiliation they convey, we manipulated androgynous neutral faces and emotionally expressive faces to appear as either men or women (Figure 2.1).

Specifically, the interior of the face contains markers of dominance and affiliation (i.e., square jaw, heavy eyebrows), whereas hairstyle is a very potent marker of sex. Thus, by combining androgynous interior faces with male and female hairstyles, apparent men and women with identical facial appearance can be created. In one study (Adams, Hess, & Kleck, 2006, Study 4), ratings of perceived emotionality were compared for apparent male and female neutral faces. In a second study (Hess, Adams, & Kleck, 2004, Study 2), emotion ratings of posed emotional displays were compared for apparent male and female expressors. Both studies yielded parallel findings. For sadness and fear, the gender stereotypical pattern obtained. That is, apparent women were rated as more likely to express these emotions, and their expressions of these emotions were rated as more intense than was the case for the apparent men who showed the identical expression. However, for anger and happiness, a pattern opposite to the gender-stereotypical pattern was found. That is, when equated for facial appearance, apparent women were seen as more likely to show anger and less likely to show happiness, and their expressions of anger were rated as more intense just as their expressions of happiness were judged as less intense.

These data are interesting for two reasons. First, the results for sadness and fear suggest that although these emotions are correlated with perceptions of dominance and affiliation, as shown in the mediational study reported herein, facial appearance effects are not pertinent for their evaluation. Rather, the simple knowledge that a person is presumed to be a man or a woman drives both the expectancy regarding their emotionality and the bias in judgment of the expressions. These data underline the fact that it is indeed a decoder bias and not a subtle encoder difference that makes women's sadness expressions appear sadder and their fear expressions more fearful because the expressions of these two emotions were identical for apparent men and women. These biases may be due to the social-learning history of the observer, which includes both social-role and gender-linked expectations. Accordingly, the bias in ratings may be induced by both the knowledge that women are physically less strong and, therefore, plausibly more afraid of a larger range of physical fear objects or, alternatively, more likely to resign in the face of aggressive adversity, and the fact that fear and sadness are more socially accepted for women.

The second interesting issue regards the observation that in both studies, the gender-stereotypical effects for anger and happiness were not nullified, as we had predicted, but rather reversed. This reversal demands an explanation because it suggests that intrinsically, all other things being equal, women are perceived as more anger prone and less likely to be happy. Specifically, it is possible that naturally occurring gender differences in facial appearance might interact with the appearance changes produced by anger and happiness expressions. That is, anger expressions emphasize some of the features that make a face appear dominant (e.g., the mouth region often appears more square, and frowning reduces the distance between eyebrows and eyes). Conversely, smiling enhances the appearance of roundness of the faces that is associated with affiliation motivation and babyishness. Due to the construction of the present stimuli, the expressive cues for anger and happiness were not "compensated for" by gender-typical appearance (i.e., the faces were chosen to be androgynous). In some ways, one could say that by depriving the inside of the face of clear gender cues, we actually amplified the expressive cues to anger in women and happiness in men, which are normally "obscured" by the gender-typical facial appearance.

What Aliens Can Tell Us about Our Emotions

The preceding argument suggests that what has generally been described as a gender stereotype for emotionality may in the case of anger and happiness more appropriately be described as a dominance/ affiliation stereotype. Yet, at the same time, there is some evidence for the influence of gender per se, which may well reflect the influence of both social roles and beliefs about gender on expectations regarding emotionality. In fact, the experiments described previously were designed to reduce social-role effects by presenting facial expressions without context. Yet, in the vignette study reported earlier, we noted that despite being described as equally dominant, women were rated as somewhat less dominant than men in the manipulation check. That is, the manipulation of dominance appearance did not fully overcome the social-role expectancies held by participants in the study.

It has been variously noted (e.g., Eagly, 1987; Hall, Carney, & Murphy, 2002; Shields, 2002) that the child-caring requirements for women entrain a need to signal more approach and nurturance. During socialization, adherence to the norm to be "a nice girl" requires that girls not show anger but rather emotions that suggest warmth and also submissive emotions such as shame and fear. In contrast, boys are encouraged to show self-affirming emotions such as anger, contempt, and pride

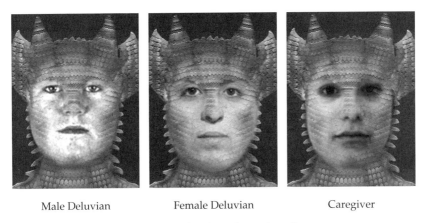

Male Deluvian   Female Deluvian   Caregiver

Figure 2.2. Examples for male, female, and caregiver aliens.

(Shields, 2002). Yet, social roles are not the only differences between sexes. Specifically, it is the case that women are physically weaker and hence should reasonably be expected to react with fear to threatening objects as well as to react with impuissance rather than aggression to antagonistic objects.

It is obviously impossible in our society to fully untangle the influence of social roles, gender, and appearance because these factors are highly correlated. Even in Western countries, men are more likely to occupy powerful social positions in politics and business; in many countries, they exclusively occupy these positions. Women not only bear children but also overwhelmingly are responsible for their upbringing, thereby assigning themselves a nurturing role.

However, it is not uncommon in science fiction to question gender roles and to imagine worlds in which these roles are different from ours. This may include the addition of genders other than male and female and the redistribution of child-rearing tasks. Therefore, we created a science fiction scenario in which a planet is inhabited by members of a race that has three genders: male, female, and caregiver. The male and female are described as exactly equal in dominant social roles, whereas the submissive and nurturing role is assigned to the caregiver, who is entirely responsible for the bearing and upbringing of the young. We varied the appearance of the members of each gender to be either high, medium, or low in dominance (Figure 2.2). Affiliation was not varied because the simultaneous manipulation of both sets of features leads to extreme-looking individuals, even in this context.

Table 2.1. *Mean Ratings for the Perceived Likelihood to Show Emotions as a Function of Facial Appearance, Social Role, and Gender*

	Dominant		Submissive		
	Mean	*SD*	*Mean*	*SD*	d
Anger	4.00	1.39	3.36	1.55	1.10
Contempt	3.53	1.75	2.92	1.68	1.33
Disgust	3.22	1.71	2.50	1.58	1.26
Happiness	3.56	3.76	3.97	1.30	0.82
Fear	2.19	1.47	2.58	1.50	0.48
Sadness	2.61	1.59	2.83	1.61	0.27
Surprise	2.67	1.33	2.78	1.27	0.25
	Agentic		Nurturing		
	Mean	*SD*	*Mean*	*SD*	d
Anger	3.68	1.35	2.36	1.61	1.93
Contempt	3.22	1.65	2.14	1.59	1.70
Disgust	2.86	1.54	2.14	1.55	1.19
Happiness	3.76	1.36	4.25	1.23	0.72
Fear	2.39	1.24	2.97	1.61	0.99
Sadness	2.72	1.38	3.25	1.44	0.71
Surprise	2.72	1.22	3.64	1.38	1.22
	Man		Woman		
	Mean	*SD*	*Mean*	*SD*	d
Anger	3.92	1.54	3.44	1.44	0.76
Contempt	3.33	1.72	3.11	1.75	0.41
Disgust	2.89	1.63	2.83	1.73	0.08
Happiness	3.53	1.48	4.00	1.41	0.64
Fear	2.31	1.39	2.47	1.59	0.20
Sadness	2.56	1.52	2.89	1.67	0.96
Surprise	2.58	1.27	2.86	1.31	0.64

When male and female participants were asked to rate the emotionality of these Aliens in terms of their likelihood to show different emotions, effects of social role, dominance, and gender emerged. Table 2.1 shows the mean ratings of the perceived likelihood to show anger, disgust, contempt, happiness, fear, sadness, and surprise. The first three are dominant, agentic, and masculine emotions, whereas the latter four are submissive, nurturing, and female emotions. The first panel of Table 2.1 compares Aliens with high-dominant facial appearance, regardless of assigned gender, to Aliens with submissive facial appearance. As expected, dominant-appearing aliens were perceived as more likely to show anger, contempt, and disgust, whereas submissive-appearing Aliens were perceived as more likely to show happiness, fear, sadness, and surprise. Effect sizes for this difference (Cohen's d) ranged from d = 0.25 for surprise to d = 1.33 for contempt. The effect sizes for the three dominant emotions were all above 1.00, thus showing the large impact of facial appearance on perceived emotionality.

The second panel of Table 2.1 shows the effect of social role. For this, ratings for the caregiver who was assigned a nurturing social role were compared with the combined ratings for male and female Aliens, regardless of dominance level. Participants rated the agentic males and females as more likely to show anger, disgust, and contempt and the nurturing caregiver as more likely to show happiness, fear, sadness, and surprise. The large effect sizes ranged from d = 0.71 for sadness to d = 1.93 for anger. Further, the largest effect sizes emerged for the agentic emotions.

Finally, we compared ratings for the male and female Aliens, regardless of facial dominance, who had both been described as agentic (see panel three of Table 2.1). The man was perceived as more likely to show anger and contempt and the woman as more likely to show happiness, fear, sadness, and surprise. Effect sizes ranged from d = 0.08 for disgust to d = 0.96 for sadness. Thus, even though both facial appearance and social role were controlled, there was still a residual impact of gender expectations. It is important that although many effect sizes for the gender effect were quite large, the average effect size for gender was only d = 0.53 compared with d = 0.79 for the facial dominance effect and d = 1.21 for the social-role effect.

These findings can only be considered suggestive of the actual variance explained by each factor. Clearly, the expectations of differing emotionality for male and female Aliens reflect the participants' learned association between gender and these emotions. Furthermore, it is, in fact, unreasonable – despite the large effect sizes for social-role expectations – to expect that these associations can be unlearned or discounted by the simple expedient of presenting a situation that presumes perfect gender equality between men and women, as was done in the previous experiment. With this caveat in mind, the results strongly suggest that in regard to expectations concerning the emotionality of our Aliens, social roles were found to be the most important factor, followed in order by dominant appearance and gender.

Equivalence Hypothesis

Results of the present research project are compatible with the notion proposed by Darwin that for behavioral traits that are pertinent to the social organism, such as dominance and affiliation, morphological and expressive features can be substituted for each other and have similar signaling functions. The results confirm a congruency between some expressive and morphological signals. The dominant individual is also an individual who has a "right" to anger displays, and the affiliative individual is expected to signal his or her approachability by smiling. However, it is clear that not all traits that a person may possess are signaled in this way. Thus, there is no evidence for facial expressions of such traits as trustworthiness or of competence even though these are also traits of great relevance to a social species. In the present context, only anger and happiness were found to be consistently signaled by morphological features. One important feature that these two emotions have in common is that they are both approach emotions. That is, the individual who is showing these emotions is displaying the intention of approaching the observer. Yet, any individual who is approached by another – especially a potentially dangerous other – has an immediate interest in discerning why exactly one is being approached.

If a conspecific is approaching affiliatively, aggressive responses to such an approach would usually be counterproductive. Likewise, not to defend oneself when the approach is aggressive in nature could be costly. If an affiliative-appearing individual approaches, one may relax one's guard; however, if a dominant individual approaches, care should be taken lest they are motivated to take away precious resources. This line of reasoning may also explain why perceptions of being prone to show fear and sadness are not influenced in the same way by perceptions of dominance and affiliation as are anger and happiness. Specifically, fear and sadness are withdrawing emotions that do not usually require immediate action by the observer.

However, as mentioned previously, both social roles and gender *category membership* have an important influence on perceived emotionality. In fact, associating fear and sadness with sex may reflect the simple fact that women, being physically less strong, are indeed more likely to be afraid in a wider variety of situations and should be more likely to withdraw from physical aggression as well. Women's social roles, which prescribe warmth and nurturance, also proscribe an aggressive stance. The degree to which emotions are susceptible to the influence of facial appearance versus social roles and gender per se was found to vary in our aliens study. Facial appearance was found to be most influential for approach emotions and to have little or no influence on withdrawing emotions. In contrast, in this study, gender per se was found to have the strongest impact on sadness.

Conclusion

Both facial appearance and gender in and of itself strongly impact our expectations regarding others' emotionality and, consequently, our perception of their emotional state. Yet, this realization also means that there are severe limits to the possible impacts of social policies on the perception of men's and women's reactions to almost all events in their lives (assuming that few things indeed are completely non-emotional in nature). In fact, although social roles (i.e., the explicit normative and socially learned rules) most amenable to rapid change seem to have the strongest impact on perceptions of emotionality, the combined impact of social-role independent gender roles and the effects of facial appearance were found to be the largest. Yet, both facial appearance and gender per se are directly or indirectly related to the physical attributes of men and women, which are unlikely to change quickly. It may be argued that we associate dominant appearance cues with male gender cues because of men's dominant social role and, conversely, women's affiliative appearance cues with female gender cues because of women's nurturing social role. However, this notion is too facile. In fact, it is unlikely that male and female gender cues are associated to dominance and affiliation because of learned expectations based on social roles. Rather, most cues to dominance that can be compared between species, such as size, posture, and gaze, are very much the same for all primates. Similarly, the two possible precursors of the human smile – the play face and the submissive bared-teeth display – both signal affiliative, nonaggressive stances in chimpanzees as does the smile. In short, the simple creation of a rule (or policy) that states that men and women are to be perceived as equal regarding their social roles is unlikely to keep people from reacting negatively to women's (affirmative) anger and to men's (affiliative) smile.

References

Adams, R. B., Jr., Hess, U., & Kleck, R. E. (2006). Emotion in the neutral face: The influence of gender-emotion stereotypes and gender-related facial appearance. Manuscript submitted for publication.

Aronoff, J., Woike, B. A., & Hyman, L. M. (1992). Which are the stimuli in facial displays of anger and happiness? Configurational bases of emotion recognition. *Journal of Personality and Social Psychology, 62*, 1050–1066.

Averill, J. R. (1997). The emotions: An integrative approach. In R. Hogan, J. A. Johnson, & S. R. Briggs (Eds.), *Handbook of personality psychology* (pp. 513–541). San Diego, CA: Academic Press.

Bauer, D. J., & Gariépy, J. L. (2001). The functions of freezing in the social interactions of juvenile high- and low-aggressive mice. *Aggressive Behavior, 27*, 463–475.

Berry, D. S., & Brownlow, S. (1989). Were the physiognomists right? Personality correlates of facial babyishness. *Personality and Social Psychology Bulletin, 15*, 266–279.

Berry, D. S., & McArthur, L. Z. (1985). Some components and consequences of a babyface. *Journal of Personality and Social Psychology, 48*, 312–323.

Berry, D. S., & McArthur, L. Z. (1986). Perceiving character in faces: The impact of age-related craniofacial changes on social perception. *Psychological Bulletin, 100*, 3–10.

Brody, L. R., & Hall, J. A. (2000). Gender, emotion, and expression. In M. Lewis & J. M. Haviland (Eds.), *Handbook of emotions, 2nd ed.* (pp. 447–460). New York: Guilford Press.

Coussi-Korbel, S. (1994). Learning to outwit a competitor in mangabeys (*Cercocebus torquatus torquatus*). *Journal of Comparative Psychology, 108*, 164–171.

Darwin, C. (1872/1965). *The expression of the emotions in man and animals.* Chicago: The University of Chicago Press. (Originally published 1872).

Deutsch, F. M. (1990). Status, sex, and smiling: The effect of smiling in men and women. *Personality and Social Psychology Bulletin 16*, 531–540.

Ding, G. F., & Jersild, A. T. (1932). A study of the laughing and smiling of preschool children. *Journal of Genetic Psychology, 40*, 452–472.

Dovidio, J. F., Brown, C. E., Heltman, K., Ellyson, S. L., & Keating, C. F. (1988). Power displays between women and men in discussions of gender-linked tasks: A multichannel study. *Personality and Social Psychology, 55*, 580–587.

Eagly, A. H. (1987). *Sex differences in social behavior: A social-role interpretation.* Hillsdale, NJ: Lawrence Erlbaum Associates.

Eagly, A. H., & Steffen, V. J. (1984). Gender stereotypes stem from the distribution of women and men into social roles. *Journal of Personality and Social Psychology, 46*, 735–754.

Fischer, A. H. (1993). Sex differences in emotionality: Fact or stereotype? *Feminism & Psychology, 3*, 303–318.

Frijda, N. (1986). *The emotions.* Cambridge, UK: Cambridge University Press.

Frijda, N. H., Kuipers, P., & ter Shure, E. (1989). Relations among emotion appraisal and emotional action readiness. *Journal of Personality and Social Psychology, 57*, 212–228.

Halberstadt, A. G., & Saitta, M. B. (1987). Gender, nonverbal behavior, and perceived dominance: A test of the theory. *Journal of Personality and Social Psychology, 53*, 257–272.

Hall, J. A., Carney, D. R., & Murphy, N. A. (2002). Gender differences in smiling. In M. H. Abel (Ed.), *An empirical reflection on the smile* (pp. 155–185). New York: The Edwin Mellen Press.

Hall, J. A., LeBeau, L. S., Reinoso, J. G., & Thayer, F. (2001). Status, gender, and nonverbal behavior in candid and posed photographs: A study of conversations between university employees. *Sex Roles, 44*, 677–692.

Haugh, S. S., Hoffman, C. D., & Cowan, G. (1980). The eye of the very young beholder: Sex typing of infants by young children. *Child Development, 51*, 598–600.

Hecht, M. A., & LaFrance, M. (1998). License or obligation to smile: The effect of power and sex on amount and type of smiling. *Personality and Social Psychology Bulletin, 24*, 1332–1342.

Henley, N. M. (1977). *Body politics: Power, sex and nonverbal communication.* New York: Prentice Hall.

Henley, N. M. (1995). Body politics revisited: What do we know today? In P. J. Kalbfleisch & M. J. Cody (Eds.), *Gender, power, and communication in human relationships* (pp. 27–61). Hillsdale, NJ: Lawrence Erlbaum Associates.

Hess, U., Adams, R. B., Jr., & Kleck, R. E. (2004). Facial appearance, gender, and emotion expression. *Emotion, 4*, 378–388.

Hess, U., Adams, R. B., Jr., & Kleck, R. E. (2005). Who may frown and who should smile? Dominance, affiliation, and the display of happiness and anger. *Cognition and Emotion, 19*, 515–536.

Hess, U., Beaupré, M. G., & Cheung, N. (2002). Who to whom and why – cultural differences and similarities in the function of smiles. In M. Abel (Ed.), *An empirical reflection on the smile* (pp. 187–216). New York: The Edwin Mellen Press.

Hess, U., Blairy, S., & Kleck, R. E. (1997). The intensity of emotional facial expressions and decoding accuracy. *Journal of Nonverbal Behavior, 21*, 241–257.

Hess, U., Blairy, S., & Kleck, R. E. (2000). The influence of expression intensity, gender, and ethnicity on judgments of dominance and affiliation. *Journal of Nonverbal Behavior, 24*, 265–283.

Hess, U., Kappas, A., & Banse, R. (1995). The intensity of facial expressions is determined by underlying affective state and social situation. *Journal of Personality and Social Psychology, 69*, 280–288.

Hess, U., Senécal, S., Kirouac, G., Herrera, P., Philippot, P., & Kleck, R. E. (2000). Emotional expressivity in men and women: Stereotypes and self-perceptions. *Cognition and Emotion*, 609–642.

Keating, C. F. (1985). Human dominance signals: The primate in us. In S. L. Ellyson & J. F. Dovidio (Eds.), *Power, dominance, and nonverbal communication* (pp. 89–108). New York: Springer Verlag.

Keating, C. F., Mazur, A., & Segall, M. H. (1981). A cross-cultural exploration of physiognomic traits of dominance and happiness. *Ethnology and Sociobiology, 2*, 41–48.

Knutson, B. (1996). Facial expressions of emotion influence interpersonal trait inferences. *Journal of Nonverbal Behavior, 20*, 165–182.

LaFrance, M., & Hecht, M. A. (1999). Option or obligation to smile: The effects of power and gender on facial expression. In P. Phillipot, R. S. Feldman, & E. J. Coats (Eds.), *The social context of nonverbal behavior* (pp. 45–70). Cambridge, UK: Cambridge University Press.

LaFrance, M., & Hecht, M. A. (2000). Gender and smiling: A meta-analysis. In A. H. Fischer (Ed.), *Gender and emotion: Social psychological perspectives* (pp. 118–142). Cambridge, UK: Cambridge University Press.

LaFrance, M., & Henley, N. M. (1994). On oppressing hypotheses: Or differences in nonverbal sensitivity revisited. In H. L. Radtke & H. J. Stam (Eds.), *Power/gender: Social relations in theory and practice. Inquiries in social construction* (pp. 287–311). London: Sage Publications.

Lewis, K. M. (2000). When leaders display emotion: How followers respond to negative emotional expression of male and female leaders. *Journal of Organizational Behavior, 21,* 221–234.

Malatesta, C. Z., Fiore, M. J., & Messina, J. J. (1987). Affect, personality, and facial expressive characteristics of older people. *Psychology and Aging, 2,* 64–69.

Malatesta, C. Z., Izard, C. E., Culver, C., & Nicolich, M. (1987). Emotion communication skills in young, middle-aged, and older women. *Psychology and Aging, 2,* 193–203.

Marsh, A. A., Adams, R. B., Jr., & Kleck, R. E. (2005). Why do fear and anger look the way they do? Form and social function in facial expressions. *Personality and Social Psychological Bulletin, 31,* 73–86.

Marsh, A. A., Ambady, N., & Kleck, R. E. (2005). The effects of fear and anger facial expressions on approach- and avoidance-related behaviors. *Emotion, 5,* 119–124.

Maybury, K. K. (1997). *The influence of status and sex on observer judgments of anger displays.* Unpublished doctoral dissertation. University of California, Davis.

Menzel, E. W., Jr. (1973). Leadership and communication in young chimpanzees. In E. W. Menzel Jr. (Ed.), *Precultural primate behavior* (pp. 192–225). Basel, Switzerland: Karger.

Menzel, E. W., Jr. (1974). A group of young chimpanzees in a one-acre field. In A. M. Schrier & F. Stollnitz (Eds.), *Behavior of nonhuman primates* (pp. 83–153). San Diego, CA: Academic Press.

Nagashima, K., & Schellenberg, J. A. (1997). Situational differences in intentional smiling: A cross-cultural exploration. *Journal of Social Psychology, 137,* 297–301.

Scherer, K. R. (1999). Appraisal theory. In T. Dalgleish & M. J. Power (Eds.), *Handbook of cognition and emotion* (pp. 637–663). Chichester, UK: John Wiley & Sons, Ltd.

Senior, C., Phillips, M. L., Barnes, J., & David, A. S. (1999). An investigation into the perception of dominance from schematic faces: A study using the World-Wide Web. *Behavior Research Methods, Instruments and Computers, 31,* 341–346.

Shields, S. A. (2000). Thinking about gender, thinking about theory: Gender and emotional experience. In A. H. Fischer (Ed.), *Gender and emotion: Social psychological perspectives* (pp. 3–23). Cambridge, UK: Cambridge University Press.

Shields, S. A. (2002). *Speaking from the heart.* Cambridge, UK: Cambridge University Press.

Zebrowitz, L. A. (1997). *Reading faces: Window to the soul?* Boulder, CO: Westview Press.

3. It Takes One to Know One Better

Controversy about the Cultural Ingroup Advantage in Communicating Emotion as a Theoretical Rather Than Methodological Issue

Hillary Anger Elfenbein

Author's Note

This chapter benefited from the helpful comments of Ursula Hess, Abigail Marsh, and Pierre Philippot, as well as from continuing debate with David Matsumoto. I thank Nalini Ambady for her many contributions over the years. Preparation of this chapter was supported by the National Institute of Mental Health Behavioral Science Track Award for Rapid Transition 1R03MH071294-1.

Correspondence can be directed to Hillary Anger Elfenbein at hillary@post.harvard.edu or by post at F-543 Haas School, University of California, Berkeley, CA 94720.

As in many areas within psychology, over time the nature-versus-nurture debate about the expression and perception of emotion has gradually given way to a more balanced perspective arguing for the importance of both nature *and* nurture – neither to the exclusion of the other. This chapter focuses on one recent and controversial area of research on universals and cultural differences in the communication of emotion: the presence of an ingroup advantage, whereby individuals can more easily and accurately understand emotional expressions originating from members of their own cultural group rather than expressions originating from members of a different cultural group.

There has been controversy about how to interpret empirical findings of the ingroup advantage. Although the controversy has often been framed in terms of a methodological debate about the underlying empirical research (Matsumoto, 2002), close examination of the issue reveals its source to be a subtle yet important theoretical divide (Elfenbein & Ambady, 2002a, 2003b). With the goal of moving the conversation forward, this chapter aims to describe the broad agreement between the theories as well as the specific area of disagreement that leads researchers to endorse differences in methodological requirements – and even, on other occasions, to endorse identical research designs and analytic strategies while differently interpreting their findings.

Two main theoretical perspectives – decoding rules and dialect theory – attempt to account for empirical findings of cultural differences in the accuracy of recognizing emotional expressions. As a starting point, both agree that there is broad universality in emotion, in that individuals across cultures are highly accurate in recognizing facial expressions of emotion. Further, both agree that there is evidence that accuracy is relatively greater when expressions and perceivers are from the same – rather than different – cultural backgrounds. Where they differ is by offering competing accounts for this ingroup advantage. According to decoding-rule theory, the ingroup advantage results from culturally acquired biases on the part of perceivers. Thus, from this perspective, on a methodological level, the appearance of emotional expressions must be equivalent across cultures when examining the ingroup advantage in order to reveal the effects of perception processes alone.

By contrast, according to dialect theory, the ingroup advantage is not an effect of perception alone but rather occurs from the matching of perceivers with culturally familiar styles of emotional expression, which they can understand more effectively than culturally unfamiliar expressive styles. Thus, from this perspective, on a methodological level, the possibility that individuals from different cultures may choose to express their emotions using subtly different styles should not be controlled away – rather, it is a noteworthy phenomenon that is part of the investigation. Indeed, the dialect explanation for the ingroup advantage relies on the presence of such differences in the appearance of emotional expressions. Simply put, the point of disagreement between the two perspectives boils down to the question of whether one considers cultural differences in the expression of emotion to be an artifact versus a phenomenon.

This chapter begins by summarizing the recent evidence for the ingroup advantage, as well as the critiques that have been made of this evidence. Outlining the nature of the controversy reveals that it follows from differences in the underlying explanation of the impact of culture on the perception of emotion. The presence of empirical results that are not accounted for by previously accepted theories – for example, decoding-rules explanations for cross-cultural differences in emotion-recognition accuracy – suggests a need for refinements to those theories.

The chapter ends with suggestions and an open invitation to join a research agenda aiming to provide a balanced foundation for further work in the area.

Initial Cross-Cultural Research on Emotion Recognition: Focusing on One Group at a Time

Broadly speaking, psychologists agree that emotional expressions can be recognized at above-chance levels across cultures, based on classic research from the 1960s demonstrating that participants around the world could make multiple-choice judgments of the intended basic emotional states portrayed in posed photographs (Ekman, 1972; Izard, 1971). Such studies contribute to the foundation of theories arguing that communicating via emotional signals is a universal phenomenon and that this skill has a basis that is at least partly evolutionary and biological rather than completely learned.

However, newer work also moves beyond establishing this basic universality and explores cross-cultural differences as well. In fact, the seeds of this work can be found in the original classic studies, given that extensive cross-cultural differences were visible in the same data used to establish universality. At the same time that numerous cultural groups achieved recognition-accuracy rates greater than that predicted from chance-guessing, these rates appeared to vary substantially across cultures. Although the original researchers were not interested in exploring these trends in their own data due to their exclusive focus on universals (Matsumoto & Assar, 1992), later reviews of this research suggested systematic differences in the accuracy levels achieved by members of various cultural groups when judging emotional expressions originating primarily from the United States (Elfenbein & Ambady, 2002b; Matsumoto, 1989; Russell, 1994).

Two initial attempts to explain this phenomenon focused exclusively on the perceiver of the emotional expressions. Matsumoto (1989) argued that members of collectivistic cultural groups use "decoding rules" (Buck, 1984) that purposely inhibit their ability to understand emotion. Such groups arguably perceive emotion universally, but they deny their comprehension, particularly of negative expressions that threaten to damage social harmony. With a different explanation also focusing on perceivers alone – noting that accuracy was lower for individuals judging members from a visibly foreign cultural group – some researchers labeled these cross-cultural differences as ethnic bias

(Kilbride & Yarczower, 1983; Markham & Wang, 1996). They argued that lesser accuracy resulted from lesser motivation to judge expressions from cultural outgroup members. Thus, until recently, cultural differences in recognition accuracy were generally interpreted via theoretical frameworks that emphasized the role of the perceiver alone and, consequently, focused on the role of one cultural group at a time.

New Perspectives: Focusing on the Interaction between Perceiver and Perceived

In contrast to explaining cultural differences in emotion-recognition accuracy by focusing exclusively on the perceiver, my colleagues and I tried to think about both the expressor and the perceiver at the same time, in terms of the match between them. This made sense to us in light of the empirical evidence we had amassed from the cumulated work of past researchers, in a meta-analysis combining the results of 97 studies with 182 different samples and a total of more than 22,000 participants (Elfenbein & Ambady, 2002b). These studies included the classic research on universality and newer work on culture and emotion, as well as cross-cultural studies inadvertently conducted by researchers who borrowed stimulus materials across cultural boundaries. First, there was a strong replication of the classic finding that emotional expressions could be recognized across cultures in multiple-choice designs at accuracy rates exceeding those due to chance-guessing alone. However, this observation alone ensures only basic rather than complete universality of the process of recognizing emotions (Russell, 1994). Further, we found a systematic ingroup advantage, in that participants were generally more accurate when making within-culture judgments than they were when making cross-cultural judgments of emotion. This is a relative finding, in that it appears when controlling for the main effects that may also exist in emotion judgments across expressor and perceiver groups. For example, certain stimuli may be universally clearer – for example, if the researchers from that culture used more extensive validation procedures or if members of certain ethnic backgrounds have facial features that make it easier to view the contours of emotional expressions.[1] Likewise, some judges may be more accurate overall in emotion recognition – for example, if the participant groups are not

---

[1] The author thanks Ursula Hess for the latter suggestion.

fully matched in terms of comfort and familiarity with experimental protocols or education levels, which might occur despite researchers' intentions to recruit equivalent samples across cultural groups. To control for such effects, the ingroup advantage is most appropriately examined as an interaction between expressor and perceiver controlling for main effects of expressor and perceiver groups.

We searched for many explanations for this ingroup-advantage effect. First, methodological differences across studies did not significantly moderate the size of the ingroup advantage. The effect replicated across any particular methodological factor – such as the research team, the spontaneous versus posed or imitated nature of stimuli, the nonverbal channel of communication (i.e., facial expressions, tone of voice, and body language) – suggesting a robust nature to the effect. Artifacts such as translation difficulties also did not appear to create the effect, given that the ingroup advantage also existed across cultural groups speaking the same language.

Suggesting the importance of the match between the expressors and the perceivers of emotional signals, the only significant moderator of the ingroup advantage was the degree of cross-cultural exposure and communication between the two groups. Cultural groups that were physically closer and that had relatively more telephone traffic between them tended also to have a lesser ingroup-advantage barrier in understanding each other's emotional expressions. Likewise, ethnic groups living together within a single nation – presumably with relatively greater daily exposure than cultural groups living in separate nations – showed much less ingroup advantage. In fact, often they did not show an ingroup advantage at all, particularly given that minority groups often showed a relative advantage in understanding the emotional expressions of outgroup majority members. Further, we stated clearly that we did not include gender differences as an element of culture. However, in light of Matsumoto's (see Chapter 7, this volume) speculation that the ingroup advantage must also incorporate gender, one would predict – given these findings – that the daily exposure and richness of cross-group contact between men and women would all but erase any ingroup advantage if one had originally existed.

Furthermore, we found that the empirical evidence did not support either of the two earlier explanations that were posited exclusively in terms of perceivers, decoding rules, and ethnic bias. To the question of decoding rules, collectivistic cultural groups did not appear to be universally poor at emotion recognition, but rather they performed poorly only when they took part in research originating elsewhere. For example, whereas Japanese participants were outperformed on American-made research tasks and stimuli (e.g., Matsumoto, 1989), they outperformed Americans and other Western groups on research tasks and stimuli created in Japan by Japanese researchers (e.g., Hatta & Nachshon, 1988; Sogon & Masutani, 1989). Such patterns argued strongly for the importance of the match between perceiver and expressor rather than a focus on the perceiver alone. Addressing concerns of ethnic bias – or even anxiety in judging foreign expressors – the ingroup advantage was also found in numerous studies in which the ethnicity of emotional expressors was not visibly different or unfamiliar: for example, in studies of facial expressions and body language including multiple Caucasian groups (e.g., Rosenthal, Hall, DiMatteo, Rogers, & Archer, 1979). In such studies, arguably there were few or no cues to suggest foreignness outside of the appearance of the emotional expressions themselves. Again, this suggested that previously hypothesized factors relating to the perceiver alone – although they could certainly exist – were not solely responsible for these cross-cultural differences in emotional-perception accuracy.

Taken together, these results were suggestive of a role for cultural learning in the understanding of emotion. The most parsimonious explanation, accounting for this body of research findings, suggested that there are subtle differences across cultures in the style of emotional expression – even though the basic expression of emotion is universal – and that individuals are better able to understand emotions expressed in a similar or otherwise familiar style. This is the core of a speculative new "dialect theory" of emotional communication: that cultures use subtly different dialects of a universal emotional language. This perspective incorporates the evidence that individuals are more accurate with emotional expressions matched from their own culture, as well as those from a culture that is more physically near or with which theirs has greater contact. This perspective also incorporates evidence that members of collectivistic cultures perform well on experimental tasks originating in their own nation, even if they perform less well in tasks originating elsewhere. Further, this perspective accounts for why the ingroup advantage is still found in research in which participants cannot even detect that the stimulus materials originate from a foreign culture, which limits the role of bias – for example, in the work conducted with multiple Caucasian groups – because the style of expression can differ subtly, whether or not the participant is aware of the source of the difference.

This background helps to make sense of the theoretical difference between dialect and decoding-rule theories. In evaluating evidence for the ingroup advantage, Matsumoto (see Chapter 7, this volume) writes, "one cannot be sure that judgment differences reflected differences in judgments or were due to differences in the stimuli being judged" (p. 147). I argue that this is a false dichotomy: Simply put, a true ingroup advantage is not a decoding effect. Rather, it results from the matching of cultural differences in decoding processes with cultural differences in emotional-expression processes. To argue that cultural differences in judgments and expressions are "inextricably confounded" with each other presupposes that there is a reason to study the two processes only in the absence of each other. To the contrary: the ingroup advantage in judgments appears to reflect greater ingroup familiarity with culturally specific forms of emotional expression. Thus, my colleagues and I do not want to avoid this so-called confound; rather, we want to embrace it.

This said, it is important to note the broad areas of common ground between dialect and decoding-rule theories, in that both argue that any differences in the appearance of emotional expressions across cultures are only subtle variations on a universal theme. Dialect theory assumes there is high consistency in emotional expressions across cultures, given that emotion is a universal language of which cultural differences are merely dialects – for example, as similar as British and American English. Thus, research findings demonstrating high correlations in the style of emotional expression across cultures are consistent with dialect theory and do not detract from it. Likewise, the ability of perceivers from different cultural groups to achieve high levels of accuracy in recognizing prototypical displays of emotion also fits comfortably within both decoding and dialect theories. Given that cultural differences in appearance are merely subtle, emotional expressions are still largely recognizable to perceivers from foreign cultures – even if the perceivers themselves might produce a slightly different display. That is, the universal *recognition* of particular expressions does not guarantee their identical and spontaneous universal *production*. After all, when listening to a person speaking a different dialect of our language, we might understand words or expressions that we would not necessarily use in our own conversations.

In addition to this meta-analysis examining the past work of others, my colleagues and I have conducted new empirical work further exploring some of these intriguing patterns. Examining the role of cultural learning in a sample of students with varying exposure to China and the United States who viewed stimuli from both regions (Elfenbein & Ambady, 2003c) – Chinese in China, Chinese in the United States, Chinese Americans, and Americans of non-Chinese ancestry – we found that participants were faster and more accurate in judging expressions with the more exposure they had to the cultural group in which the expressions originated. That is, the relative advantage in perceiving U.S. stimuli was greatest for Americans of non-Chinese ancestry, next for Chinese Americans, next for Chinese in the United States, and least for Chinese in China. Along the same lines, Tibetans residing in China were faster and more accurate when judging Chinese rather than U.S. expressions, and Africans residing in the United States were faster and more accurate when judging U.S. rather than Chinese expressions. In both of these cases, then, groups more efficiently judged emotions originating in their host versus non-host society. A corresponding effect even extended across generations for Chinese Americans, in that participants who themselves had immigrated from China showed only a small advantage in judging stimuli from the United States rather than China, whereas those whose families had been in the United States for decades showed a much larger advantage when judging U.S. stimuli. It is worth noting that to provide a valid test according to dialect theory, we paired stimuli representing prototypical expressions developed within the United States (Ekman & Friesen, 1976) with those developed within China (Wang & Markham, 1999) to provide the potential for stimulus nonequivalence in that the style of emotional expressions could contain culturally acquired dialects.

Other work addressed the hypothesis that subtle cross-cultural differences in emotional-expression style are responsible for the ingroup advantage in recognition accuracy. In Elfenbein, Mandal, Ambady, Harizuka, and Kumar (2004), we used facial expressions from India, Japan, and the United States that were composites created from the left and right facial hemispheres of a single set of photographs. Results showed that the ingroup advantage was greater for left than for right hemifacial composites. The only plausible explanation for such a finding is that the ingroup advantage results from subtle differences in the appearance of stimuli because, presumably, perceiver biases and other perceiver attributes are all held constant when a person judges both sides of another person's face. Certainly, observers could be more anxious when judging the faces of expressors who are foreign or unfamiliar (see Matsumoto, current volume). However, such an effect should be equally strong when judging both sides of another person's face and, therefore, would be controlled for by using such a research design. Any effects or artifacts associated with the posers themselves – such as ethnic facial features, hairstyle, jewelry, and skin pigmentation – are also controlled in that they should be equivalent for both sides of the same person's face. Because the appearance of facial expressions was the only factor that changed across the two hemifacial conditions, the appearance of facial expressions must be related to the cross-cultural differences in their judgment.

These findings also fit with data from other researchers showing that the ingroup advantage disappears in cases when stimulus materials from different groups are constrained to have an identical appearance across cultures. For example, Biehl et al. (1997) did not find the ingroup advantage when using the Japanese and Caucasian Facial Expressions of Emotion (JACFEE) set of stimuli in which Caucasian Americans, Japanese Americans, and Japanese posers were all instructed to move precisely the same muscles rather than to pose unconstrained emotional expressions. Although the JACFEE is a valid portrayal of universal prototypes of emotional expression, by its very design the careful process of ensuring identical portrayals of emotions across cultural groups erases cross-cultural differences in expressive style. Likewise, Beaupré and Hess (2005) did not find the ingroup advantage when they collected facial expressions from French, Chinese, and African Canadians using a directed facial-action task that resulted in identical expressions from members of all three cultural groups. If one takes a theoretical perspective such as decoding-rules theory – in which the ingroup advantage is a perceptual bias originating from the perceivers alone – then such empirical findings would appear to cast doubt on the ingroup advantage. However, to the contrary, when adopting a dialect perspective, such findings do not argue against the existence of the ingroup advantage; rather, they support the explanation that the ingroup advantage results from cross-cultural differences in the style of emotional expression. Without such differences in style, the apparent mechanism – the ingroup advantage – disappears. Thus, research that has null findings for the ingroup advantage when stimuli are identical across cultures supports the notion that the ingroup advantage results from subtle cross-cultural differences in the appearance of emotional expressions. Furthermore, such work speaks against the idea that the ingroup advantage results from processes on the part of perceivers alone, such as bias or lesser motivation to understand members of a visibly different culture. After all, such factors – which would explain the ingroup advantage using a different mechanism other than that posited by dialect theory – do not appear empirically to cause a noticeable ingroup advantage in studies that use the JACFEE or other stimuli that erase cultural differences in expression.

The dialect theory of emotion is still new and emerging, driven mainly by the need to account for the empirical data on the ingroup advantage. The evidence strongly suggests that cultural differences in expressive style drive cultural differences in judgment accuracy – thus, explaining findings that relate to the perception of emotion also casts the expressor as an essential actor.

Controversy about the Ingroup Advantage: Theory, Not Methods

The emerging dialect theory – and, indeed, the ingroup advantage phenomenon more broadly – has not been without controversy. In fact, the meta-analysis documenting the ingroup advantage (Elfenbein & Ambady, 2002b) was published along with a critique (Matsumoto, 2002), as well as a rejoinder to the critique (Elfenbein & Ambady, 2002a). In his critique, Matsumoto (2002) focused on three asserted "methodological requirements" to believe the evidence for the ingroup advantage. First, he argues that studies should use balanced designs, in which members of each culture view stimuli equally from members of their own and each other group in the study. The second requirement is "stimulus equivalence"; that is, stimuli from different cultures should express emotion identically. The third is that a meta-analysis of such studies should include a measure of the clarity or intensity level of stimuli.

Referring to these features as "requirements" suggests a certain level of agreement about the methods that are necessary and desirable for investigating cultural differences in the understanding of emotion. However, there are, indeed, widely varying opinions about the optimal methods for use more generally in the scientific study of nonverbal behavior (e.g., Ekman, 1994; Izard, 1994; Nowicki & Duke, 2001; Rosenthal et al., 1979; Russell, 1994). Given this diversity in opinion, referring to any set of opinions as requirements can create confusion and misinterpretations for readers interested in understanding the state of evidence – in this case, for the ingroup advantage. Arguing, for example, that "researchers interested in promoting such claims should give consideration to these methodological requirements to test for it" (Matsumoto, this volume, p. 178) implies that the scientific evidence to date is not sufficient to document the key finding that individuals are more accurate in understanding emotional expressions originating from members of their own cultural group.

In fact, as described herein, the first and third of these features are already met by the larger body of research findings, and the second feature is the subject of theoretical disagreement. To the first feature, balanced designs appear to demonstrate perceivers' relative advantage in understanding emotional expressions originating from members of their own cultural group. Further, my colleagues and I took precautions (described in detail in the original paper) to ensure that the unbalanced designs examined served to replicate the results we found with their balanced counterparts (Elfenbein & Ambady, 2002b). These precautions included a statistical test confirming no significant difference between the size of the ingroup advantage in balanced versus unbalanced designs. Thus, we concluded that the limited use we made of unbalanced studies did not account for the finding of a relative ingroup advantage in emotion recognition. To the third feature, the issue of examining stimulus-clarity levels, we coded the closest variable reported by the original researchers – whether or not authors used a consensus sample to ensure a minimum level of stimulus clarity, and this variable did not make a difference in the size of the ingroup advantage. Further, we used a heterogeneity analysis to document that there was not excessive variance left to require explanation via additional moderating variables.

As for the second feature, stimulus equivalence, I argue that referring to the opinion that this is necessary – or, indeed, desirable – as a methodological requirement is troublesome and obscures the underlying issue. It distracts attention by focusing the debate about the ingroup advantage on methods rather than the related theoretical differences among researchers that drive them as a consequence to use different methods. Researchers who rely on subtly different models of emotion can disagree about which methods are optimal to address which questions. Matsumoto argues that an ingroup advantage results from bias on the part of perceivers – that is, from decoding rules alone. If the ingroup advantage is exclusively a bias on the part of perceivers, then certainly any difference in the appearance of emotional expressions across cultural groups represents a confounding factor when studying the effect. Thus, it makes sense from Matsumoto's perspective that one must have stimulus equivalence as a methodological requirement in studying the ingroup advantage. By contrast, my colleagues and I have argued that the ingroup advantage is a consequence of perceivers being more accurate when they judge emotions expressed in a more familiar style. The ingroup advantage results from matching norms for displays with norms for decoding. Thus, from this perspective, stimulus equivalence is detrimental rather than necessary to examine the phenomenon. Requiring stimuli to be equivalent across cultures would deny the possibility that people from different cultures may express their emotions differently. If the ingroup advantage results from differential familiarity with expressive styles, then requiring expressive styles to be identical should dissipate the effect. For this reason, arguing that cultural differences in the perception of emotion result directly from cultural differences in the expression of emotion, researchers adopting dialect theory would attempt to ensure the opposite: stimulus nonequivalence.

These competing theoretical accounts help to explain why researchers taking different theoretical perspectives can also endorse the same research designs yet offer different interpretations of particular findings. As described earlier, Biehl et al. (1997) and Beaupré and Hess (2005) did not find an ingroup advantage in studies using stimulus materials that were constrained to have an identical appearance regardless of the cultural background of the posers. Whereas Matsumoto's (2002) interpretation would regard such data as evidence that the ingroup advantage does not exist, as described earlier, my colleagues and I interpret these data as evidence that the ingroup advantage is caused by cross-cultural differences in emotional-expression style. Thus, the two theoretical perspectives share the common ground of agreeing that stimulus nonequivalence is the likely cause of the ingroup advantage. However, based on the perspective taken, one can conclude that this is either a methodological artifact, as Matsumoto has argued, or a core finding, as my colleagues and I have argued. Thus, at its core, this is a conversation about theory. With issues of theory and methods intertwined, arguing about the soundness of methods alone serves as a distraction and tends to hinder further understanding and development in this area.

Alternate Perspectives to Account for Cultural Differences in Emotion Recognition

Because currently accepted theories of the communication of emotion do not yet fully account for the body of empirical evidence discussed previously, it is a worthwhile pursuit to refine these theories in light of this evidence. The door is wide open, and the field would benefit from fresh contributions in this area.

Empirical Observations That Alternate Theories Must Explain

The only constraint on new theoretical development is that it must account for the existing data. In particular, there were two central empirical findings relating to the ingroup advantage, discussed previously, that inspired the initial development of a dialect theory. The first is that any explanation of an ingroup advantage must address not only the perceiver but also the match between the perceiver and the expressor of emotion. After all, evidence on the ingroup advantage demonstrates that accuracy is relatively higher when individuals judge expressions from members of their own cultural group; therefore, it matters not only who is doing the judging but also their match or mismatch with who is being judged.

The second empirical finding to be explained by any new theoretical perspective is that the cultural differences that cause the ingroup advantage must somehow be contained within the appearance of the emotional expressions themselves. Because studies have demonstrated that the ingroup advantage is impacted by changes only in the properties of stimulus materials, then logically the ingroup advantage must result from cues contained within these materials. In the example discussed earlier regarding multiple Caucasian groups judging American facial expressions and body language (e.g., Rosenthal et al., 1979), Americans could only have outperformed other groups if there was something particularly American about the stimuli.

No Evidence for a Decoding-Rules Explanation
of Cross-Cultural Differences in Accuracy

Although the door is wide open to alternative accounts other than dialect theory, there is evidence arguing against some of the particular alternatives already proposed. Specifically, the current body of data argues strongly against a decoding-rules explanation of cross-cultural differences in emotion-recognition accuracy. Decoding rules surely exist in many contexts and circumstances and they may explain other phenomena, but they simply cannot provide an explanation for the ingroup advantage.

First, when focusing only on the perceiver, evidence on decoding rules breaks down. As discussed previously, the same collectivist groups supposedly employing decoding rules to depress their emotion-recognition performance actually outperform others when taking part in studies developed by researchers within their home country. Further, a decoding-rules explanation cannot explain results in terms of the match between perceiver and expressor. To use decoding rules to explain an ingroup advantage would require that these performance-reducing rules operate more strongly when judging members of a foreign cultural group. However, the theoretical framework behind decoding rules would suggest exactly the *opposite*: that the goal of preserving harmony fostered by overlooking the negative expression of emotion is *more* salient and valuable within an ingroup context. In fact, our own empirical findings documented an ingroup advantage alongside a tendency to attribute greater *positivity* when making judgments of outgroup members (Elfenbein, Mandal, Ambady, Harizuka, & Kumar, 2002), further arguing that the hypothesized form of decoding rules does not appear to explain the ingroup advantage. Even studies attempting to connect decoding rules and emotion-recognition accuracy across cultural groups appear to depend on the artifact of using data primarily collected using stimuli from the United States. In Matsumoto (1989), significant correlations were found between emotion-recognition accuracy and cultural profiles by country (Hofstede, 2001). However, in Elfenbein and Ambady (2003a), we found that these correlations did not vary across individual emotions nor across positive versus negative valence – a central prediction of decoding-rules theory, which argues that specific profiles on cultural dimensions are associated with specific sensitivity to particular types of emotion (Matsumoto, 1989; Schimmack, 1996). Rather, the pattern of correlations in Elfenbein and Ambady (2003a) was more consistent with a cultural similarity argument, whereby emotion-recognition accuracy was greater for groups that were more similar in their cultural profile to that of the group in which the research stimuli originated.

Although the decoding-rules explanation frequently appears in discussions on the topic of cross-cultural differences in emotion-recognition accuracy, empirical research has not tested directly that the presence or absence of such rules predicts differences in accuracy. Rather, supporters generally infer the rules from the lower performance frequently attained by participants from cultures visibly different from the United States and Europe. Given an alternative explanation for this empirical observation – that of cultural match versus mismatch between emotional expressors and perceivers, along with the generation of most research tasks in the United States and Europe – it is time for empirical data to support directly the claims made in the name of decoding rules or else for an alternative explanation to supersede them.

Future Directions

As stated previously, there is an open door for further theoretical development to refine current theories on universals and cross-cultural differences in order to account for the current body of empirical data. The following suggestions for further research are only that – suggestions – and the area would benefit from a diversity of new research angles and approaches.

To develop greater credibility, the new dialect theory needs to be supported by additional empirical work, testing each link proposed by the theory. In particular, it is necessary to reveal which particular cues and patterns contained within the emotional dialects vary across cultures. Further, it is necessary to map the presence or absence of those cues and patterns in stimuli to the emotion-recognition judgments made of those stimuli. Current work in progress attempts to tackle these goals. For example, with collaborators Ursula Hess, Martin Beaupré, and Manon Leveque (Elfenbein, Beaupré, Leveque, & Hess, in press), in a study examining naturalistic expressions among North Americans from Quebec and Africans from Gabon, we found suggestive evidence of subtle dialects in the basic emotions as well as more noticeable dialects in secondary emotions. In future work, we hope to use computerized animation to simulate the effect of having members of each culture pose their own expressive style as well as that of the other group. It is interesting that this mirrors one of Matsumoto's (see Chapter 7, this volume) suggestions for future empirical work in the area, with the goal of demonstrating that the ingroup advantage does not result from perceivers being more accurate merely when judging other *people* from their own culture – but rather that perceivers are more accurate when judging culturally familiar *expressions*, regardless of the apparent ethnicity of the person posing the expression. Such designs would further emphasize the ingroup advantage as a result of social-psychological processes such as cultural familiarity and learning rather than physical similarity factors such as race. Accordingly, additional research could examine the cultural learning of these cues and patterns over time to support the argument that familiarity with culturally specific elements of emotional style aids in the communication of emotion across cultures.

Another worthwhile area for further research is to examine whether there are corresponding findings to the cultural ingroup advantage across the personal styles that vary among individuals within a culture.

On the one hand, some evidence suggests not: Research examining whether interpersonal acquaintance and familiarity increase emotion-recognition accuracy has been mixed (for a review, see Elfenbein, Marsh, & Ambady, 2002). However, suggesting the value of reopening this question, there is new evidence for "relationship effects" among unacquainted individuals within a single culture. That is, when judging each other's facial expressions, some dyads uniquely understand each other well or poorly, even controlling for individual differences in perception and expression skill (Elfenbein, Foo, Boldry, & Tan, 2006). This suggests the intriguing possibility that the cross-cultural phenomenon of subtle differences in expressive style better understood with greater familiarity could perhaps replicate itself within a single culture. This also suggests a cautious approach to research on "emotional intelligence" (Mayer, Salovey, & Caruso, 2000), in which accuracy in expressing and perceiving emotion is a major component. If individuals are more accurate when judging the emotions of some expressors but not others, then this calls into question whether emotional intelligence is a "one-size-fits-all" phenomenon and poses difficulty on a practical level for the creation of valid test instruments of individual differences.

Overall, the study of cross-cultural universals and differences in the communication of emotion has benefited from the controversy and attention that it has received. It will likely continue to be a topic of great interest to researchers. The goals of this chapter have been to put into context the nature of the current controversies and to issue a warm welcome to others who may be interested in getting involved with this topic. Much work remains to be done, and fresh and balanced perspectives will continue to benefit the field.

References

Beaupré, M., & Hess, U. (2005). Cross-cultural emotion recognition among Canadian ethnic groups. *Journal of Cross-Cultural Psychology, 36*, 355–370.
Biehl, M., Matsumoto, D., Ekman, P., Hearn, V., Heider, K., Kudoh, T., & Ton, V. (1997). Matsumoto and Ekman's Japanese and Caucasian facial expressions of emotion (JACFEE): Reliability data and cross-national differences. *Journal of Nonverbal Behavior, 21*, 3–21.
Buck, R. (1984). *The communication of emotion*. New York: Guilford Press.
Ekman, P. (1972). Universals and cultural differences in facial expressions of emotion. In J. Cole (Ed.), *Nebraska Symposium on Motivation, 1971* (Vol. 19, pp. 207–282). Lincoln: University of Nebraska Press.
Ekman, P. (1994). Strong evidence for universals in facial expressions: A reply to Russell's mistaken critique. *Psychological Bulletin, 115*, 268–287.

Ekman, P., & Friesen, W. V. (1976). *Pictures of facial affect*. Palo Alto: Consulting Psychologists Press.

Elfenbein, H. A., & Ambady, N. (2002a). Is there an ingroup advantage in emotion? *Psychological Bulletin, 128*, 243–249.

Elfenbein, H. A., & Ambady, N. (2002b). On the universality and cultural specificity of emotion recognition: A meta-analysis. *Psychological Bulletin, 128*, 203–235.

Elfenbein, H. A., & Ambady, N. (2003a). Cultural similarity's consequences: A distance perspective on cross-cultural differences in emotion recognition. *Journal of Cross-Cultural Psychology, 34*, 92–110.

Elfenbein, H. A., & Ambady, N. (2003b). Universals and cultural differences in recognizing emotions. *Current Directions in Psychological Science. 12*, 159–164.

Elfenbein, H. A., & Ambady, N. (2003c). When familiarity breeds accuracy: Cultural exposure and facial emotion recognition. *Journal of Personality and Social Psychology, 85*, 276–290.

Elfenbein, H. A., Beaupré, M., Leveque, M., & Hess, U. (in press). Toward a dialect theory: Cultural differences in the expression and recognition of posed facial expressions. *Emotion.*

Elfenbein, H. A., Foo, M. D., Boldry, J. G., & Tan, H. H. (2005). Dyadic effects in nonverbal communication: A variance partitioning analysis. *Cognition and Emotion, 20*, 149–159.

Elfenbein, H. A., Mandal, M. K., Ambady, N., Harizuka, S., & Kumar, S. (2002). Cross-cultural patterns in emotion recognition: Highlighting design and analytical techniques. *Emotion, 2*, 75–84.

Elfenbein, H. A., Mandal, M. K., Ambady, N., Harizuka, S., & Kumar, S. (2004). Hemifacial differences in the ingroup advantage in emotion recognition. *Cognition and Emotion, 18*, 613–629.

Elfenbein, H. A., Marsh, A., & Ambady, N. (2002). Emotional intelligence and the recognition of emotion from the face. In L. F. Barrett & P. Salovey (Eds.), *The wisdom of feelings: Processes underlying emotional intelligence* (pp. 37–59). New York: Guilford Press.

Hatta, T., & Nachshon, I. (1988). Ear differences in evaluating emotional overtones of unfamiliar speech by Japanese and Israelis. *International Journal of Psychology, 23*, 293–302.

Hofstede, G. (2001). *Culture's consequences (2nd ed.)*. Thousand Oaks, CA: Sage Publications.

Izard, C. E. (1971). *The face of emotion*. New York: Appleton-Century-Crofts.

Izard, C. E. (1994). Innate and universal facial expressions: Evidence from developmental and cross-cultural research. *Psychological Bulletin, 115*, 288–299.

Kilbride, J. E., & Yarczower, M. (1983). Ethnic bias in the recognition of facial expressions. *Journal of Nonverbal Behavior, 8*, 27–41.

Markham, R., & Wang, L. (1996). Recognition of emotion by Chinese and Australian children. *Journal of Cross-Cultural Psychology, 27*, 616–643.

Matsumoto, D. (1989). Cultural influences on the perception of emotion. *Journal of Cross-Cultural Psychology, 20*, 92–105.

Matsumoto, D. (2002). Methodological requirements to test a possible ingroup advantage in judging emotions across cultures: Comments on Elfenbein and Ambady and evidence. *Psychological Bulletin, 128,* 236–242.

Matsumoto, D., & Assar, M. (1992). The effects of language on judgments of universal facial expressions of emotion. *Journal of Nonverbal Behavior, 16,* 85–99.

Mayer, J. D., Salovey, P., & Caruso, D. R. (2000). Models of emotional intelligence. In R. J. Sternberg (Ed.), *Handbook of intelligence* (pp. 396–420). Cambridge, England: Cambridge University Press.

Nowicki, S., Jr., & Duke, M. P. (2001). Nonverbal receptivity: The diagnostic analysis of nonverbal accuracy (DANVA). In J. A. Hall & F. J. Bernieri (Eds.), *Interpersonal sensitivity theory and measurement* (pp. 183–198). Mahwah, NJ: Lawrence Erlbaum Associates.

Rosenthal, R., Hall, J. A., DiMatteo, M. R., Rogers, P. L., & Archer, D. (1979). *Sensitivity to nonverbal communication: The PONS test.* Baltimore: Johns Hopkins University Press.

Russell, J. A. (1994). Is there universal recognition of emotion from facial expression? A review of the cross-cultural studies. *Psychological Bulletin, 115,* 102–141.

Schimmack, U. (1996). Cultural influences on the recognition of emotion by facial expressions: Individualistic or Caucasian cultures? *Journal of Cross-Cultural Psychology, 27,* 37–50.

Sogon, S., & Masutani, M. (1989). Identification of emotion from body movements: A cross-cultural study of Americans and Japanese. *Psychological Reports, 65,* 35–46.

Wang, L., & Markham, R. (1999). The development of a series of photographs of Chinese facial expressions of emotion. *Journal of Cross-Cultural Psychology, 30,* 397–410.

4. Beauty Is in the Eyes of the Perceiver

The Impact of Affective Stereotyping on the Perception of Outgroup Members' Facial Expressions

Pierre Philippot, Yanélia Yabar, and Patrick Bourgeois

Authors' Note

The writing of this chapter has been facilitated by grants from the "Fonds National de la Recherche Scientifique de Belgique" 8.4510.99 and 8.4510.03 and by a grant ARC 96/01-198 from the University of Louvain. The authors appreciate the helpful comments of Ursula Hess on earlier drafts of this chapter. Correspondence regarding this chapter should be addressed to Pierre Philippot, Faculté de Psychologie, Université de Louvain, place du Cardinal Mercier, 10, B-1348 Louvain-la-Neuve, Belgique. Electronic mail may be sent via Internet to Pierre.Philippot@psp.ucl.ac.be.

Introduction

A crucial role of facial expressions is to convey one's feeling to facilitate interpersonal or intergroup understanding and interactions (Kirouac & Hess, 1999; Philippot, Feldman, & Coats, 1999). Indeed, the exchange of nonverbal information in human interactions serves not only to inform interaction partners of each other's emotional (Ekman, Friesen, & Ellsworth, 1982; Hess, Kappas, & Scherer, 1988; Noller, 1985; Russell, 1994) or intentional states (Frijda, 1986; Frijda & Tcherkassof, 1997; Tcherkassof, 1999) but also to regulate aspects of social relationships (Kirouac & Hess, 1999).

In this context, a small body of research has established that facial expressions of emotions (e.g., anger, disgust, fear, happiness and sadness) affect decoders' interpersonal trait inferences, such as inferences of dominance, affiliation or romantic interest (Eibl-Eibesfeldt, 1989; Hess, Blairy, & Kleck, 2000; Keating, 1985; Keltner, Young, Oemig, Heerey, &

Monarch, 1998; Knutson, 1996) or of perceived intelligence, attractiveness and sociability (Matsumoto & Kudoh, 1993; Riggio & Friedman, 1986). Of course, such inferences are expected to affect reactions toward the partner (Patterson, 1999).

Another body of research has addressed the role of nonverbal behavior in the regulation of interactions via motor mimicry (Hess, Philippot, & Blairy, 1999). The tendency to synchronize one's nonverbal behavior with those of another person induces a corresponding emotion in the decoder (Hatfield, Cacioppo, & Rapson, 1993; Laird, Alibozak, Davainis, Deignan, Fontanella, et al., 1994; Strayer, 1993). Some have proposed that such 'emotional contagion' might help the decoder to infer the expressor's emotional state (McHugo, Lanzetta & Bush, 1991; Levenson & Ruef, 1992; Wallbott, 1991), which should increase the perception of empathy and, as such, the intimacy of the relationship (Ickes, 1984). This latter part of the causal path, however, has not found support in much empirical data (e.g., Blairy, Herrera, & Hess, 1999; Hess & Blairy, 2001).

It is quite surprising that the social context of the recognition of facial expressions has received little attention from researchers (Fernández-Dols, 1999; Kirouac & Hess, 1999; Wagner & Lee, 1999). Indeed, nonverbal research has mainly focused on the impact of social context on encoding aspects of facial expressions rather than on aspects of decoding such expressions. For instance, nonverbal research has investigated display rules or cultural norms that determine what kind of facial expressions can be displayed by whom and under which circumstances (Ekman, 1993; Kupperbusch, Matsumoto, Kooken, Loewinger, Uchida, Wilson-Cohn, & Yrizarry, 1999). Nonverbal research has also focused on the impact of the audience on the expression of emotion. It has been observed that the intensity of positive and negative emotional facial displays increases in the presence of a real or imagined audience, demonstrating the sociality dimension of emotion displays (Fridlund, 1991; Manstead, Fischer, & Jacobs, 1999; Wagner & Lee, 1999; Wagner & Smith, 1991).

However, the impact of the expressor's social group membership – in the social-psychological meaning of this notion – on the recognition of facial expressions has been addressed by only a few studies. This chapter attempts to fill in this gap by presenting a series of studies from our laboratories that have focused on the impact of intergroup context on the decoding of facial expressions. We argue that the decoding of facial expressions is affected by the intergroup status of the expressor and, in particular, by the social-role expectations associated with the expressor's group membership. For instance, in a European context, expecting male North Africans to be aggressive may foster the attribution of anger to male North Africans' facial displays. In other words, we predict that the interpretation of outgroup members' facial displays is biased by the stereotype of that outgroup. Such influences are likely to bias intergroup communication, especially in the affective domain, and to reinforce stereotypes. To support this claim, we first review the relevant literature and develop a theoretical framework specifying the processes by which the expressor's group membership might affect the decoding of facial expressions. Then, we present recent findings from our laboratories.

Group Membership in Facial Expression Decoding: A Review

In the literature, the influence of the group membership of the expressor on the accuracy of emotional decoding has been investigated for gender, social and ethnic/racial memberships. Because the effects of gender and ethnic/racial memberships are reviewed in other chapters of this volume, we focus on the few studies that examined the effects of the social group to which the expressor belongs on facial expression decoding by a member of a similar or different social group. In this context, some studies have reported that stereotypes about the group of the expressor affect the intensity of emotion attributed to facial expression, and other studies have observed an effect on the decoding accuracy of facial expressions.

For instance, Priest (1997) showed that the social group membership of the expressor (an executive versus an interior designer) did not influence the accuracy of the emotion attributed to his facial expression but rather the overall emotional-intensity ratings. These results are congruent with the observation that executives are stereotypically judged as being conservative and uptight, which results in attributions of less expressivity and more inhibition to such targets (McArthur, 1981; Sanbonmatsu, Sherman, & Hamilton, 1987).

On the other hand, Gallois and Callan (1986) showed that when Australians had to attribute an emotion on the basis of a videotape displaying a content-ambiguous message delivered by either an Australian, British, or Italian speaker, Italian speakers were decoded less accurately than the others. Gallois and Callan's interpretation was that because of their negative attitude toward Southern European immigrants, Australians allocated more attention to social markers such as accent and less to emotional markers such as facial expressions or message contents. Consequently, the emotional decoding process of the communication was less efficient for prejudiced outgroup members and more influenced by their negative stereotype.

Apart from these few studies, little work has empirically tested the influence of the group membership of the expressor on the decoding of facial expressions. Furthermore, these pioneering studies suffer from several limitations. For instance, the study by Priest (1997) used full-blown facial expressions of basic emotions as stimuli, presenting little ecological validity. Indeed, most everyday facial expressions tend to be relatively weak and ambiguous (Motley & Camdem, 1988), and some have argued that the expressor's group membership is likely to influence specifically the decoding of weak expressions (Kirouac & Hess, 1999).

Also, no attention has been given to the decoding of facial expressions in terms of action tendencies (i.e., intentions to behave in a certain way following an emotion-eliciting situation; Frijda, 1986) in an intergroup setting. This latter concern is important for several reasons. First, some have argued and raised evidence indicating that action tendencies are more easily attributed to facial expressions than emotion categories because facial expressions might represent one's relational activity to the environment more than one's inner state (Frijda & Tcherkassof, 1997; Tcherkassof, 1999). Second, in an intergroup context, indications regarding one's relational activity are more important and adaptive than indications regarding one's inner state (Dijker, 1987). Thus, showing an impact of stereotypes on the attribution of action tendencies in an intergroup context bears direct consequences for the efficacy of communication between members of different social groups (Kirouac & Hess, 1999).

Why and How Should Social Group Membership Influence Facial Expression Decoding?

Few theoretical developments have been proposed to specify the nature of the impact that the social-group membership of expressors and the stereotype attached to it might have on the decoding of their facial expressions. Unfortunately, most of the social-psychological literature has focused on personality-trait stereotypes (Gilbert, Fiske, & Lindzey, 1996); little attention has been devoted to emotional-trait stereotypes.

However, three lines of research have documented the notion that emotional characteristics might be as important as personality characteristics in terms of stereotype content.

One line of research has documented that people hold stereotypes about the frequency with which certain emotional states or emotional-action tendencies are attributed to specific outgroups. For instance, Yabar and Philippot (2000) have shown that Belgian natives stereotypically believe that migrant North African males (i.e., the outgroup) experience anger more often and show more aggressive action tendencies than Belgian natives (i.e., the ingroup). These authors suggested that more than personality traits, these emotional features of the outgroup stereotype are determinants in accounting for the prejudicial attitude of Belgians toward North African migrants.

Another line of research (Leyens, Paladino, Rodrigues-Torres, Vaes, Demoulin, Rodriges-Perez, & Gaunt, 2000) has shown that feelings are stereotypically denied to the outgroup. The rationale underlying this research is that people believe that feelings are a typically 'human' feature (as opposed to bestial). Consequently, overattributing feelings to the ingroup and denying them to the outgroup would constitute a form of ingroup favoritism and outgroup prejudice. According to this hypothesis, subtle feelings (e.g., tenderness and sadness) would be attributed to the ingroup, whereas raw, animal-like emotions (e.g., joy and anger) would be attributed to the outgroup.

Still another line of research (Pennebaker, Rimé, & Blankenship, 1996) has documented that all over the world, people hold stereotypes about the emotional expressivity of outgroups. More specifically, people believe that other groups, living closer to the equator and thus in warmer regions, are more emotionally expressive than they are. Conversely, they hold the opposite stereotype for people living closer to the poles than they are.

In sum, several lines of research support the notion that emotion stereotypes do exist, perhaps to the same extent as personality stereotypes. However, much is still unknown about these stereotypes. One hypothesis is that specific emotions would be attributed to specific outgroups; for instance, in a Northern European context, anger would be stereotypically attributed to North African migrants, whereas joy would be attributed to Southern Europeans. Another hypothesis is that feelings would be attributed to the ingroup but denied to outgroups. In contrast, basic, animal-like emotions would be stereotypically attributed to outgroups. Finally, a third hypothesis is that it would not really be the nature of the emotion that would matter but rather its intensity. Some outgroups would be stereotypically believed to experience and express more intense emotions than others. These three hypotheses hold different predictions on how outgroup stereotypes might bias the decoding of facial expressions of emotion.

Still, the very notion that facial expression decoding will be biased by stereotypes has yet to be established empirically. One might even question whether stereotype biases apply to the decoding of emotional facial expression. Indeed, humans have a special expertise and an innate ability in the processing of faces (Russell & Fernández-Dols, 1997), in terms of both identity and expressivity. Some have even advocated that facial expressions of emotion (at least expressions of threat) are innate unconditioned stimuli (Öhman, 1999). It might thus be that such routinized automatic processes remain uninfluenced by the activation of outgroup stereotypes.

An intermediate theoretical position is that social stereotypes would not bias full-blown emotional facial expressions but rather would only exert an influence on the decoding of ambiguous or weak facial expressions. This view is consistent with an observation by Ekman, Friesen, and Ellsworth (1982), who showed that facial expressions generally dominate contextual information in determining emotion attribution, with the exception of ambiguous or weak facial expressions. When facial expressions are prototypical and intense, the context does not affect emotion attribution (Boucher & Carlson, 1980), whereas it intervenes when facial expressions are ambiguous or weak (Shaver, Wu, & Schwartz, 1992). This argument is important because in everyday life, emotional display tends to be weak and ambiguous as compared to the intense and prototypical stimuli generally used in emotion-recognition research (Motley & Camdem, 1988). When the expressor belongs to another ethnic group, facial expression may be even more ambiguous because of differences in physiognomies and/or because of the nonfamiliarity of the perceiver with such physiognomies. When facial expressions are ambiguous, decoders would refer more frequently to information from the social context, such as knowledge concerning the expressor or the stereotype associated to the expressor's group (Hess & Kirouac, 1997).

In sum, several lines of research have shown that social stereotypes comprise emotional features and that these features might be influential in the process of prejudice. However, the exact nature of emotional stereotypes is not well established, and at least three models have been proposed. On the other hand, one might question whether emotional stereotypes would bias the decoding of facial expression of emotion. Indeed, several authors have proposed and raised empirical evidence that emotional facial expressions are strong and that innate signals are not very sensitive to contextual noise. The biasing potential of emotional stereotypes might well apply to weak or ambiguous facial expressions but not to full-blown expressions.

Do Emotional Stereotypes Bias the Decoding of Facial Expression?

We designed a research program to investigate whether emotional stereotypes bias the decoding of facial expression, while attempting to overcome limitations from previous studies. This research program investigated the impact of the expressor's social-group membership and related stereotypes on the decoding of neutral as well as emotional facial displays, in terms of both emotions and action tendencies. Specifically, participants were exposed to facial expressions displayed by a member of their group or by a member of another group for which they held a negative stereotype. Our hypothesis was that emotional stereotypes would bias the attribution of emotions and action tendencies to facial expressions, at least when these expressions are weak or ambiguous. To the contrary, the decoding of full-blown emotional expression of out-group members should not be biased by the emotional stereotypes.

Stereotype Biases in the Decoding of Outgroup Members' Neutral Faces

In our first experiment, we investigated the situation in which emotional stereotype biases are the most likely to occur: the decoding of neutral facial expressions displayed by prejudiced outgroup members. Specifically, Belgian participants had to infer the action tendencies possibly felt by an individual whose face they were shown. The facial stimuli were neutral faces of either North African or Belgian young males. One could expect participants to endorse an action tendency more frequently when that item is stereotypical of the expressor's group than when it is nonstereotypical. In this particular instance, because Belgians stereo-typically believe that young North African males are aggressive (Yabar & Philippot, 2000), one might expect participants to attribute aggressive action tendencies more frequently to North African expressors than to Belgians.

More specifically, Belgian participants were exposed to eight neutral faces of young Belgian males and eight neutral faces of young North African males. Both groups differ in terms of morphological features, and a pretest ascertained that Belgian and North African expressors were unambiguously recognized as such. Participants rated each face that appeared during 500 ms. on a computer screen on fifteen items: five action tendencies stereotypical of Belgians, five action tendencies stereotypical of North Africans, and five nonstereotypical action tendencies. Each face was presented three times, each time with a different type of action tendency (i.e., nonstereotypical, stereotypical of Belgians, or stereotypical of North Africans). Participants were told that their task consisted of interpreting spontaneous facial expressions displayed by either Belgian or North African expressors. The cover story was that photographs had been taken from actual situations in which expressors were looking at emotion-eliciting video excerpts and that the judgment items corresponded to what they had reported feeling in those situations. Participants were also told that the photographs and correspondent judgment items were mixed and that they had to judge whether the judgment items presented corresponded to facial expressions.

As expected, action tendencies stereotypical of North Africans were more frequently attributed to North African expressors than to Belgian expressors. Action tendencies stereotypical of Belgians were equally attributed to both groups. This effect may result from the fact that stereotypical Belgian action tendencies are clearly of an introverted nature, which is more compatible with the neutral expression of the stimulus faces than the extraverted North African stereotypical action tendencies. There was no main effect of the expressor's group on the overall attribution of action tendencies.

In sum, these results document that a prejudiced stereotype can bias the attribution of action tendencies to outgroup members' neutral faces. Would this observation be replicated for the attribution of emotions rather than action tendencies? Indeed, action tendencies (or behavioral intentions in the context of attitudes; see Fishbein & Ajzen, 1975) can be described as the situational counterparts of personality traits, and previous research has long demonstrated the influence of stereotypes on the description of outgroup members in terms of personality traits (for a review, see Fiske, 1998). Thus, stereotyping appears to be more likely to affect the attribution of action tendencies than to affect the attribution of emotions.

The relationship of emotion categories to stereotypes may be quite different from that of personality traits or action tendencies. Indeed, some researchers have argued that emotions and emotional displays are universal and, therefore, do not differ as a function of cultural or group membership (Ekman, 1993; Frijda, 1986; Izard, 1994). Such an assumption is shared by 'naive theories' of lay people (Saarni & Weber, 1999), which would imply that there would be no cognitive representations about which emotions are stereotypical of specific outgroups.

Despite the arguments just developed and because stereotypes about emotions typical of different groups have been evidenced in a previous study (Yabar & Philippot, 2000), we proposed that these stereotypes should also affect the decoding of facial expressions. Study 1 was thus replicated using emotions rather than action tendencies as judgment items. Based on the study by Yabar and Philippot (2000), six items were selected for the present study: two emotions stereotypical of Belgians (i.e., fear and sadness); two emotions stereotypical of North Africans (i.e, anger and contempt); and two nonstereotypical emotions (i.e., admiration and desire).

Congruent with our hypothesis, emotions stereotypical of North Africans were more often attributed to North African faces and emotions stereotypical of Belgians were more often attributed to Belgian faces. Emotion items thus seem to respond quite similarly to personality traits or action tendencies in the stereotyping process. In addition, there was an overall over-attribution of emotional items to Belgian faces as compared to North African faces. This observation differs from the results of the first experiment (i.e., no effects of stereotypes were reported for ingroup members' facial expressions) or in relation to previous research (i.e., the perceptual or informational processing initiated for ingroup members is supposed to be analytic and stereotype-inconsistent; Fiske & Taylor, 1991; Koomen & Dijker, 1997). This aspect of our results is further discussed in the context of the next experiment.

Stereotype Biases in the Decoding of Outgroup Members' Emotional Faces

As argued in a preceding section, stereotype biases are more likely to occur in the decoding of weak or ambiguous facial expressions than in the decoding of full-blown facial expressions. This possibility was investigated in the next experiment. It replicated Experiment 1 with the additional factor that half of the facial expression stimuli in each expressor's group were neutral and the other half were clearly emotional, displaying either anger, joy, fear or sadness.

The results indicated that when facial expressions were neutral, action tendencies stereotypical of North Africans were more often attributed to North African expressors than to Belgian expressors. In contrast, when facial expressions were emotional, all action tendencies were systematically more often attributed to Belgians, with the exception of action tendencies stereotypical of Belgians, which were equally attributed with respect to the expressor's group membership.

These observations suggest two phenomena. First, stereotypes appear to bias facial-expression decoding only when facial expressions are neutral. Second, there is an over-attribution of action tendencies to ingroup members. Such an ingroup over-attribution had also been observed in Experiment 2. It could reflect two distinct processes. A first possibility is that participants experienced more difficulties in decoding facial expressions of outgroup members because they had less in-depth contact with the outgroup (Kilbride & Yarczower, 1983). This lack of contact might have generated an impression of unfamiliarity with outgroup members' faces, resulting in an uncertainty in decoding their facial expressions. A second possibility is that participants merely wanted to favor ingroup members by attributing fewer feelings to outgroup members. Indeed, displaying an emotion – specifically, a complex feeling – is perceived as a positive and typically human feature (Leyens et al., 2000).

Thus, attributing more feelings to an ingroup member's facial expression as opposed to an outgroup member's facial expression might represent a form of implicit prejudice toward outgroup members: They would be less human than ingroup members because they would have fewer feelings.

In summary, results of Experiment 3 provide reasonable support for the idea that stereotype-driven biases in the decoding of facial expression vary as a function of the emotionality of the stimulus (Ekman, Friesen, & Ellsworth, 1982; Shaver, Wu, & Schwartz, 1992; Wallbott, 1988). When facial expressions are neutral, the decoding process would preferentially be based on contextual features, whereas when facial expressions are emotional, the decoding process would preferentially be based on facial features per se.

An Effect of Outgroup Membership or of Differences in Morphology?

In the three experiments described previously, outgroup facial expressions were displayed by young North African men. It should be noted that North Africans differ sensibly from Northern Europeans (and, thus, Belgians) in terms of their morphological features and physiognomy. Thus, these three experiments present confounds between the expressor's group membership per se and the unfamiliarity and difference in physiognomy of the stimulus face. The fact that stereotype-driven biases were observed, at least for neutral faces, could indeed be explained by a difference between North African and Belgian expressors in terms of physiognomies (Deregowski, Ellis, & Shepherd, 1975; Kilbride & Yarczower, 1983; Malpass & Kravitz, 1960; Shepherd, Deregowski, & Ellis, 1974). One could question whether the effects we observed would maintain for cases in which outgroup faces would not differ from ingroup faces in terms of physiognomy and thus of familiarity (Fiske & Taylor, 1991; Koomen & Dijker, 1997; McArthur, 1981; Sanbonmatsu, Sherman, & Hamilton, 1987).

Experiment 4 was designed to replicate the results of Experiment 3 with respect to the effect of the emotional nature of the stimuli and to test whether the activation of stereotypes is directly initiated by the expressor's group membership or indirectly by a difference in morphology. For that reason, the same facial stimuli from Caucasian expressors were presented to the French-speaking Belgian participants as being the faces of either Walloon (i.e., French-speaking) or Flemish (i.e., Dutch-speaking) Belgian nationals. Belgium is divided into two main linguistic areas: the French-speaking area situated in the South known as Wallonia and the Dutch-speaking area situated in the North known as Flanders. Members of French- and Dutch-speaking communities present identical ethnic features but hold relatively conflictive relations that trigger prejudice (Bourhis, Giles, Leyens, & Tajfel, 1979; Yzerbyt, Leyens, & Bellour, 1995) and different stereotypes in terms of global expressiveness (Pennebaker, Rimé, & Blankenship, 1996). Consequently, if a difference in group membership constitutes a sufficient condition for stereotype-driven biases in facial expression decoding, such an effect should be observed in Experiment 4.

Because for geographical and historical reasons most Walloons have roots and contacts with both the Walloon and the Flemish communities, actual outgroup contacts were controlled for in this experiment. Indeed, intergroup contacts have been shown to be an important moderator of prejudice and stereotyping under certain conditions (Brown, 1996; Pettigrew, 1998; Tzeng & Jackson, 1994). A measure of outgroup contacts offers a reliable means to control for the participants' links to Flemish and Walloon communities independently of their group membership (Tzeng & Jackson, 1994).

The procedure of Experiment 4 was identical to the one used in Experiment 3, except that the expressor's group membership was now either Walloon or Flemish (as opposed to Belgian or North African). Participants were told that their task consisted of interpreting facial expressions displayed by either a Walloon or a Flemish expressor. The group identity of each stimulus person was indicated by the label "Flemish" or "Walloon" appearing just before the display of the facial expression. As in the previous studies, participants were made to believe that the photographs were taken from actual situations in which expressors were looking at emotion-eliciting video excerpts and that the judgment items corresponded to what expressors had reported feeling. Half of the participants were presented with neutral facial expressions and the other half with emotional expressions. All facial stimuli were taken from the Caucasian subset of the JACFEE (Matsumoto & Ekman, 1988).

Again, the results clearly showed that when facial expressions were neutral, action tendencies stereotypical of the outgroup (here, Flemish people) were more often attributed to outgroup (Flemish) faces, whereas nonstereotypical action tendencies or action tendencies stereotypical of the ingroup (here, Walloon people) were more often attributed to ingroup (Walloon) faces, provided that contact with the outgroup was controlled for. In contrast, when facial expressions were emotional, the attribution of action tendencies was not modulated by the expressor's group membership. Finally, there was a statistically nonsignificant tendency to over-attribute action tendencies to the emotional expression of the ingroup faces.

The results of Experiment 4 support the hypothesis that stereotype-driven biases in facial-expression decoding occur specifically when facial expressions are neutral. This effect was observed for faces of members of groups with no differences in morphology, which also corroborates the assumption that the expressor's group membership can directly initiate the application of stereotypes. In other words, knowing that an expressor belongs to a specific outgroup is a sufficient condition for applying a stereotype in the decoding of neutral facial expressions.

Differences in physiognomies are not a necessary condition for such a bias to interfere with the decoding of facial expressions, at least when facial expressions are neutral. On the other hand, when facial expressions are clearly emotional, this latter feature takes over the decoding process and seems to suppress influences from the stereotype. It might be that in the case of emotional faces, prejudice would take another face and would consist in the denial of emotion – or at least feelings – to the outgroup (Leyens et al., 2000). However, this interpretation must be taken cautiously because this effect did not reach statistical significance in the results of the present experiment. However, Beaulieu (2001) reported evidence in agreement with that notion. Participants, who were either basketball players or not, had to rate the facial expressions of two groups of people who were identified either as basketball players or nonplayers. In addition, half the stimulus persons were Caucasian and half were African. Caucasian basketball players rated the facial expressions of anger and happiness shown by purported Caucasian basketball players as less angry and happier, respectively, than the same expressions when shown by a purported nonplayer. Yet, no effects emerged for African stimulus persons, which suggests that participants rated the facial expressions of a presumed ingroup member more positively than one of an outgroup member. Yet, for individuals who were members of one ingroup (i.e., basketball players) but also a member of an ethnic outgoup, this ingroup favoritism was not observed.

The Role of Prejudice for Stereotype-Driven Biases in Facial Expression Decoding

In Experiment 4, an effect of intergroup contact was observed. Indeed, stereotype-driven biases in the decoding of facial expression were fully observed only after controlling for intergroup contact. It is well known that positive outgroup contacts alleviate prejudice (Bourhis & Leyens, 1994), which suggests that these stereotype-driven biases might be modulated by individual differences in terms of a prejudicial attitude toward outgroup members.

Experiment 5 was designed to test whether stereotype-driven biases in facial expression decoding are affected by individual differences in reported prejudice. Specifically, it was assumed that low-prejudice individuals display different patterns of evaluation, either because they inhibit the application of stereotype (Devine, 1989) or because different stereotype contents are activated (Lepore & Brown, 1997). Following one perspective, low- and high-prejudice people have access to the same stereotypical negative attributes associated with a prejudiced outgroup but endorse different beliefs about it. Low-prejudice people would inhibit spontaneously activated attribution of negative traits to outgroup members (Devine, 1989; Devine & Elliot, 1995). Following the other perspective, low- and high-prejudice people would hold different representations. Low-prejudice people would reject negative stereotypes to endorse positive stereotypical features. In the long term, the activation of positive stereotypical features would become automatic (Lepore & Brown, 1997).

The first perspective implies that low- and high-prejudice people are differentiated on both judgment contents and judgment latencies because inhibition of spontaneous negative-traits attribution involves a cognitive cost. To the contrary, the second perspective implies that low- and high-prejudice people are differentiated only on judgment contents because positive-traits attribution is automatically activated and involves no inhibition or cognitive cost. Empirical evidence has been reported at an automatic level (i.e., stereotype activation) supporting one perspective or the other (Devine, 1989; Lepore & Brown, 1997; Kawakami, Dion, & Dovidio, 1998). Experiment 5 aims at differentiating the two perspectives at a controlled level (i.e., stereotype application) and in the field of facial expression decoding.

The procedure was similar to the procedure for Experiment 2, with emotion labels as judgment items. The experimental task included the presentation of five Belgian neutral faces and five North African neutral faces. Each face was presented three times with different types of emotion-response items: nonstereotypical, stereotypical for Belgians, or stereotypical for North Africans. In addition, participants (i.e., French-speaking Belgians) were asked to fill out a French translation of a scale developed by Tzeng and Jackson (1994). This scale was developed from existing 'modern and subtle racism' measures (e.g., Jacobson, 1985; McConahay, Hardee, & Batts, 1981; Pettigrew & Meertens, 1995) and assessed how much one likes (and thus is susceptible to favor) one's ingroup. Based on a median split of this questionnaire, participants were distributed in a high- or low-prejudice group.

Consistent with the literature, results showed that high-prejudice participants attributed more emotions stereotypical for North Africans to North Africans than low-prejudice participants. This effect was reversed in low-prejudice participants. Moreover, results also showed that high-prejudice participants attributed emotions more rapidly than low-prejudice participants in a controlled context. These observations are consistent with Devine's (1989) perspective: A cognitive cost is expected for low-prejudice participants because they activate the same representation as high-prejudice participants but inhibit its application because of personal beliefs.

Social Context and Facial Mimicry

The experiments reported in the previous section demonstrate that one does not react in the same manner to ingroup as compared to outgroup members' facial displays. The attribution of emotion and action tendencies on the basis of facial signals is modulated by group stereotypes, at least for weak or ambiguous facial expressions. The attribution of inner states, however, is just one aspect of the responses triggered by facial expressions. As mentioned in the introduction of this chapter, there is another type of reaction to an interaction partner's facial expression: facial mimicry (Hess, Philippot, & Blairy, 1999). This tendency to synchronize one's nonverbal behavior with those of another person is assumed to induce a corresponding emotion in the decoder (Hatfield, Cacioppo, & Rapson, 1993; Laird, Alibozak, Davainis, Deignan, Fontanella, et al., 1994; Strayer, 1993), which would increase the perception of empathy and the intimacy of the relationship (Ickes, 1984). In an intergroup context, it might be that more facial mimicry is observed when interacting with ingroup members than with outgroup members.

In line with this assumption, McHugo, Lanzetta, and Bush (1991) observed facial-mimicry and emotional-contagion effects in American students who supported then-president Reagan when they saw facial displays by him but not when they saw facial displays by his political adversary, Senator Hart. Conversely, nonsupporters of Reagan showed lower mimicry levels. In this context, Reagan might be considered an ingroup member by his supporters, whereas Hart might be considered an outgroup member.

Still, one limitation of that study is that the two politicians differed in their general appeal. Reagan was a much more charismatic and expressive person than Hart. It is possible that nonsupporters of Reagan found him fake or overly flamboyant when comparing his displays and Senator Hart's, especially as counter-mimicry effects were observed only to strong expressions by Reagan and only when expressions by Hart were also shown. Although seeing expressions by Hart makes political attitudes more salient, it may also serve as a baseline against which Reagan's expressions then seem less convincing to his nonsupporters.

We designed an experiment to replicate the McHugo et al. (1991) study but by comparing facial reactions to two political leaders who were both considered charismatic and good communicators. Specifically, we investigated observers' facial reactions toward smiles and frowns by two prominent Quebec politicians, Lucien Bouchard and Jean Charest, who, at the beginning of the 1998 elections, both received 40.7 percent support in a poll. Participants in the present study were in support of Bouchard. They viewed twelve short video sequences of facial expressions displayed by either Bouchard or Charest. The sequences were taken from a pre-electoral debate and were selected because either a frown or a smile was displayed. Participants' facial reactions as they were watching the video clips were recorded by facial electromyography (EMG) of their *Orbicularis Oculi* and *Zygomaticus Major* muscles to assess smiling and of their *Corrugator Supercilii* muscle to assess frowning. In addition, participants had to rate the emotional expression of the politician by choosing one term from a list of emotion labels.

The results globally supported our hypothesis. Specifically, Bouchard's supporters showed congruent muscle activity to his anger displays, while they showed no clear muscle pattern when judging Charest's anger displays. For happiness displays – despite a less clear pattern – results also leaned slightly in favor of the impact of attitude on mimicry behavior. In this case, participants showed global patterns of mimicry for both Bouchard and Charest. In sum, and despite the less clear pattern of results for responses to smiles, more mimicry was observed as a response to a display by an ingroup member (in the present case, a supported politician) than by an outgroup member (here, a political opponent). The observations of McHugo et al. (1991) are thus replicated and extended to expressors who did not differ in terms of expressivity and charisma. There is, therefore, empirical support for the notion that people mimic the facial expressions of ingroup than of outgroup members more.

As part of the study on basketball players reported previously (Beaulieu, 2001), facial EMG was recorded as well (Bourgeois & Hess, 2006). The results suggest that, again, happiness expressions by members of all four groups (i.e., basketball players and nonplayers of both African and Caucasian appearance) were mimicked equally. However, for sadness expressions, a different pattern emerged. Specifically, participants mimicked as a function of group status. The strongest evidence for mimicry was found for the 'double' ingroup (i.e., the Caucasian basketball players); some evidence also emerged for both single outgoups (i.e., African basketball players and Caucasian nonplayers); and expressions by members of the double outgroup (i.e., African nonplayers) were not mimicked. No evidence for anger mimicry emerged. Bourgeois and Hess (2006) explain this finding by referring to the social cost of mimicry. In fact, to the degree that mimicry is an affiliative social signal aimed at group cohesion, mimicking different emotions entrains different costs. Thus, happiness is a positive emotion that signals that all is well and seeing happy people makes others feel good. Therefore, happiness mimicry should have low social costs and only be found to be absent in explicitly competitive contexts (Lanzetta & Englis, 1989). In contrast, anger is a threat signal and mimicking anger may lead to the unwanted signaling of threat. Also, mimicking anger directed toward oneself would defeat the notion of affiliative intent. Yet, it may be affiliative to mimic anger when the expression is valid and clearly directed elsewhere, as was the case for the study of politicians described previously. Finally, sadness is an emotion which is associated with a demand for succor. Mimicking sadness also implies signaling understanding and hence may entail a cost in terms of providing social support. This notion is supported by the close parallel between levels of mimicry and degrees of closeness that were found in this study.

Thus, one important factor in deciding whether someone will mimic another person may be the anticipated social cost of that 'decision.' Therefore, mimicking outgroup members in many situations may be too costly.

General Conclusion

In this chapter, we developed the idea that the manner with which an individual interprets and reacts to a facial display might be modulated by the social-group status of the expressor. We presented converging evidence from several studies, mostly from our laboratories, that outgroup stereotypes bias the interpretation of facial expressions that are weak or ambiguous. However, such biases are not observed when unambiguous facial expressions of emotion are displayed. Furthermore, this bias seems to occur more particularly in people who are prejudiced against outgroup members.

Thus, the data presented clearly support the notion that stereotypes might affect the type of emotions that are attributed to weak or ambiguous expression. Such a specification of the conditions under which stereotypes affect facial expression decoding does not greatly restrict the implications of our results. Indeed, in everyday life, emotional displays tend to be weak and ambiguous as compared to the intense and prototypical facial stimuli generally used in emotion-recognition research (Motley & Camdem, 1988). Furthermore, during interactions with outgroup members, people might have fewer cognitive resources to fully process facial displays because they have to regulate the strategic and sensitive aspects of outgroup communication. This lack of cognitive resources might favor the influence of stereotypes on the decoding process. This latter hypothesis, however, needs to be empirically tested.

Some aspects of our data also suggest that more emotional meaning is attributed to facial expressions of ingroup members. This finding, although it was not systematically observed in all our studies, is congruent with the hypothesis of Leyens and collaborators (2000) that one aspect of prejudice against outgroups might be to deny them feelings because feelings are believed to be a specifically human and positive characteristic.

Finally, the social group status of the expressor not only affects the interpretation of facial expression, but it also seems to modulate the extent to which social interaction partners mimic each other. The last experiment we reported, together with the results of McHugo and collaborators (1991), suggests that people tend to mimic ingroup members but not outgroup members. This latter observation, however, needs to be further replicated.

In sum, the different lines of research reviewed in this chapter show that there is more than one way by which the social group status of the expressor modulates the responses to facial expressions. The type and intensity of the emotions attributed to the facial expression might be altered; a process of mimicry might be initiated or inhibited according to whether one interacts with an outgroup or an ingroup member. Such modulations in the flow of emotional communication are likely to affect the relationship among interaction partners and to reinforce stereotypes. Therefore, our understanding of prejudice might greatly benefit from a more systematic study of how nonverbal communication might be biased by outgroup stereotypes.

References

Beaulieu, N. (2001). L'impact de la similarité perçue sur la perception des émotions de différents groupes ethniques. Unpublished honors thesis. University of Quebec at Montreal.

Blairy, S., Herrera, P., & Hess, U. (1999). Mimicry and the judgment of emotional facial expressions. *Journal of Nonverbal Behavior, 23*, 5–41.

Boucher, J. D., & Carlson, G. E. (1980). Recognition of facial expression in three cultures. *Journal of Cross-Cultural Psychology, 11*, 263–280.

Bourgeois, P., & Hess, U. (2006). *The impact of social context on mimicry*. Manuscript submitted for publication.

Bourhis, R. Y., Giles, H., Leyens, J.-P., & Tajfel, H. (1979). Psycholinguistic distinctiveness: Language divergence in Belgium. In H. Giles & R. St. Clair (Eds.), *Language and social psychology* (pp. 158–185). Oxford, England: Basil Blackwell.

Bourhis, R. Y., & Leyens, J.-P. (Eds.) (1994). *Stéréotypes, discrimination et relations intergroupes*. Liège: Mardaga.

Brown, R. (1996). *Social psychology* (2nd ed.). New York: Free Press.

Deregowski, J. B., Ellis, H. D., & Shepherd, J. W. (1975). Description of white and black faces by white and black participants. *International Journal of Psychology, 10*, 119–123.

Devine, P. G. (1989). Stereotype and prejudice: Their automatic and controlled components. *Journal of Personality and Social Psychology, 56*, 5–18.

Devine, P. G., & Elliot, A. J. (1995). Are racial stereotypes really fading? The Princeton trilogy revisited. *Personality and Social Psychology Bulletin, 21*, 1139–1150.

Dijker, A. J. M. (1987). Emotional reactions to ethnic minorities. *European Journal of Social Psychology, 17*, 305–325.

Eibl-Eibesfeldt, I. (1989). *Human ethology*. New York: Aldine de Gruyter Press.

Ekman, P. (1993). Facial expression and emotion. *American Psychologist, 48*, 384–392.

Ekman, P., Friesen, W. V., & Ellsworth, P. (1982). *Emotion in the human face*. Cambridge, England: Cambridge University Press.

Fernández-Dols, J. M. (1999). Facial expression and emotion: A situationist view. In P. Philippot, R. S. Feldman, & E. J. Coats (Eds.), *The social context of nonverbal behavior* (pp. 242–262). Cambridge, England: Cambridge University Press.

Fishbein, M., & Ajzen, I. (1975). *Belief, attitude, intention and behavior: An introduction to theory and study*. Reading, MA: Addison-Wesley Publishing Company,

Fiske, S. T. (1998). Stereotyping, prejudice and discrimination. In D. T. Gilbert, S. T. Fiske, & G. Lindsey (Eds.). *The handbook of social psychology* (4th ed.). New York: McGraw-Hill.

Fiske, S. T., & Taylor, S. E. (1991). *Social cognition* (2nd ed.). New York: McGraw-Hill.

Fridlund, A. J. (1991). The sociality of solitary smiling: Potentation by an implicit audience. *Journal of Personality and Social Psychology, 60*, 229–240.

Frijda, N. H. (1986). *The emotions*. Cambridge, England: Cambridge University Press.

Frijda, N. H., & Tcherkassof, A. (1997). Facial expression and modes of action readiness. In J. A. Russell & J. M. Fernández-Dols (Eds.), *The psychology of facial expression* (pp. 78–102). Cambridge, England: Cambridge University Press.

Gallois, C., & Callan, V. J. (1986). Decoding emotional messages: Influence of ethnicity, sex, message type and channel. *Journal of Personality and Social Psychology*, *51*, 755–762.

Gilbert, D., Fiske, S. T., & Lindzey, G. (Eds.) (1996). *Handbook of social psychology*. New York: McGraw-Hill.

Hatfield, E., Cacioppo, J. T., & Rapson, R. L. (1993). *Emotion contagion*. Madison, WI: C. W. Brown.

Hess, U., & Blairy, S. (2001). Facial mimicry and emotional contagion to dynamic emotional facial expressions and their influence on decoding accuracy. *International Journal of Psychophysiology*, *40*, 129–141.

Hess, U., Blairy, S., & Kleck, R. E. (2000). The influence of expression intensity, gender, and ethnicity on judgments of dominance and affiliation. *Journal of Nonverbal Behavior*, *24*, 265–283.

Hess, U., & Kirouac, G. (1997). Group membership and the decoding of nonverbal behavior. In P. Philippot, R. Feldman, & E. Coats (Eds.), *The social context of nonverbal behavior*. Cambridge, England: Cambridge University Press.

Hess, U., Kappas, A., & Scherer, K. R. (1988). Multi-channel communication of emotion: Synthetic signal production. In K. R. Scherer (Ed.), *Facets of emotion: Recent research* (pp. 161–182). Hillsdale, NJ: Lawrence Erlbaum Associates.

Hess, U., Philippot, P., & Blairy, S. (1999). Mimicry: Facts and fiction. In P. Philippot, R. S. Feldman, & E. J. Coats (Eds.), *The social context of nonverbal behavior* (pp. 213–242). Cambridge, England: Cambridge University Press.

Ickes, W. (1984). Compositions in black and white: Determinants of interaction in interracial dyads. *Journal of Personality and Social Psychology*, *47*, 330–341.

Izard, C. E. (1994). Innate and universal facial expressions: Evidence from developmental and cross-cultural research. *Psychological Bulletin*, *115*, 288–299.

Jacobson, C. K. (1985). Resistance to affirmative action: Self-interest or racism? *Journal of Conflict Resolution*, *29*, 306–329.

Kawakami, K., Dion, K. L., & Dovidio, J. F. (1998). Racial prejudice and stereotype activation. *Personality and Social Psychology Bulletin*, *24*, 407–416.

Keating, C. F. (1985). Human dominance signals: The primate in US. In S. L. Ellyson & J. F. Dovidio (Eds.), *Power, dominance, and nonverbal behavior* (pp. 89–108). New York: Springer-Verlag.

Keltner, D., Young, R. C., Heerey, E. A., Oemig, C., & Monarch, N. D. (1998). Teasing in hierarchical and intimate relations. *Journal of Personality and Social Psychology*, *75*, 1231–1247.

Kilbride, J. E., & Yarczower, M. (1983). Ethnic bias in the recognition of facial expressions. *Journal of Nonverbal Behavior*, *8*, 27–41.

Kirouac, G., & Hess, U. (1999). Group membership and the decoding of nonverbal behavior. In P. Philippot, R. S. Feldman, & E. J. Coats (Eds.), *The social context of nonverbal behavior* (pp. 182–213). Cambridge, England: Cambridge University Press.

Knutson, B. (1996). Facial expressions of emotion influence interpersonal trait inferences. *Journal of Nonverbal Behavior*, *20*, 165–182.

Koomen, W., & Dijker, A. (1997). In-group and out-group stereotypes and selective processing. *European Journal of Social Psychology, 27*, 589–601.

Kupperbusch, C., Matsumoto, D., Kooken, K., Loewinger, S., Uchida, H., Wilson-Cohn, C., & Yrizarry, N. (1999). Cultural influences on nonverbal expression of emotion. In P. Philippot, R. S. Feldman, & E. J. Coats (Eds.), *The social context of nonverbal behavior* (pp. 182–213). Cambridge, England: Cambridge University Press.

Laird, J. D., Alibozak, T., Davainis, D., Deignan, K., Fontanella, K., Hong, J., Levy, B., & Pacheco, C. (1994). Individual differences in the effects of spontaneous mimicry on emotional contagion. *Motivation and Emotion, 5*, 139–154.

Lepore, L., & Brown, R. (1997). Category and stereotype activation: Is prejudice inevitable? *Journal of Personality and Social Psychology, 72*, 275–287.

Levenson, R. W., & Ruef, A. M. (1992). Empathy: A physiological substrate. *Journal of Personality and Social Psychology, 63*, 234–246.

Leyens, J. P., Paladino, P. M., Rodriguez-Torres, R., Vaes, J., Demoulin, S., Rodriquez-Perez, A., & Gaunt (2000). The emotional side of prejudice: The attribution of secondary emotions to ingroups and outgroups. *Personality and Social Psychology Review, 4*, 186–197.

Malpass, R. S., & Kravitz, J. (1960). Recognition for faces of own and other race. *Journal of Personality and Social Psychology, 13*, 330–334.

Manstead, A. S. R, Fischer, A. H., & Jacobs, E. B. (1999). The social and emotional functions of social displays. In P. Philippot, R. S. Feldman, & E. J. Coats (Eds.), *The social context of nonverbal behavior* (pp. 287–317). Cambridge, England: Cambridge University Press.

Matsumoto, D., & Ekman, P. (1988). *Japanese and Caucasian facial expressions of emotions (JACFEE) and neutral faces (JACNeuf)*. San Francisco: San Francisco State University.

Matsumoto, D., & Kudoh, T. (1993). American-Japanese cultural differences in attributions of personality based on smiles. *Journal of Nonverbal Behavior, 17*, 231–243.

McArthur, L. (1981). What grabs you? The role of attention in impression formation and causal attribution. In E. Higgins, C. Herman, & M. Zanna (Eds.), *Social cognition: The Ontario Symposium, 1*, 201–246. Hillsdale, NJ: Lawrence Erlbaum Associates.

McConahay, J. B., Hardee, B. B., & Batts, V. (1981). Has racism declined in America? It depends on who is asking and what is asked. *Journal of Conflict Resolution, 25*, 563–579.

McHugo, G. J., Lanzetta, J. T., & Bush, L. K. (1991). The effect of attitudes on emotional reactions to expressive displays of political leaders. *Journal of Nonverbal Behavior, 15*, 19–41.

Motley, M. T., & Camdem, C. T. (1988). Facial expression of emotion: A comparison of posed expressions versus spontaneous expressions in interpersonal communications settings. *Western Journal of Speech Communication, 52*, 1–22.

Noller, P. (1985). Video primacy – a further look. *Journal of Speech Communication, 9*, 28–47.

Öhman, A. (1999). Distinguishing unconscious from conscious emotional processes: Methodological consideration and theoretical implications. In

T. Dalgleish & M. J. Power (Eds.), *Handbook of cognition and emotion* (pp. 765–782). Chichester, England: John Wiley & Sons.

Patterson, M. L. (1999). The evolution of a parallel process model of nonverbal communication. In P. Philippot, R. S. Feldman, & E. J. Coats (Eds.), *The social context of nonverbal behavior* (pp. 317–348). Cambridge, England: Cambridge University Press.

Pennebaker, J. W., Rimé, B., & Blankenship, V. E. (1996). Stereotypes of emotional expressiveness of northerners and southerners: A cross-cultural test of Montesquieu's hypothesis. *Journal of Personality and Social Psychology, 70,* 372–380.

Pettigrew, T. F. (1998). Intergroup contact theory. *Annual Review of Psychology, 49,* 65–85.

Pettigrew, T. F., & Meertens, R. W. (1995). Subtle and blatant prejudice in Western Europe. *European Journal of Social Psychology, 25,* 57–75.

Petty, R. E., & Cacioppo, J. T. (1986). *Communication and persuasion: Central and peripheral routes of attitude change.* New York: Springer-Verlag.

Philippot, P., Feldman, R. S., & Coats, E. J. (1999). *The social context of nonverbal behavior.* Cambridge, England: Cambridge University Press.

Priest, R. L. (1997). *The effect of group membership on the perception of emotion.* Unpublished manuscript.

Riggio, R. E., & Friedman, H. S. (1986). Impression formation: The role of expressive behavior. *Journal of Personality and Social Psychology, 50,* 421–427.

Russell, J. A. (1994). Is there universal recognition of emotion from facial expression? A review of the cross-cultural studies. *Psychological Bulletin, 115,* 102–141.

Russell, J. A., & Fernández-Dols, J. M. (1997). What does a facial expression mean? In J. A. Russell & J. M. Fernández-Dols (Eds.), *The psychology of facial expression* (pp. 3–30). New York: Cambridge University Press.

Saarni, C., & Weber, H. (1999). Emotional display and dissemblance in childhood: Implications for self-presentation. In P. Philippot, R. S. Feldman, & E. J. Coats (Eds.), *The social context of nonverbal behavior* (pp. 262–287). Cambridge, England: Cambridge University Press.

Sanbonmatsu, D., Sherman, S., & Hamilton, D. (1987). Illusory correlation in the perception of individuals and groups. *Social Cognition, 5,* 1–25.

Shaver, P. R., Wu, S., & Schwartz, J. C. (1992). Cross-cultural similarities and differences in emotion and its representation: A prototype approach. In M. S. Clark (Ed.), *Emotion, review of personality and social psychology* (pp. 175–212). Newbury Park, CA: Sage Publications.

Shepherd, J. W., Deregowski, J. B., & Ellis, H. D. (1974). A cross-cultural study of recognition memory for faces. *International Journal of Psychology, 9,* 205–211.

Strayer, J. (1993). Children's concordant emotions and cognitions in response to observed emotions. *Child Development, 64,* 188–201.

Tcherkassof, A. (1999). Les indices de préparation à l'action et la reconnaissance des expressions émotionnelles faciales. *Revue Européenne de Psychologie Appliquée, 49,* 99–105.

Tzeng, O. C. S., & Jackson, J. W. (1994). Effect of contact, conflict, and social identity on interethnic group hostilities. *International Journal of Intercultural Relations, 18*, 259–276.

Wagner, H., & Lee, V. (1999) Facial behavior alone and in the presence of others. In P. Philippot, R. S. Feldman, and E. J. Coats (Eds.), *The social context of nonverbal behavior* (pp. 262–286). New York: Cambridge University Press.

Wagner, H. L., & Smith, J. (1991). Facial expressions in the presence of friends and strangers. *Journal of Nonverbal Behavior, 15*, 201–214.

Wallbott, H. G. (1988). In and out of context: Influences of facial expression and context information on emotion attributions. *British Journal of Social Psychology, 27*, 357–369.

Wallbott, H. G. (1991). Recognition of emotion from facial expression via imitation? Some indirect evidence for an old theory. *British Journal of Social Psychology, 30*, 207–219.

Yabar, Y. C., & Philippot, P. (2000). Caractéristiques psychosociales et réactions émotionnelles dans l'application des stéréotypes: Prédicteurs, médiateurs et modérateurs. *Cahiers Internationaux de Psychologie Sociale, 47*, 42–56.

Yzerbyt, V. Y., Leyens, J.-P., & Bellour, F. (1995). The ingroup over-exclusion effect: Identity concerns in decisions about group membership. *European Journal of Social Psychology, 25*, 1–16.

5. The Perception of Crying in Women and Men

Angry Tears, Sad Tears, and the "Right Way" to Cry

Leah R. Warner and Stephanie A. Shields

Authors' Note

Portions of this chapter were presented in a poster at the meeting of the International Society for Research on Emotions in Cuenca, Spain, in July 2002. We thank Randy Cornelius, Ursula Hess, and Pierre Philippot for their valuable comments on the manuscript. We also thank the undergraduate research assistants involved in collecting data: Susie Balazik, Maegan Dillman, Traci Lynn Frye, Lauren Kleha, and Dan Petrosky. We are grateful to Alice Eagly for providing access to her data on national stereotypes.

Correspondence regarding this chapter should be addressed to Leah R. Warner, Department of Psychology, The Pennsylvania State University, University Park, PA 16802. Email: lrw138@psu.edu.

> Cell phones. You never know what news a call might bring. And in a public place it can be difficult to get a handle on the roller-coaster of emotions that ensues. Chris is upset. News of the divorce is surprising, yet not totally unexpected. Making matters worse, the phone call comes at a restaurant while Chris sits with friends at the table, surrounded by a roomful of strangers. The news is too much. And then it happens – along with the growing anger, tears well up in Chris's eyes.

Adults' tears can be powerful elicitors of concern and sympathy. Tears can also elicit scorn or suspicion regarding the crying person's motives. Crying prompts others to pay attention, which makes tears a powerful form of persuasion. However, tears can also be deemed suspect if the tearful individual's motives are questioned, especially because people have a remarkable capacity to control weeping. So, what determines whether tears are valued or are suspect?

In this chapter, we consider the paradoxical nature of crying, focusing on questions of why and how evaluations of tears differ – depending on who sheds the tears, how the crying is done, and the context in which the crying occurs. We begin with a review of research on the perceptions of tears, specifically on what contributes to the power and ambiguity of tears as communicative signals. We then focus specifically on the influence that the crying person's gender has on how their crying is evaluated by others. We do this through examining the role played by the eliciting emotion, the role played by the type of tears cried, and the assumptions that observers make about the crier in context. We then report the results of a vignette study in which we investigated the extent to which people find different intensities of angry versus sad tears appropriate and the extent to which judgments of their appropriateness depend on the gender and race of the person shedding the tears. In the concluding section, we discuss the significance of the observer and the context for predicting how crying will be evaluated.

Evaluating Tears: Powerful but Ambiguous Signals

Tears are powerful stimuli that produce strong reactions in the observer, such as empathy and a willingness to comfort (Cornelius & Lubliner, 2003). In addition, those who cry are aware that their tears are likely to be evaluated. For example, public weeping can lead to negative affect or embarrassment for the weeper (Hoover-Dempsey, Plas, & Wallston, 1986). Because tears have such powerful effects on others, researchers are converging on the idea that adult crying is not only a reflection of an internal state of feeling but also a form of social communication.

Vingerhoets, Cornelius, Van Heck, and Becht (2000) observe that tears, by communicating a variety of needs, serve an instrumental purpose by influencing others to change the situation to the crier's liking. Thus, tears signal that others should pay attention and respond according to the message that the tears convey. In this regard, tears serve as a "distance regulator" in relationships (Kottler & Montgomery, 2001). For example, in one study, when participants were asked to describe the signal function of emotional expressions on faces, they were significantly more likely to say that faces shown with tears signified "help me" or "leave me alone" compared to nontearful faces (Cornelius, Nussbaum, Warner, & Moeller, 2000).

What makes the message of tears so powerful? Tears offer a way to express genuine emotion without the necessity of identifying the emotion behind them. Kottler (1996) describes tears as a "paralanguage" that serves the purpose of asking for help or surrender without being expected to engage in the reciprocal behaviors that accompany direct requests. Crying is a condensed way to say, "I am feeling intensely." As Kottler and Montgomery (2001) observe, there are few other means to express so much about the intensity of one's feeling in so little time. Katz (1999, p. 197) captures the essence of the power of tears when he describes them as "a personally embodied form of expression that transcends what speech can do." In other words, tears demonstrate the profundity of a person's feelings when speech fails. Thus, paradoxically, tears express strong feelings while neither specifying exactly what those feelings are nor precisely what others present are supposed to do about them.

The status of tears as a distinctly *emotional* communication complicates judgments about the degree and nature of the tearful person's needs. Cornelius et al. (2000) found that images of tearful faces were rated as more emotional than were the same faces with the tears digitally removed. This was true regardless of observer gender or target gender. Tears reveal that the crier is experiencing something significant. By signaling that something important has occurred, tears have the potential to elicit concern for the crier, thereby signaling that the crier requires help. At the same time, however, tears can signal loss of control in a situation (Vingerhoets et al., 2000). In situations where someone is expected to act but does not and instead cries, tears may signal failure.

Even though tears signal that the crier requires help from others, tears by themselves do not necessarily signal what help is needed. For example, Cornelius et al. (2000) found that participants' opinions diverged over whether they thought that the images of tearful faces signaled "help me" or "leave me alone." Thus, there is ample room for multiple interpretations of a single tearful event. The degree of distance or comforting that the tearful individual requires, the perceived degree of distressful dependency of the tearful individual, and the tearful individual's perceived capacity for self-control all depend on the observer's reading of the situation. The ambiguity of tears thus opens the possibility for the observer's own biases – such as his or her attitude toward the target – to contribute to his or her evaluations of the tearful individual.

To complicate matters, humans have a remarkable capacity to control their weeping (e.g., Kraemer & Hastrup, 1988), so tears can be interpreted as deliberate and manipulative. Therefore, another contentious dimension of reading tears is the evaluation of whether they are genuine. Frijda (1997) asserts that tears will be evaluated as suspect if one's motive for crying is questioned, and thus tears will be read as a form of extortion. Katz (1999) suggests that certain motives are associated with different quantities and qualities of tearing. Controlled tears stand for compassion, concern, sorrow, and so on, but too many tears make the expression too blatantly emotional and can signal that the tears are deliberate. Although these observations intuitively make sense regarding adult tears and their interpretation, we have found no empirical evidence to support them.

The fact that tears can be associated with so many emotions and intensities contributes to their ambiguity. Tears can occur with various emotions, including sadness, joy, anxiety, surprise, and anger (Vingerhoets et al., 2000). Tears also occur in varying amounts, from as little as a moist eye to streams of visible tears. Nonetheless, all tears signal feelings of intense emotion (Kottler & Montgomery, 2001). The social value of tears, however, depends on the specific emotion with which they are associated. Katz (1999) suggests that a moist eye in a sad context is a way to genuinely and appropriately express sadness. The moist eye signals that a strong emotion is being expressed in response to an uncontrollable loss but also that the emotion is sufficiently under control so as to not produce an overflow of emotion and full-blown crying. On the other hand, angry tears of any amount have been described as ineffective because they do no more than express frustration with stronger forces, preventing one from achieving certain goals (Crawford, Kippax, Onyx, Gault, & Benton, 1990). Crawford et al. point out the powerlessness that angry tears express: The individual is so frustrated by forces that allow no effective action that only one reaction seems possible – crying and admitting failure. These angry tears have low social value because the weakness associated with them calls into question the legitimacy of the original feeling of frustration.

Gender and Evaluation of Tears

Different types of tears may have different signal value depending on who shows them. The type of tears expressed and the situation in which crying occurs can affect the way that men's and women's tears are evaluated by others. In fact, studies of adult crying have assumed that the gender of the crier is the main variable driving the valence of tear evaluation. Studies in the 1980s found that women's tears were seen as more acceptable than men's. Cited extensively in recent reviews (e.g., Cornelius & Labott, 2001; Vingerhoets et al., 2000), these early studies concluded that people perceived men's tears to be inappropriate, whereas they believed that women's tears were more acceptable. In addition, people were more likely to indicate that they wanted to give sympathy and help to women. Notably, these studies rarely focused on the amount of crying or on the social context of crying.

The results of more recent work, in contrast, suggest that women's tears are not necessarily more valued than men's. Lewis (2000) found that both male and female actors who dabbed at their eyes and sniffled were given an equally negative evaluation in terms of their effectiveness when the respondents were told that the actors were leaders. Also, Zammuner (2000) found that men and women believe crying to be equally appropriate for themselves in a sad context, such as the death of a family member or a pet. Consistent with Zammuner's findings, Fischer, Manstead, Evers, Timmers, and Valk (2004) report – based on findings from a vignette study – that people perceive hypothetical men's and women's tears to be equally warranted when the situation is extreme (e.g., the death of an intimate or the breakup of a romance). However, traditional beliefs about men's and women's tears persisted when the situation was less severe (e.g., a burglary or a computer crash).

In some contexts, men's tears even may be valued more than women's (Labott, Martin, Eason, & Berkey, 1991). Labott and colleagues measured participants' evaluations of trained confederates' reactions (i.e., crying, laughter, or no expression) to an emotional movie. They found that the male confederates were better liked by the respondents when they wept than when they did not, whereas the female confederates were liked better when they were nonreactive than when they wept. Participants' evaluations of the confederates' laughter, however, yielded no gender difference. This pattern of results suggests that the evaluation of women's and men's crying was not based on an overall difference in the evaluation of men's and women's expressiveness.

One possible reason as to why recent studies are more likely to find positive evaluations of men's crying than those published in the 1980s is that some norms for men and crying are changing (Labott et al., 1991). Although some traditional norms still persist (Fischer et al., 2004), there may be certain types of expressions that were socially proscribed for men in the past but are now becoming more acceptable. One study has addressed this possibility, albeit indirectly. Gray and Heatherington (2003) found that men tended to express more verbal and nonverbal sad feelings in the presence of another man who was also expressive of sad feelings compared to one who was inexpressive. Men verbally expressed sad feelings to an even greater extent when the other man demonstrated that he was accepting of sad feelings. In sum, these findings suggest that men's expressivity is susceptible to changes in norms for a particular situation (Gray & Heatherington, 2003).

A common social-psychological explanation for why women are moved to tears more often than men is that tears violate social norms for masculinity (Bekker & Vingerhoets, 2001). Several studies have found that traditional men report that they avoid crying because they think crying is associated with weakness (e.g., Lombardo, Cretser, & Roesch, 2001; Ross & Mirowsky, 1984). Fischer (1993) proposes that masculinity is associated with displaying power and assertiveness, making men more likely than women to express "powerful" emotions, such as anger. She suggests that women, in contrast, are less concerned with demonstrating power and, therefore, more likely than men to report showing emotional expressions that reveal vulnerability or powerlessness, such as crying (see Bekker & Vingerhoets, 2001, for a review). Timmers, Fischer, and Manstead (2003) found that people believe that men display more powerful emotional behavior than women, lending support to the idea that tears expressing weakness are viewed as incompatible with conventional masculinity. Yet, it may be that certain types of tears are no longer associated with powerlessness and thus no longer conflict with assertions of masculinity. Recent findings of the acceptability of men's tears would reflect this change in meaning.

Even if the norms for the acceptability of some emotional behaviors may be changing, self-reports regarding the intensity and frequency of crying have not. Lombardo, Cretser, and Roesch (2001) found that gender differences in the self-reported frequency and intensity of crying were comparable in a 1983 and a 2001 sample. One complicating factor in interpreting whether and how norms are changing is the tendency for emotion self-reports about general, nonspecific situations to conform to gender stereotypes even when behavioral measures do not (Robinson, Johnson, & Shields, 1998).

Research has pointed to apparent gender differences in the frequency of crying to explain why men's tears may be viewed more favorably than women's in some contexts (Fischer et al., 2004; Labott et al., 1991). It has consistently been shown that women report being more prone to cry. Both self-report and observational data demonstrate that women are much more likely than men to be moved to tears and to cry more intensely, especially when angry (see Bekker & Vingerhoets, 2001, for a review). Labott and colleagues suggest that because men's tears are unusual, observers might think that something genuinely important must have happened for adult men to cry. On the other hand, women's relatively more frequent crying suggests to an observer that women cry in response to more mundane issues as well as in response to important ones. Because women are believed to cry more frequently than men, women's tears may be regarded as more suspect. For example, Lutz (1999) cites numerous historical anecdotes of women's tears being regarded suspiciously and perceived as shed only to obtain a desired outcome.

If men's tears are more likely than women's to be evaluated positively because men cry less often and the norms for men's tears are changing, then we must ask why the general belief persists that men's crying is negatively evaluated. There may simply be a discrepancy between what people believe about gender and crying in general and what actually happens when specific targets in specific situations are evaluated. In other words, implicit norms about men's tears may be changing, but this change is not yet reflected in explicit knowledge. Consequently, in self-report measures, individuals refer to traditional beliefs that men's tears are rare and that they signal weakness.

If norms are changing, what does the new ideal form of expression look like? What type of tears no longer signals weakness? In the following section, we propose an explanation for the evaluation of women's and men's tears that is contingent on the manner and the context in which the tears are expressed.

Manly Emotion: An Account of Gendered Evaluation of Tears

Shields (2002) proposed that in contemporary U.S. society, one type of "ideal" emotional expression is construed as controlled expression that conveys deep and authentically felt emotion. This expressive style is celebrated in popular culture and exemplified in dramatic movie heroes such as Russell Crowe in *Gladiator* or Vigo Mortensen as Aragorn in the *Lord of the Rings* trilogy. It conveys the individual's emotion as one of authentic feeling and self-control: "I can control my emotion (i.e., my self), and I can competently harness my emotion to control the situation."

Shields (2002) referred to this expressive style as "manly emotion" because it derives its value from and defines (as well as is defined by) a particular version of white heterosexual masculinity. Greater cultural value is placed on manly emotion through its connection to the expression of rationality and self-control. As a standard, this style is elusive or only partially attainable for the individual. Like other cultural standards, such as those for beauty, it may be completely and ideally expressed only in films and other works of fiction. It is important to note that manly emotion is not equivalent to men's emotion per se. In fact, it is a standard that women are expected to adhere to in many situations as well.

Men in the United States and Northern Europe report that they are concerned with possessing the competence necessary for manly expression of emotion. Timmers, Fischer, and Manstead (1998) argued that because men are reluctant to express feelings that show vulnerability, they are more concerned with the instrumentality of emotional expression. In other words, they want to be able to change the situation or the behavior of another person to demonstrate that they are in control of themselves. Timmers and colleagues tested this idea by instructing participants to read a series of vignettes about individuals expressing powerful versus powerless emotions. Participants were instructed to imagine whether they would express the emotion in the same way as described in the vignette. Timmers et al. (1998) found that the men were more likely to report that they would express their anger to be seen as self-confident. On the other hand, the women were more likely to report that they would express their anger because they expected it to be a relief or because the anger was out of their control. In addition, these researchers found that men were less likely to say they would express their sadness than women, especially through crying.

Other work corroborates Timmers et al.'s (1998) results by demonstrating a connection between masculinity and anger expression. For example, Kinney, Smith, and Donzella (2001) used the Bem Sex Role Inventory (Bem, 1974), a measure of the extent to which people endorse gender stereotypes as descriptive of themselves, and the anger-in and anger-out portions of the State Trait Anger Expression Inventory (Spielberger et al., 1985) in a correlational study to explore this association. They found that the endorsement of masculine stereotypical traits as self-descriptive positively predicted the degree to which individuals report expressed anger (i.e., anger-out). Conversely, endorsement of feminine stereotypical traits as self-descriptive negatively predicted reports of expressed anger. Moreover, endorsing stereotypical masculine traits was negatively related to the degree to which individuals repressed anger (i.e., anger-in). Thus, the more masculine stereotypes the respondents endorsed, the more they reported that they express anger and the less they reported that they repress anger.

These two studies demonstrate a link between masculinity and emotional expressions that signal competence. However, because women are also held to competence standards, manly emotion may be expected of them, too. For example, women are just as negatively evaluated for expressing "weak" emotions in positions of leadership as men are (Lewis, 2000), but because manly emotion is associated with men, individuals tend to assume that men are able to uphold competence standards more than women are. For example, Timmers, Fischer, and Manstead (2003) found that their participants believed men are better than women in situations where sensitivity is required for competence (e.g., in nursing). Indeed, Timmers and colleagues concluded, "For men, emotions still seem to be more associated with ability, with good social and emotional skills, whereas for women emotions remain linked to stereotypical femininity, that is, to their vulnerability, and thus to their loss of control and power" (p. 58). Both men and women were held to competency standards, but it was assumed that men handled their emotions better than women. Men were still seen as more competent than women even though situations requiring sensitivity are stereotypically associated with women's work (Fabes & Martin, 1991).

Returning to our discussion of tears, how does the concept of manly emotion help us understand why men's tears may be valued more than women's in some contexts? Contrary to assertions that all crying is undesirable, the moist eye in a sad context may be a valued emotional expression, especially for men, because it fits the criteria for manly emotion expression. As discussed previously, a moist eye in a sad context reveals intense feeling while demonstrating the ability to control those feelings (Katz, 1999). Such a display can demonstrate the competence prescribed by manly emotion norms. Another feature that may affect the acceptability of tears is the degree to which the person is believed to have some control over the situation. For example, in a work context, sad news regarding a colleague's health (something that the person could not have influenced) warrants more reaction than that colleague's failure to be promoted (something that the person could have influenced and, therefore, something of a personal failure). In Lewis's (2000) study described earlier, participants evaluated leaders' reactions to a poor financial year in a work context. Sad reactions (e.g., tearful displays and a quiet, pleading voice) were compared to angry reactions (e.g., looking stern, raising one's voice, and pounding fists) and to nonreactions (e.g., unemotional expression and a neutral voice). Men's sad reactions were seen as less competent than either no reaction or an angry reaction, whereas there was no difference in the evaluation of women's sad and angry reactions.

Although evidence suggests that subtle tears in a sad context may meet the standards for manly emotion, angry tears are more problematic. Thomas's (2003) qualitative study of men's attitudes toward their own anger revealed that men strive to maintain a manly emotion version of their anger. Competence and minimal expression were central themes that emerged in her interviews of nineteen predominantly middle-class white men. Thomas found that "right anger," or the appropriate expression of anger, was described as "proportionate to the offense and successful in making its point" (p. 168). For example, one respondent said, "You are going to work for justice and people are going to know what your point is, but you're not going to yell at them" (p. 168). "Wrong anger," on the other hand, involved overreaction and failing to act: "Men became angry when they did not have the ability to control or 'fix' things" (p. 168). In other words, the desired expression of anger is one that competently addresses the cause of anger and resolves the conflict but employs minimal expression of anger to achieve this goal. It is interesting that the men in Thomas's study said that, as they grew older, they became better able to express anger in a manly emotional style. Respondents reported that, as they matured, they tended to "have more realistic expectations, make finer distinctions, and display less volatile responses" (p. 171). Thomas reported that the men recalled decades of conflict regarding how to express their anger in a way that maximized competence without overreaction.

In summary, if minimal expression and appearance of competence are indicators of manly emotion, it would be extremely difficult for angry tears to meet this standard. It appears that in terms of how the quantity and quality of tears influence evaluations of women's and men's tears, the most positively evaluated may be a moist eye in a sad context, most notably if the one who emotes is a man. Furthermore, what is read as manly emotion is susceptible to observer interpretation (Shields, 2005). The crier's emotional state, communication intent, self-control, and authenticity are all open to interpretation. The expressor's gender also influences how observers interpret the expressor's emotional behavior and feeling (e.g., Hess et al., this volume, Chapter 2; Shields & Crowley, 1996), which are evident in tears (e.g., Shields & Crowley, 2000).

Race, Gender, and Manly Tears

The research summarized herein demonstrates that in situations demanding competence, masculine norms of competence set the standard for tearful expression for both men and women. This would seem to be the end of the story. However, the apparent simplicity of describing emotional, tearful expression in terms of gender difference masks important questions: Which man? Which woman? Before turning to our study of manly emotion in men's and women's tears, we consider here how another dimension of social identity – namely, race – might interact with gender in influencing the evaluation of a person's tears.

As we noted earlier, the manly emotion standard is not simply based on masculinity; rather, it is based on *white* (i.e., white European American) masculinity. Few investigators have addressed the way in which gender and race mutually affect beliefs about emotion. The scant evidence available suggests that white participants believe that white men conform to manly emotion standards more successfully than white women or women and men from other racial or ethnic groups. That said, we expect that the ways in which non-white men and women are believed to deviate from these standards are different from the ways that white women are believed to deviate.

Evidence from studies that have addressed stereotype content more generally indicates that, across races, women are believed to be more emotional than men. The degree to which this is so, however, depends on the race of the target. Shields and Crowley (2000) asked research participants to read a single scenario in which a white, black, or latina/o target learned that she or he had been denied a promotion. After reading the scenario, participants answered a short series of questions about the likely reactions of the target and the target's suitability for the job. Participants (not just white participants) rated the white female target as significantly less in control, sadder, and more frequently emotional than the male target. Answers to an open-ended question corroborated this pattern. Participants were asked to "Imagine [the target] after reading the letter [and] describe [the target's] reaction to the news." The terms "sad" and "disappointed" were more often used for the female target than for the male target, and "angry" or "angry and disappointed" were more often used for the male target. Tears or weeping were mentioned more often for the female target. Gender effects, however, differed by target race. Relevant here is the frequency with which the participants referenced tears or weeping in their description of the target's reaction to the news about the missed promotion. Tears were mentioned more frequently for women than for men for all three ethnicities, but the proportion of responses that mentioned tears for white women (15.5 percent) was greater than for latinas or black women (7.2 and 9.4 percent, respectively).

In a study of stereotypes held by white women, Landrine (1985) also found differences in emotion stereotypes of black women and white women. Black women were rated as significantly more "dirty," "hostile," and "superstitious" than white women, whereas white women were rated as significantly more "dependent," "emotional," and "passive." Landrine's study specifically suggests that negatively valenced words that signal uncontrolled anger are associated with black women, whereas emotion is more generally associated with white women.

Additional evidence that being emotional is associated particularly with white American women comes from a study of national stereotypes. Eagly and Kite (1987) examined national stereotypes of twenty-eight nations held by U.S. college students (race was not reported). The participants used a scale of 0 to 100 to indicate the percentage of men, women, and persons in general (gender unspecified) of each nationality that they believed possessed each of forty-one attributes. Ethnicity of men, women, and persons *within* nations remained unspecified. Eagly and Kite found that, for any nation, the stereotypes for persons were significantly closer to stereotypes for men than for women. This finding is consistent with the idea that the stereotypes of dominant members in a category tend to be overrepresented in the stereotype content of the category as a whole (see Schneider, 2004, for a review). Eagly and Kite also found that the percentage of American women estimated as "emotional" was higher than any other target from any nation (i.e., in the United States, person = 68.0 percent, man = 57.0 percent, and woman = 72.5 percent). If we assume that the same category-dominance effects occur with race, the stereotype that American women are emotional may be closer to the stereotype for American white women than for women of color. In addition, dampened or controlled emotion may be more of a white male stereotype than a stereotype about men of color.

In summary, the few studies that pertain to emotion stereotypes across racial or national groups suggest that in the United States, the emotional female/unemotional male stereotype may be a dimension of stereotypes of whites/European Americans, and that emotional behavior may not be a developed component of stereotypes of blacks. There is simply too little data to speculate on the quality or importance of emotion stereotypes for other racial and ethnic groups. If it is the case that there are few or weak emotion stereotypes of blacks, whites' ratings of blacks' tears would not be based on consistent beliefs about black women's or men's emotions. The resulting evaluations of their tears would thus be mixed.

In the next section, we describe a vignette study that provides an initial demonstration of manly emotion standards as applied to the evaluation of tears. In this study, we primarily considered target gender. Because we believe there is a need to examine gender effects in relation to other aspects of social identity, we also included a race of the target condition as an exploratory component of the study. We were particularly interested in comparing how black targets (women and men) would be evaluated in terms of the quantity and quality of crying in context.

An Empirical Investigation of Manly Emotion's Role in Tear Evaluation

We investigated the extent to which people find different intensities of angry versus sad tears appropriate in an uncontrollable situation and the extent to which judgments of appropriateness of tears depend on the gender and race of the person displaying them. As noted previously, little attention has been given to the effect of the intensity of tears in comparing evaluations of men's and women's tears. Rather, conclusions about the value of tears have been based on the presence or absence of tears (Cornelius & Labott, 2001). Our discussion of manly emotion, however, suggests that tear intensity and gender should be central to determining evaluation. Specifically, we predict that moist eyes will be more favorably evaluated than open tears and that moist eyes displayed by men will be evaluated most favorably overall.

In addition, the relation among gender, tears, and the kind of emotion evoking the tears has not been considered in empirical work. Scholars have suggested that angry tears of any kind are negatively evaluated (e.g., Shields, 2002), whereas tears are more acceptable in sad situations (e.g., Katz, 1999); however, these proposals have yet to be empirically tested. The acceptability of sad tears, however, is qualified by the situation such that tears are deemed appropriate only when the situation is truly not under one's direct control. Our work on manly emotion suggests that in situations outside of one's control, positive evaluations will depend not only on the type of emotion associated with the tears but also on the gender of the individual who is crying. Specifically, we predict that a male target's tears will be more positively evaluated than a female target's tears in a sad context. This prediction follows from previous research showing that emotion is associated with ability and competence to a greater degree in men than women. Because manly emotion is hypothesized to be particularly desirable in situations where individuals are motivated to express competence, we developed vignettes describing situations in which people were in a public place and strangers as well as friends were present. We included race as an exploratory component to examine how black targets' tears would be evaluated by whites.

The vignettes included key words to indicate gender, race, emotion type, and tear type. Vignettes were varied on four two-level factors: 2 (target gender: woman or man) by 2 (target tear type: moist eye or visible tears) by 2 (target emotion type: sad or angry) by 2 (target race: black or white). To vary gender and race, we used the subtle tactic of using different names of the main character.[1] We varied emotion type by describing the target as becoming either "sadder" or "angrier" in response to the experience described in the vignette. We varied tear-type intensity by describing the target as beginning to "tear up" for subtle tears, while describing the target as beginning to "cry" for more intense tears. Our manipulation checks indicated that participants recognized the distinctions in emotion type and in tear intensity.[2]

---

[1] Our gender and race manipulation was achieved by using names that are conventionally associated with a particular gender and race in the United States. Previous research concluded that some names are commonly identified as designating one or the other gender (Kasof, 1993; Van Fleet & Atwater, 1997). For our study of tears, we used four names we had identified as race and gender typical. As a manipulation check, participants rated a longer list of names individually on (a) the likelihood that the names were African American versus European American (1 = African American, 4 = either, 7 = European American), and (b) the likelihood that the names were male versus female (1 = male, 4 = either, 7 = female). The names we used in our study of tears (i.e., Latisha, Jamal, Jennifer, and Daniel) were all found to be gender and race specific. We found a significant difference in the predicted direction between mean ratings of the two white targets (Jennifer, $M = 5.63$, $SD = 1.28$; Daniel, $M = 5.35$, $SD = 1.34$) and the two black targets (Latisha, $M = 1.73$, $SD = 1.02$; Jamal, $M = 1.59$, $SD = 0.96$, $t(282) = 38.83$, $p < 0.001$). We also found a significant difference in the predicted direction between mean ratings of the two female targets (Jennifer, $M = 6.98$, $SD = 0.13$; Latisha, $M = 6.90$, $SD = 0.60$) and the two male targets (Daniel, $M = 1.08$, $SD = 0.36$; Jamal, $M = 1.31$, $SD = 1.15$, $t(283) = 125.12$, $p < 0.001$).

[2] As a manipulation check for emotion type we asked, "How angry is [the target]?" and "How sad is [the target]?" In comparison to targets described as becoming "sadder," targets described as becoming "angrier" were rated as more angry ($M = 5.86$, $SD = 1.00$

Participants responded to one of two vignettes, one about break-ing up with a significant other or one about parental divorce.[3] Because the participant responses to each topic were similar (i.e., did not differ statistically), results for the two vignettes were combined; those com-bined results are reported herein. The following sample vignette tem-plate shows in italics the words that were varied.

Latisha and her boyfriend have been dating for almost one year and have been considering living together. One week before their one-year anniversary, they meet several friends at a busy restaurant for lunch as planned. During the meal, it accidentally comes out that *Latisha's* boyfriend has been seeing someone else. He says he still loves her, but *Latisha* only becomes *sadder* and begins to *cry*.

In this study, 284 university undergraduates participated. Our sample included 69 percent women and 31 percent men. Because nearly all participants indicated that they were white (i.e., 94 percent), we are limited to comparing white women's and men's responses.[4]

We tested the participants in groups. Participants first read the vignette and then completed a questionnaire packet that included the Positive Evaluation Scale, a five-item scale created for this study to

---

versus $M = 4.98$, $SD = 1.43$, $t(287) = 6.05$, $p < 0.001$) and less sad ($M = 5.99$, $SD = 1.03$ versus $M = 6.37$, $SD = 0.78$, $t(287) = -3.45$, $p = 0.001$). As a manipulation check for tear intensity we asked participants, "How intense did you imagine [the target's] tears to be?" Respondents answered the question using a 1 to 4 scale (1 = "no actual tears," 2 = "a moist eye," 3 = "visible tearing," 4 = "weeping") to see if our two tear descriptors were considered to be of different intensities. Targets described as beginning to "cry" ($M = 3.06$, $SD = 0.60$) were rated as displaying more intense tears than targets described as beginning to "tear up" ($M = 2.71$, $SD = 0.60$, $t(287) = 5.01$, $p < 0.001$).

[3] We constructed the vignette template taking into account five considerations. First, we emphasized the uncontrollability of the situations by describing situations that could not be avoided by the protagonist. Second, to emphasize the public nature of the situa-tion, the vignettes described the presence of strangers in a public space. The presence of friends was described so that the tears could not be thought of as unnoticed or anony-mous. We did not use private or intimate situations because such situations may call for expressive rules that entail displays of nurturance rather than manly emotion (Shields, 2002). Third, we constructed the vignette template such that it was relevant to both sad-ness and anger. Because only the emotion words were changed and not the content of the story, the situation had to be constructed such that tears from both sadness and anger were plausible reactions. Fourth, the vignettes described events that were upsetting but were also ambiguous in nature, such that room for interpretation of the protagonist's emotional response was possible. Fifth, the vignettes concerned topics relevant to the participant population: students enrolled in an introductory psychology course.

[4] We deleted data for participants who did not pass our manipulation checks (i.e., more than 2.5 standard deviations away from the mean on tests of the vignette variables); this left 284 participants in our final sample.

measure how positively participants evaluate targets' emotional expression (e.g., "How likely is it that you would react in the same way as [the target]?"). For these items as well as for all other close-ended questions, the respondents indicated their level of agreement on a seven-point scale. Higher numbers indicated a more positive evaluation of the target's behavior. The scale reliability was computed via Chronbach's alpha, $r = 0.65$.

The emotion evaluation data were analyzed by means of a 2 (emotion type) by 2 (tear type) by 2 (target gender) by 2 (race) between-subjects ANOVA on the Positive Evaluation Scale. First, as noted previously, we predicted that a moist eye would be evaluated more positively than visible tears, especially for males. Consistent with this prediction, we found a significant tear type by gender interaction. Notably, all means were above the 4.0 mark, which indicates that all the targets were rated more positively than negatively; however, males in the tear-up condition were evaluated more positively than targets in any other condition. In addition, regardless of gender, targets were evaluated more positively the less intense their tear display (Figure 5.1).

Second, we hypothesized that sad tears would be evaluated more positively than angry tears, especially for males. This prediction was supported by a significant emotion type by target gender interaction. Male targets described as sad were evaluated more positively than sad female targets, angry male targets, and angry female targets. Again, all means were above the 4.0 mark, which indicates that all targets were rated more positively than negatively but that sad males were evaluated most positively (Figure 5.2).

Third, we hypothesized that participants would justify the male targets' (positive) ratings and the female targets' (negative) ratings by implying that the women's tears were less genuine than the men's. In addition to the Positive Evaluation Index, we asked two questions pertaining to the participants' beliefs about the targets' ability to control their tears: "How much is [the target] able to control his or her emotions in this situation?" and "How hard is it for [the target] to handle his or her emotions in this situation?" Higher numbers indicated lower levels of ability to control emotions. Indeed, we found that female targets ($M = 3.48$, $SD = 1.50$) were judged as more able to control their emotions than male targets ($M = 3.00$, $SD = 1.35$), $F(1, 267) = 9.38$, $p = 0.002$. Also, female targets ($M = 3.02$, $SD = 0.57$) were perceived as displaying more intense tears than male targets ($M = 2.76$, $SD = 0.65$), $F(1, 267) = 12.96$, $p < 0.001$. Females were more likely to be described as displaying "visible

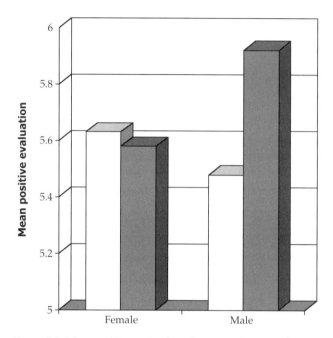

Figure 5.1. Mean positive evaluation of tears as a function of gender and tear type, $F(1, 267) = 3.77$, $p = 0.05$.

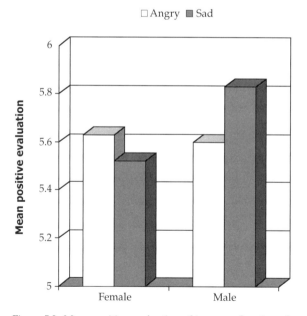

Figure 5.2. Mean positive evaluation of tears as a function of gender and emotion type, $F(1, 267) = 3.70$, $p = 0.05$.

tearing," whereas males were more likely to be described as displaying "a moist eye" – regardless of the actual tearing condition in the vignette. Thus, while women were believed to cry more intensely, they were also judged better able to control their tear flow, perhaps suggesting that they purposely displayed more intense tears than men.

The results of this study inform us of the participants' strength of opinions on male and female tears. The results also indicate that the scenarios were intense; a breakup or a divorce is not trivial. In all the vignette-rating conditions, the participants believed that because of the strong situation, the targets had a good reason to react emotionally. Even though all the participants had a good reason for emotion, some targets seem to have been credited with a better reason for tears. Specifically, the male targets were rated more positively than the female targets when they reacted with a subtle tear or were sad.

Finally, we treated race as an exploratory variable because there are several possible competing predictions for the role that race plays in the evaluations of tears. If our idea is correct that whites believe that blacks' angry tears deviate from manly emotion, then we would expect especially negative evaluations of blacks' angry tears compared to the evaluation of their sad tears. On the other hand, if it is more likely that whites' beliefs about blacks' emotion expression are underdeveloped, then we would expect inconsistent findings or no findings due to race. Our findings in this initial study suggest the latter. Indeed, all effects due to race were not significant except for one. This finding, a significant race by emotion type interaction, $F(1, 267) = 4.20$, $p = 0.04$, produced results opposite to what we would have expected based on our argument about blacks' angry tears. Specifically, blacks described as displaying angry tears ($M = 5.76$, $SD = 0.62$) were rated significantly more *positively* than whites who were described as displaying angry tears ($M = 5.42$, $SD = 0.93$). However, the evaluations of blacks' sad tears ($M = 5.64$, $SD = 0.79$) did not differ from the evaluations of blacks' angry tears or the evaluations of whites' sad tears ($M = 5.70$, $SD = 0.67$). This initial finding suggests that there is more to the story in understanding whites' evaluations of blacks' tears. Thus, we need a better understanding of where emotion fits into stereotypes of black targets, both female and male, and other subgroup stereotypes. Future studies should compare blacks' evaluations of whites' and blacks' expressive behavior, including tears, to better understand how dimensions of social identity intersect in producing target-group and specific gender-emotion stereotypes.

The Paradoxical Nature of Manly Tears

There is a positive value to the nonverbal expression of sad emotion via publicly shed tears, but our results suggest that men are more likely to receive this positive evaluation than women. If this is the case, it reveals a paradox: If sadness is a "weak" emotion (as suggested by some researchers), why are men's sad tears evaluated positively? If anger is a "strong" emotion, why are angry tears seen as less positive in men than sad tears? These seeming contradictions may be explained in part by the context-driven social meaning of emotion. By this, we mean that specific emotions (or emotions more generally) in themselves are not inherently strong or weak; rather, the value placed on them depends in part on the circumstances in which they are felt or expressed, how they are expressed, and by whom.

As discussed earlier in this chapter, angry tears and open tears sug-gest frustration with stronger forces (Crawford, Kippax, Onyx, Gault, & Benton, 1990); therefore, anger displayed in association with tears is perceived as ineffective rather than effective and would be evaluated negatively. In addition, in our vignettes, sadness is not associated with ineffectiveness because the protagonist is not directly responsible for the situation. This understanding of anger and sadness in the context of tears contrasts with the position that anger necessarily conveys higher status and competence than sadness does (Tiedens, 2001). Expressions of sad, moist eyes can convey competence (in this case, self-control) if one does not have personal responsibility for the negative situation. Thus, results of our study might suggest that the context, not the emo-tion per se, dictates whether an emotion is associated with high or low competence.

It remains for us to account for why men are evaluated most posi-tively in the sad, moist-eye context. It may be that women's reactions are evaluated less positively than men's here because men in general are believed to display more expressions of competence than women (Timmers, Fischer, & Manstead, 2003). If an expression signals weak-ness in the situation, as do angry or open tears, women and men will not be evaluated differently because the ineffectiveness is clear. However, if the expression has the potential to signal effectiveness, such as moist eyes in a sad context, then other beliefs about effec-tiveness can inform one's evaluation of a target's emotion. Because the short vignettes in our study left some ambiguity as to how the emotions were expressed, the participants could have inferred that the male targets' expressions were more competent than the female targets' expressions.

In addition to the belief that men express their emotions more effectively than women, another belief about effectiveness that may contribute to the evaluations of men's and women's tears in the sad, moist-eye context is the extent to which participants believed that women targets controlled or "manipulated" their tears. Men's and women's emotions were rated as having the same intensity of feeling, but there appeared to be some implied manipulation of the appearance of tears by women. Women targets were estimated as displaying more intense tears and being more able to control their emotion than men protagonists. Together, we interpret these results as reflecting our participants' belief that women targets may have intentionally displayed more intense expressions than the men targets. If this is the case, it converges with Cretser, Lombardo, Lombardo, and Mathis's (1982) finding that female respondents reported believing that society views females' crying as manipulative (to a greater degree than did male respondents about females' crying).

It is plausible that some of our effects were intensified due to the fact that the vignettes described situations involving important personal relationships. In Lombardo and colleagues' (2001) comparison of 1981 and 1993 data on the frequency of men's tears, the only significant change between their two studies was an increase in male crying as a result of a "breakup of a romance," indicating that tears in situations involving close relationships may be more acceptable than tears in other situations. Fischer and colleagues (2004) also reported that participants indicated approval of men's tears when the tears occurred in response to the breakup of a romantic relationship. It is possible that our findings are limited to changing relationship norms. However, the public nature of the situation in our vignettes suggests a change in standards more pervasive than the romantic relationships context because men traditionally report that they avoid crying in front of strangers (Lombardo et al., 2001). Future research would benefit from comparing different types of public situations to discover how widely the positive regard for men's crying extends.

Taking a broader view, our study bears out the conclusion that perceptions of crying are embedded in particular cultural timeframes. Several authors (e.g., Labott et al., 1991; Vingerhoets et al., 2000; Cornelius & Labott, 2000; Shields, 2002) have asserted that attitudes toward men compared to women criers have changed substantially in the United

States during the past thirty years, from the "sensitive man" of the early 1970s to a "hard bodies" political backlash in the 1980s (Jeffords, 1994) to the "new fatherhood" of the 1990s. The events of September 11, 2001, seem to have brought about yet another change in the criteria for public displays of intense sadness by men, including crying. Visible and sometimes profuse tears were shed by various powerful men in the immediate aftermath of the terror attack, the most famous perhaps being veteran CBS news anchor Dan Rather's intense weeping on David Letterman's late-night television talk show. The general suspension of the prohibitions on open weeping in the short run seems to have altered expectations for what is deemed appropriate since then.

Conclusion: The Meanings of Tears

How crying is evaluated depends on how it is done and who sheds the tears. There is a positive value for nonverbal expression of sad emotion via tears in situations that require competence, but the results of our study suggest that men are more likely to receive this positive evalua-tion than women. In this chapter, we emphasized that the tearful expres-sion (both type and amount) and characteristics of the target interact to inform whether an observer's evaluation will be positive or negative. In other words, observers do not uniformly accept or reject certain expres-sions of emotion based on target gender. Their beliefs about the gender and race of the target work in conjunction with their beliefs about the appropriateness of the type and quantity of tears as the basis for evalu-ating others' tears. Controlled yet deeply felt manly emotion is valued in many displays of tears, and those who adhere to this standard are more positively evaluated than those who do not. Because competence and instrumentality are stereotypically associated with masculinity, they are also associated with manly emotion, fostering the belief that men are better at adhering to manly emotion than women.

The ambiguity of tears contributes to the role that beliefs related to gender, race, and other social groups play in determining evaluation valence. Tears can be controlled to a greater extent than many other nonverbal behaviors, but they can also be seen as a signal of uncon-trolled emotion. Thus, tears alone do not clearly indicate whether a per-son is genuinely and justifiably upset. This is especially the case when the situation is extreme (Hutson-Comeaux & Kelly, 2002) or unclear. Such ambiguity leaves room for biases to influence the evaluation of another's tears. In addition to reliance on beliefs about social groups, the ambiguity of tears increases the chance that other types of observer biases will affect evaluation of this expressive behavior. Factors such as the observers' social values, attitudes toward the target, and likeability of the target all can affect their evaluation of tears.

The power and ambiguity of tears as a signal of felt emotion make them susceptible to the observer's Biased Emotion Evaluation, the term we apply to the observer's use of a target's emotional behavior as evidence for or against that target's legitimacy (Shields, Simon, Warner, & Scott, under review). We argue that, unlike other forms of biased social perception, emotion-relevant information carries special weight in the evaluations of others. Facial expressions of emotion and nonverbal movements are believed to be more difficult to control than language or actions (Gilbert & Krull, 1988; Morgan & Averill, 1992). Also, emotions have an immediate visibility in real-time behavior that other characteristics influenced by biased perception, such as honesty or moral character, do not. Thus, the observer may weigh heavily the value of judgments about emotion in judging the authenticity or worth of the target because he or she believes emotion is both visible and difficult to control and, therefore, a reflection of the target's subjective state.

Indeed, previous work indicates that lay people may link emotion with authenticity, even though this link may be inaccurate. Averill (1983) argued that authenticity is defined by lay people as a conjunction between internal experience and external expression. Internal experience is supposedly representative of who one truly is, a manifestation of one's core beliefs and values (Hochschild, 1983; Morgan & Averill, 1992), and emotion is viewed as a more direct expression of internalized experience than other target characteristics such as nonemotive personal attributes or observable actions (Johnson & Boyd, 1995). Although people may believe that emotions and their expression are unequivocal indicators of a target's authenticity, the salience and complexity of emotionally expressive behavior also make it susceptible to multiple interpretations (Shields, 2005). Thus, if emotions are perceived to be reflections of authenticity, and if observer biases influence the evaluations of the targets' emotions as inappropriate, such evaluations may provide particularly persuasive justification for negative actions toward those targets.

Throughout our discussion of crying, we have been concerned with the consequences that the evaluation of crying has for the target. We conclude with the proposal that what is at stake in crying is no less than the perceived authenticity and legitimacy of the felt emotion of the person who sheds the tears. Our results also reveal a particular double bind for women. When facing an emotion-evoking event, men may be expected to adhere more strictly to competence standards for tearful expression than women. However, even if women adhere to competence standards when they cry, they are likely to be less positively evaluated than men who are behaving comparably. As the saying goes, "It takes a real man to cry," but the right *man* must cry the right way at the right time.

References

Averill, J. R. (1983). Studies on anger and aggression: Implications for theories of emotion. *American Psychologist, 38,* 1145–1160.

Bekker, M. H. J., & Vingerhoets, A. J. J. M. (2001). Male and female tears: Swallowing versus shedding? The relationship between crying, biological sex, and gender. In A. J. J. M. Vingerhoets & R. R. Cornelius (Eds.), *Adult crying: A biopsychosocial approach* (pp. 91–114). Philadelphia: Taylor & Francis.

Bem, S. L. (1974). The measurement of psychological androgyny. *Journal of Consulting and Clinical Psychology, 42,* 155–162.

Cornelius, R. R., & Labott, S. M. (2001). The social psychological aspects of crying. In A. J. J. M. Vingerhoets & R. R. Cornelius (Eds.), *Adult crying: A biopsychosocial approach* (pp. 159–176). Philadelphia: Taylor & Francis.

Cornelius, R. R., & Lubliner, E. (2003, October). The what and why of others' responses to our tears: Adult crying as an attachment behavior. Third International Conference on The (Non)Expression of Emotions in Health and Disease; Tilburg, The Netherlands: Tilburg University Press.

Cornelius, R. R., Nussbaum, R., Warner, L. R., & Moeller, C. (August 2000). "An action full of meaning and of real service": The social and emotional messages of crying. International Society for Research on Emotion, Quebec City, Quebec, Canada.

Crawford, J., Kippax, S., Onyx, J., Gault, U., & Benton, P. (1990). Women theorizing their experiences of anger: A study using memory-work. *Australian Psychologist, 25,* 333–350.

Cretser, G. A., Lombardo, W. K., Lombardo, B., and Mathis, S. (1982). Reactions to men and women who cry: A study of sex differences in perceived societal attitudes versus personal attitudes. *Perceptual and Motor Skills, 55,* 479–486.

Eagly, A. H., & Kite, M. (1987). Are stereotypes of nationality applied to both men and women? *Journal of Personality and Social Psychology, 53,* 451–462.

Fabes, R. A., & Martin, C. L. (1991). Gender and age stereotypes of emotionality. *Personality and Social Psychology Bulletin, 17,* 532–540.

Fischer, A. H. (1993). Sex differences in emotionality: Fact or stereotype? *Feminism & Psychology, 3,* 303–318.

Fischer, A. H., Manstead, A. S. R., Evers, C., Timmers, M., & Valk, G. (2004). Motives and norms underlying emotion regulation. In P. Philippot & R. S.

Feldman (Eds.), *The regulation of emotion* (pp. 187–210). Mahwah, NJ: Lawrence Erlbaum Associates.

Frijda, N. H. (1997). On the functions of emotional expression. In A. J. J. M. Vingerhoets, F. J. Van Brussel, & A. J. W. Boelhouwer (Eds.), *The (non) expression of emotions in health and disease* (pp. 1–14). Tilburg, the Netherlands: Tilburg University Press.

Gilbert, D. T., & Krull, D. S. (1988). Seeing less and knowing more: The benefits of perceptual ignorance. *Journal of Personality and Social Psychology, 54,* 193–202.

Gray, S. M., & Heatherington, L. (2003). The importance of social context in the facilitation of emotional expression in men. *Journal of Social and Clinical Psychology, 22,* 294–314.

Hochschild, A. R. (1983). *The managed heart.* Berkeley, CA: University of California Press.

Hoover-Dempsey, K. V., Plas, J. M., & Wallston, B. S. (1986). Tears and weeping among professional women: In search of new understanding. *Psychology of Women Quarterly, 10,* 19–43.

Hutson-Comeaux, S. L., & Kelly, J. R. (2002). Gender stereotypes of emotional expression: How we judge an emotion as valid. *Sex Roles, 47,* 1–10.

Jeffords, S. (1994). *Hard bodies: Hollywood masculinity in the Reagan era.* New Brunswick, NJ: Rutgers University Press.

Johnson, J. T., & Boyd, K. R. (1995). Dispositional traits versus the content of experience: Actor/observer differences in judgments of the "authentic self." *Personality and Social Psychology Bulletin, 21,* 375–383.

Kasof, J. (1993). Sex bias in the naming of stimulus persons. *Psychological Bulletin, 113,* 140–163.

Katz, J. (1999). *How emotions work.* Chicago: University of Chicago Press.

Kinney, T. A., Smith, B. A., and Donzella, B. (2001). The influence of sex, gender, self-discrepancies, and self-awareness on anger and verbal aggressiveness among U.S. college students. *The Journal of Social Psychology, 141,* 245–263.

Kottler, J. A. (1996). *The language of tears.* San Francisco: Jossey-Bass.

Kottler, J. A., & Montgomery, M. J. (2001). Theories of crying. In A. J. J. M. Vingerhoets & R. R. Cornelius (Eds.), *Adult crying: A biopsychosocial approach* (pp. 1–18). Philadelphia: Taylor & Francis.

Kraemer, D. L., & Hastrup, J. L. (1988). Crying in adults: Self-control and autonomic correlates. *Journal of Social and Clinical Psychology, 6,* 53–68.

Labott, S. M., Martin, R. B., Eason, P. S., & Berkey, E. Y. (1991). Social reactions to the expression of emotion. *Cognition and Emotion, 5,* 397–419.

Landrine, H. (1985). Race × class stereotypes of women. *Sex Roles, 13,* 65–75.

Lewis, K. M. (2000). When leaders display emotion: How followers respond to negative emotional expression of male and female leaders. *Journal of Organizational Behavior, 21,* 221–229.

Lombardo, W. K., Cretser, G. A., & Roesch, S. C. (2001). For crying out loud: The differences persist into the '90s. *Sex Roles, 45,* 529–545.

Lutz, T. (1999). *Crying: The natural and cultural history of tears.* New York: W. W. Norton.

Morgan, C., & Averill, J. R. (1992). True feelings, the self, and authenticity: A psychosocial approach. In D. D. Franks & V. Gecas (Eds.), *Social perspectives on emotion* (pp. 95–123). Greenwich, CT: JAI Press.

Robinson, M. R., Johnson, J. T., & Shields, S. A. (1998). The gender heuristic and the database: Factors affecting the perception of gender-related differences in the experience and display of emotions. *Basic and Applied Social Psychology, 20*, 206–219.

Ross, C. E., & Mirowsky, J. (1984). Men who cry. *Social Psychology Quarterly, 47*, 138–146.

Schneider, D. J. (2004). *The psychology of stereotyping*. New York: Guilford Press.

Shields, S. A. (2002). *Speaking from the heart: Gender and the social meaning of emotion*. Cambridge, England: Cambridge University Press.

Shields, S. A. (2005). The politics of emotion in everyday life: "Appropriate" emotion and claims on identity. *Review of General Psychology, 9*, 3–15.

Shields, S. A., & Crowley, J. C. (1996). Appropriating questionnaires and rating scales for a feminist psychology: A multi-method approach to gender and emotion. In S. Wilkinson (Ed.), *Feminist social psychologies* (pp. 218–232). Buckingham, Great Britain: Open University Press.

Shields, S. A., & Crowley, J. C. (August 2000). Stereotypes of "emotionality": The role of the target's racial ethnicity, status, and gender. In U. Hess and R. Kleck (Chairs), *The influence of beliefs regarding men's and women's emotions on the perception and self-perception of emotions*. Symposium conducted at the meeting of the International Society for Research on Emotions, Quebec City, Canada.

Shields, S. A., Simon, A., Warner, L. R., & Scott, R. (under review). Biased emotion evaluation: Naming a winner influences observers' evaluation of debaters' emotion.

Spielberger, C. D., Johnson, E. H., Russell, S. F., Crane, R. J., Jacobs, G. A., & Worden, T. J. (1985). The experience and expression of anger: Construction and validation of an anger expression scale. In M. A. Chesney & R. H. Rosenman (Eds.), *Anger and hostility in cardiovascular and behavioral disorders* (pp. 5–30). Washington, DC: Hemisphere.

Thomas, S. (2003). Men's anger: A phenomenological exploration of its meaning in a middle-class sample of American men. *Psychology of Men & Masculinity, 4*, 163–175.

Tiedens, L. Z. (2001). Anger and advancement versus sadness and subjugation: The effect of negative emotion expressions on social status conferral. *Journal of Personality and Social Psychology, 80*, 86–94.

Timmers, M., Fischer, A. H., & Manstead, A. S. R. (1998). Gender differences in motives for regulating emotions. *Personality and Social Psychology Bulletin, 24*, 974–985.

Timmers, M., Fischer, A. H., & Manstead, A. S. R. (2003). Ability versus vulnerability: Beliefs about men's and women's emotional behavior. *Cognition and Emotion, 17*, 41–63.

Van Fleet, D. D., & Atwater, L. (1997). Gender neutral names: Don't be so sure! *Sex Roles, 37*, 111–123.

Vingerhoets, A. J. J. M., Cornelius, R. R., Van Heck, G. L., & Becht, M. C. (2000). Adult crying: A model and review of the literature. *Review of General Psychology, 4*, 354–377.

Zammuner, V. L. (2000). Men's and women's lay theory of emotion. In A. H. Fischer (Ed.), *Gender and emotion: Social psychological perspectives* (pp. 48–70). London: Cambridge University Press.

6. Tell Me a Story

Emotional Responses to Emotional Expression during Leader "Storytelling"

Kristi Lewis Tyran

Author's Note

Kristi Lewis Tyran is Associate Professor of Management, College of Business and Economics, Western Washington University. The author would like to thank Ursula Hess and Pierre Philippot for their helpful comments and suggestions.

Organizations are often thought to be nonemotional venues where serious work is done. Goals are set and accomplished, daily tasks checked off, and goods and services are produced – emotion is generally assumed to be absent or at least unnecessary in the work setting. Recently, scholars have acknowledged what workers have long known: that the workplace is far from a nonemotional environment (Fineman, 1993, 2003). Both positive and negative emotions are experienced and expressed daily, and the quality of these emotional experiences varies from elation and celebration when goals are accomplished to sadness or anger when expectations are not met (Rafaeli & Sutton, 1987, 1989; Sutton, 1991). Emotional expression can also be a required part of the job role, as in customer service (Hochschild, 1979, 1983; Rafaeli & Sutton, 1990; Sutton & Rafaeli, 1988). As such, emotion can play a role in all facets of work life. In this chapter, I focus on the worker's emotional reaction to a leader's emotional expression. A leader's expression of emotion in interpersonal interaction may occur incidentally or purposefully. The consequences of emotional expression by a leader in interpersonal communication are complex to predict and vary based on the follower audience. Nevertheless, if communication is conducted with a goal or purpose of influence, then understanding the impact of a leader's intentional or unintentional emotional expression on followers is important.

This chapter intends to build on the existing leadership literature by enhancing our knowledge of how gender and emotional expression during leader "storytelling" influences, motivates, and inspires a positive emotional response in others. Storytelling in organizations is defined as communicating and describing events for the construction of a collective sense of meaning and interpretation of those events (Boje, 1991; Spicochi & Tyran, 2002). Storytelling is a common method of communication in organizations and is often conducted as a dialogue with participants – effective storytelling involves listening as well as speaking. As participants participate in the dialogue and identify with the leader and her or his story, they make sense of events collectively through their own frame of reference (Greenberg, 1995). The purpose of storytelling versus traditional communication or information exchange is to establish a connection among those participating in the story so that, collectively, all participants gain a deeper sense of meaning within the shared experience. Because the objective of storytelling is to inspire collective interpretation of events, leader emotional expression and gender may play a crucial role in how individuals perceive the leader's story and thus make sense of complex and challenging events (Gioia & Thomas, 1996).

The exploration of leader emotional expression during storytelling requires the integration of three streams of literature: effective leadership styles and emotional expression, the emotional experience of those who observe male and female leaders' emotional expression, and leader storytelling as a part of effective leadership. To put the research in context, I begin with a brief discussion and overview of how leadership relates to emotions in organizations in general, followed by a discussion of each of these three research areas, and then move on to integrate these literatures through a discussion concerning the ways that leader gender and emotional expression may influence the audience's emotional experience during leader storytelling. The chapter concludes with recommendations for enhancing leader effectiveness when storytelling is employed to help followers cope with and understand challenging events.

Emotions in Organizations: A Leader's Perspective

Many economists and business people would argue that the workplace is a rational and nonemotional place where people are clearly guided by self-interest and the bottom line. But, research on emotions in organizations suggests that the workplace is a very emotional place, and leaders know this all too well. In the workplace, people experience joy when successful, sadness in failure, and anger when thwarted by others. Indeed, emotions are an integral part of the work experience for workers and customers, and leaders are not only aware of these emotions but also can manage, motivate, and respond to the emotions of the workplace on many levels.

Within the workplace, there are norms for emotional experience and expression and expectations for which emotions are appropriate to express in specific situations (Rafaeli & Sutton, 1989). Some jobs require emotional expression as part of the job description (Hochschild, 1983). For example, flight attendants are expected to be positive and happy, whereas bill collectors are expected to be gruff and mean (Hochschild, 1983; Sutton, 1991). Most customer-service employees are trained in maintaining positive affect even when the customer is expressing anger (Grandey, Fisk, Matilla, Jansen, & Sideman, 2005). In a recent study on the impact of affect and authenticity of affective expression in customer-service encounters, Grandey and her colleagues (2005) found that a service professional's authenticity in affect was equally as important as positive affect in customer satisfaction with the service they received. So, employees are not only expected to express positive emotion but also to do it authentically. Some workers take on an emotional persona so as to embed this emotional experience and expression in their job tasks, as in the case of adventure-travel guides (Sharpe, 2005). The emotional labor of adventure guides is an integral part of the adventure fantasy participants pay to have when going on an adventure-travel vacation. The research on emotional labor indicates, however, that incongruence (i.e., emotional dissonance) between felt and expressed emotion can lead to employee burnout and dissatisfaction (Hochschild, 1983).

As employees experience and express emotion, so do those in leadership roles. A leader can influence the quality of workers' emotional lives in many important ways. Leaders can provide guidance as to norms for emotional experience and expression; they can also model emotional norms. Recent research has focused on how emotional intelligence in leaders can improve many aspects of the work life of employees (Mandell & Pherwani, 2003). In addition, leaders who are considered "authentic" – that is, self-aware and true to their values, identities, preferences, and emotions – are argued to be more effective (Avolio, Gardner, Walumbwa, Luthans, & May, 2004). Thus, leaders model how to effectively manage and express emotions not only through their own emotional expression but also through their empathy and awareness of others' emotions. Leaders who empathize with the emotional labor of workers can structure policies and strategies to ease the burden of emotional dissonance and other negative consequences of emotional labor.

Leader communication – both one-way (i.e., directive) and two-way (i.e., dialogue) – is an area in which leader emotional expression and response to emotional experience is particularly salient in the workplace. In his book, *Toxic Emotions at Work* (2003), Peter Frost argues that leaders who demonstrate compassion when responding to follower expressions of pain, anger, and other negative emotions can reduce the negative effects that experiencing toxic emotions can bring. Compassion and empathy are important aspects of effective leader communication (Frost, 2004). A leader's communication when followers are experiencing change, crisis, or other negative situations can be extremely important in determining how followers respond to such upheaval (Spicochi & Tyran, 2002). Most important, a leader's ability to listen as well as talk can influence the emotional responses of followers. A leader's communication style is related to his or her leadership style, and in the next section, this is related directly to leader emotional expression.

Effective Leadership Styles and Emotional Expression

> "Before you can inspire with emotion, you must be swamped with it yourself. Before you can move their tears, your own must flow. To convince them, you must yourself believe." (Winston Churchill)

There are as many different definitions of leadership as there are contexts for leading (Bass, 1990; Vecchio, 1997). For our purposes, leadership is defined as the social-influence process that occurs between and among individuals working toward a common goal. Leaders frequently influence followers as a way to motivate them to behave in ways that benefit the organization. For instance, desired organizational outcomes may include higher levels of work performance, increased commitment to the organization's mission, and higher job satisfaction. In the influence process, emotional expression may enhance or suppress the motivation of individual followers (House, Spangler, & Woycke, 1991). For example, a leader expressing anger and blame may cause followers to feel guilt and shame, whereas a leader's enthusiasm and encouragement may inspire newfound energy and enthusiasm in followers as they work toward the organization's goals (Brief & Weiss, 2002). To understand the role of emotion in leader storytelling, it is useful to consider a leadership style associated with emotion and storytelling: transformational leadership.

Early research on leadership identified outstanding leaders and their common traits (Bass, 1990). Later research focused on leader behaviors and their consequences (Kanungo & Mendonca, 1996). As leadership research has developed, ideas of what constitutes effective leadership have changed over time (Dess & Picken, 2000). Previously, effective leadership was assumed to be authority-driven: Leaders gave explicit directions and monitored results. Based on the results, workers were allowed to keep their jobs or were fired for failure to achieve the desired outcomes. This type of directive and authoritative leadership style was thought to be the norm up until the last twenty or thirty years. More recent research indicates that effective leadership is now viewed as – among other things – motivational, participative, inspirational, and authentic (Avolio, Gardner, Walumbwa, Luthans, & May, 2004; Bass & Steidlmeier, 1999). This view of leadership involves communicating a large, systemic vision to others in an inspirational and convincing way (Fullan, 2001). As such, emotional expression is now considered by many researchers to be part and parcel of more effective leadership styles (Pitcher, 1997).

Consistent with this new view of effective leadership, research conducted by Bass and Avolio (1994) identified three alternative leadership styles: transformational (i.e., sets high standards and inspires others to adopt a vision for achieving those goals), transactional (i.e., reacts to follower behaviors with rewards or punishments), and laissez-faire (i.e., generally fails to take responsibility for leading or managing). Transformational leadership is frequently argued as the most effective leadership style in today's rapidly changing and dynamic organizational environment because it focuses on intrinsically motivating individuals (Bono & Judge, 2003). Transformational leadership is characterized by a variety of behaviors designed to fit the situation (Lowe, Kroeck, & Sivasubramaniam, 1996). These behaviors may include communicating a vision with which followers may internalize and identify; mentoring and developing followers; displaying optimism and excitement for future goals; and motivating attitudes of respect, pride, and ownership for the work performed by followers (Ackoff, 1999; Bass & Avolio, 1994). Recent research has provided strong support for the argument that transformational leaders motivate followers to view their work as more important and congruent with their own values (Bono & Judge, 2003).

Authentic leaders are keenly self-aware; thus, their actions directly reflect their most deeply held values, their beliefs, and their emotions (Avolio et al., 2004). Authentic leaders go beyond transformational leadership to see their transformational behavior as stemming directly from their moral and principled center (May, Chan, Hodges, & Avolio, 2003). Thus, authentic leaders are deeply committed to authenticity in both action and emotion. This authenticity is argued to be motivational to followers who believe that their leader is committed to the best interests of the organization and followers, even at their own expense (May et al., 2003).

> "Whenever I . . . asked a class what qualities define an 'A player,' it always made me happiest to see the first hand go up and say, 'Passion.' For me, intensity covers a lot of sins. If there's one characteristic all winners share, it's that they care more than anyone else. No detail is too small to sweat or too large to dream. Over the years, I've always looked for this characteristic in the leaders we selected. It doesn't mean loud or flamboyant. It's something that comes from deep inside. Great organizations can ignite passion." (Welch, 2001)

Authentic transformational leaders motivate followers by communicating and describing the work required of the followers in ideological terms (Burns, 1978). Using emotional expression while communicating is a part of how transformational leaders inspire and motivate followers to internalize the leader's vision and see their work as consistent with their own values (Shamir, House, & Arthur, 1993). Although emotion is theorized to play a key role in transformational leadership behavior, few theoretical and empirical studies concerning the role of emotional expression in leader–follower interaction have been conducted. In addition, few studies have considered the role of leader and follower gender in how emotional expression by leaders is interpreted. Although research is limited, Winston Churchill's quote provides support to the conclusion that emotion may play a key role with respect to the emotional responses of followers to transformational leaders (Lewis, 2000). In the following section, we explore how emotional expression of leaders may emotionally affect followers.

Emotional Responses to Emotional Expression in Leaders

Followers often attribute charismatic behavior to those leaders who are seen as transformational (Conger & Kanungo, 1994, 1998). Charismatic attributions are frequently made based on a leader's attitude, emotional expression, and communication style. When followers attribute charisma to a leader, they identify with that leader and have a desire to do what that leader asks of them. Leaders that followers see as charismatic have a profound effect on follower performance, attitudes, and mood (Groves, 2005; Lowe, Kroeck, & Sivasubramaniam, 1996). Attributions of charisma are made based in part on a leader's emotional expression when communicating (McHugo et al., 1985). A leader's emotional intelligence in understanding the impact of emotional expression in others is an important factor in leader effectiveness (Goleman, 2000). Leaders who are effective at communicating emotion consistent with their message (Goleman, 1998) and whose positive emotion is inspiring, motivating, and contagious (Hatfield, Cacioppo, & Rapson, 1994; Verbeke, 1997) are perceived as more transformational and effective (Groves, 2005). Followers are motivated by emotional expression that they perceive is appropriate and positive (Staw, Sutton, & Pelled, 1994). Not only are followers motivated, but they also can "catch" the leader's mood and translate it into a group mood as well (Sy, Cote, & Saavedra, 2005). Sy and colleagues (2005) found that when the group leader's mood was positive, groups also experienced a more positive mood and exhibited more coordination and less expended effort. Leaders influence followers' moods – and, therefore, their performance – through their own mood; their empathy; and, in particular, how they communicate information, direction, and attitude.

The circumplex model of affect can help us to interpret and understand how followers will respond to a leader's emotional display in all types of communication but particularly during storytelling (Burke, Brief, George, Roberson, & Webster, 1989; Larsen & Diener, 1992). In this model, positive and negative affect can vary from active to passive. Transformational leaders are viewed as expressing both active and passive positive emotions, which can result in active and positive affective responses in followers. Positive active emotions include enthusiasm and excitement; positive passive emotions include a sense of relaxation and calm confidence. Research demonstrates that the consequences of positive affect in the workplace are generally positive (Isen, Daubman, & Nowicki, 1987; Brief & Weiss, 2002; Fredrickson & Joiner, 2002). Thus, to the extent that leaders can promote or motivate positive emotions in followers, they are likely to see positive consequences in terms of mood (Sy, Cote, & Saavedra, 2005), performance (Gaddis, Connelly, & Mumford, 2004), coordination (Sy, Cote, & Saavedra, 2005), attitude (Frost, 2004), and customer-service quality (George, 1995).

Expressing positive emotion is an integral part of transformational leadership behaviors. Negative emotion can also be important but only when it is perceived as appropriate to the situation and context. Indeed, a leader who is perceived as "happy" after a negative event befalls a follower may be perceived as lacking empathy. For example, if a follower has been the victim of another person's unethical behavior, the follower may perceive the appropriate emotional response from the leader as empathetic anger and sadness at the situation. Cognitively and emotionally, followers will analyze cues from both the situation and the leader's expression as they try to make sense of the emotional experience. In addition to the cognitive analysis of a leader's emotional expression, an internal emotional response will be initiated through emotional contagion (Izard, 1977; Izard, Kagan, & Zajonc, 1984; Lewis, 2000; Sy, Cote, & Saavedra, 2005). Both social and environmental-context factors will influence how the follower's emotional experience is interpreted. Particularly during leader storytelling, these cues will be important (Crawford, Kippax, Onyx, Gault, & Benton, 1992).

Situational cues that followers may focus on include the leader's role in the situation, the uncertainty associated with the situation, the leader's gender, and the role expectations that they have for a leader in that specific situation. As followers engage and involve themselves in the storytelling process, they will cognitively process the information surrounding the events they experience and the story they are told and will experience emotional contagion (Frijda, 1986; Hatfield et al., 1994; Verbeke, 1997). Thus, the follower's emotion will be influenced by the leader's emotional display during the storytelling process. We know that both positive and negative emotions or moods at work are related to important employee outcomes, including absenteeism, turnover, and satisfaction (George, 1989; George & Jones, 1997; Staw, Sutton, & Pelled, 1994). For example, Staw et al. (1994) found that feeling positive emotions is associated with later evaluations of work achievement (i.e., higher pay and favorable evaluations of work). The goal of transformational leadership is to intrinsically inspire and motivate followers so that they see accomplishing the leader's vision as a way to find meaning and purpose in their work life. Therefore, inspiring positive affect and emotional experience – both passive (i.e., relaxation and calm) and active (i.e., enthusiasm and excitement) – is an appropriate goal for a leader. Using positive emotional expression in storytelling with the intention of inspiring positive emotional experience and increased understanding of events is done within an organizational and societal context that impacts interpretation. Therefore, in the next section, I address the implications of gender, emotional expression, and a transformational leadership style on the impact of leader storytelling on the audience.

Leader Storytelling: The Role of Emotion

Storytelling is described as a form of communication that constructs a collective sense of meaning, with the goal of having a deeper understanding of the meaning of experienced events (Boje, 1991; Boyce, 1995). A storytelling organization has a culture of sharing stories to help members interpret and understand all of the complex events that compose that organizational experience. For example, Boje (1995) discusses how storytelling at Disney helped those inside (and outside) the organization to understand the history and goals of the organization. The stories explained, for instance, how Walt Disney developed his ideas for various Disney characters and the Disney theme parks. Because people socially construct their perceptions of reality, many of the social cues for these perceptions come from those we admire or look to for guidance: our leaders (Berger & Luckmann, 1966). Leaders use storytelling to create the opportunity for more consistent and optimistic interpretation of events – in effect, helping individuals make better sense of what they have collectively experienced. Storytelling is initiated to enhance effective "sensemaking," where sensemaking is defined as individual efforts to cognitively create order out of ambiguous experiences and information through reflection (Hill & Levenhagen, 1995; Weick, 1995). Those who listen and participate in storytelling are interested in reducing their uncertainty through greater understanding of how the story relates to their own life and perceptions. However, leaders may be more or less effective in telling their story, as reflected in this quote from Jack Welch's book, *Straight from the Gut*:

> At the end, the reaction in the room made it clear that this crowd thought they were getting more hot air than substance. One of our staffers overheard one analyst moan, "We don't know what the hell he's talking about." I left the hotel ballroom knowing there had to be a better way to tell our story. Wall Street had listened, and Wall Street yawned. The stock went up all of 12 cents. I was probably lucky it didn't drop. (Welch, 2001)

Examples of leader storytelling can easily be found both throughout history and in current events (Weil, 1998). Leader storytelling is particularly salient when organizations and individuals experience challenging events and when ambiguity in events leads individuals to seek out guidance and help from leaders as to how they can make sense of what they have experienced. For example, after the tragedies of September 11, 2001, citizens of the world looked to their leaders at home and abroad for guidance in interpreting the terrorist attacks. People asked questions about who was responsible, who the victims were, how they should respond, and what it meant for their future. Leaders of countries and organizations affected by the tragedies, including (among others) the military offices in the Pentagon, companies located in the World Trade Center, the airline industry, and the Red Cross, all used storytelling to help people answer these questions and interpret and make sense of the events.

One example of post–September 11 storytelling comes from a prominent New York citizen, former Senator Daniel Patrick Moynihan. Moynihan used storytelling to help inspire the citizens of New York City to work together toward a new vision after the World Trade Center tragedies. He told a story about New Yorkers working together to maintain a thriving, vibrant, and successful city, one where people participated and cooperated enthusiastically in this effort. His story argued that this was a healthy and preferred response to the tragedies they had experienced. An excerpt from one of his speeches, aimed at inspiring and motivating individuals to identify with a vision (in this case, the vision of rebuilding the city of New York, beginning with the rehabilitation of Penn Station), reflects this message:

> "This is not a moment to be intimidated," Moynihan went on. "It's worth keeping in mind how the British behaved during the Blitz. They kept those theaters and music halls going the whole time. People didn't change their way of life. The only way these terrorists can win is to change the way we live. And we live in cities." (Judge, 2001)

Emotions expressed during storytelling may emphasize a point or express the leader's true emotions regarding a subject. Moynihan was very passionate about his vision, and his "zeal" seemed to positively affect the audience (Judge, 2001). This contagious positive emotion is instrumental in motivating others to adopt a vision. In this case, Moynihan inspired the vision of New York City as a thriving city where new structures enhanced the lifestyle of its citizens. Moynihan tapped into people's emotional response to the tragedies through positive passive emotions, including empathy, and demonstrated that he shared their shock, anger, and sadness. He also expressed positive active emotions by communicating enthusiasm and energy for the new Penn Station renovation project and emphasizing the positive impact the project would have on people's emotional responses to the tragedies and their city.

In this illustration of storytelling, Moynihan used emotional expression to inspire and motivate others toward a common goal. Leader expression of emotion in storytelling, however, can focus on a variety of positive outcomes for followers. For example, leaders may want to reduce followers' negative affect associated with change, uncertainty, or hurtful experiences by expressing empathy and sensitivity (Frost, 2004). Emotionally aware leaders will respond to followers who are experiencing "toxic" situations by telling stories that restore a person's confidence and inspire hope for the future (Frost, 2004). One of the classic examples of this is the response of Malden Mills' owner, Aaron Feuerstein, to the disastrous 1995 fire in his textile mill. Feuerstein insisted on maintaining his payroll and rebuilding the mill after the fire, but it required a great deal of storytelling to convince employees that the company would endure and eventually employ them all again. He did this through storytelling and action, as is reflected in the following quote:

> From this moment on, it is just a question of doing more rapidly what people are used to doing more slowly. We will rebuild in record time; what some consider impossible, we will figure out how to do. (Perkins, 2000)

After the fire, Feuerstein committed to paying his employees' salaries and health benefits even though the plant was closed. Feuerstein continued to communicate with employees, sometimes visiting them in person, to tell his story that a "miracle" was going to happen and that he had confidence in their ability to make it happen. He displayed courage, empathy, and commitment to his employees, and the employees responded. They worked around the clock to rebuild their manufacturing lines and, through hard work and expertise, the production crew restored the first line within ten days of the fire. All of the employees, as inspired by Feuerstein, responded to his story of how their response to this tragedy would make a difference: They knew that he felt their pain, and they could see it in his response to their success in restoring the line:

> I went over and shook hands with each one of them, and they were all crying. I let myself cry on that day because it was a cry of joy and satisfaction. One worker said, "Aaron, we're going to pay you back tenfold," and they did. (Perkins, 2000)

Perceptions of Leaders: Emotional Responses to Leader Gender, Storytelling, and Emotion

The story of Malden Mills and Aaron Feuerstein illustrates how followers can respond positively to a leader's example and emotional expression during storytelling. In addition to understanding the emotional impact of storytelling on followers, another important contribution of this chapter is to expand our understanding of follower emotional response to a male and a female leader's emotional expression. Recent research has indicated that gender may be a factor in perceptions of effective leadership and, in particular, transformational leadership style (Eagly & Johnson, 1990; Eagly, Karau, & Makhijani, 1995; Carless, 1998). Studies using the Multifactor Leadership Quotient, the most common measure of transformational versus transactional leadership styles, show that women are more frequently perceived as using a transformational style, whereas men are perceived as more frequently using a transactional style (Eagly & Johannesen-Schmidt, 2001; Eagly, Johannesen-Schmidt, & van Engen, 2003). Transformational leadership is associated with emotional intelligence, and leaders who are higher in emotional intelligence are more aware of their own emotions and more empathetic to others' emotions (Mandell & Pherwani, 2003). In their study exploring emotional intelligence, transformational leadership, and gender, Mandell and Pherwani (2003) found that although female leaders were significantly higher in emotional intelligence and emotional intelligence was significantly related to transformational leadership, women leaders did not differ from men in their transformational style. Transformational leaders use more positive emotional expression, even in the face of challenging circumstances (Conger & Kanungo, 1994). These positive emotions are frequently associated with a female leadership style (Stephens, 2003).

In addressing the question of why women leaders are perceived as using transformational leadership more frequently, the role of emotional expression may be key. Perhaps women use emotional expression as a way to identify with followers and engender their support and commitment to organizational goals. In her exploration of the role of rhetoric in women's leadership style, Stephens (2003) argues that women leaders use language to connect to others, identify with others, engage others in conversation, and learn more about those with whom they are interacting, thereby connecting others to the common thread of purpose they share. The behaviors that Stephens outlines are, by definition, transformational and consistent with the findings of Eagly and her colleagues (Eagly & Johannesen-Schmidt, 2001; Eagly et al., 2003). When women leaders engage in storytelling, they are using language to engage others in dialogue with the purpose of helping them to better understand recent shared events. Using positive emotional expression is consistent with transformational leaders as storytellers. One example of how a female leader uses storytelling in dialogue with others is Myrtle Potter, currently the COO of Genentech, who has received many honors and recognition as a rising female executive. She describes her leadership style as "managing by walking around":

> If there's somebody walking beside me, I'll ask, "Where do you work? What are you working on? How is it going?" People often tease me because I'm the one holding the elevator door open while I finish a conversation. So I really do work to open myself up and make sure the organization knows that I'm accessible. (Madell, 2000)

In our study of leader storytelling in the health-care industry, we found that positive and negative emotional expression – both text-based and in person – influenced the interpretation of events in the process of sensemaking (Spicochi & Tyran, 2002). In our study, we compared two leaders as they embarked on a significant change in their health-care organizations. Through storytelling, the leaders sought to help employees understand and support what promised to be difficult changes to the organization. For example, one leader spoke enthusiastically and positively about employees, promising to engage and include them in the proposed organizational changes, thereby creating a vision of inclusion. This positive emotion was expressed as the leader helped employees make sense of the changes in a positive way, as illustrated in the following quote:

> Evolution, however, is never an easy process, and there are always growing pains along the way. While we don't know right now what changes we may have to make to remain a viable institution in the future, I promise that we will endeavor to keep employees informed about the process at each step. (Spicochi & Tyran, 2002)

The leader made an effort to relate the change to the employees' experience so that the employees can see how they could participate in achieving the organization's vision. The response of employees to this positive story was renewed commitment to the organization. This contrasts with some leaders who focus only on informational, one-way communication to employees about the logistical changes to be implemented, ignoring the story as a way of engaging others. In one instance, this resulted in increased turnover and labor-relations problems (Spicochi & Tyran, 2002). As employees lost faith in the organization's commitment to their best interest, they focused on increasing their power through unionization. Good employees left for organizations that they saw as more committed to keeping employees happy while competing in a changing health-care industry.

Positive emotions such as excitement and enthusiasm – as well as empathy and sympathy as expressed by the leader discussed previously – enhance engagement of others in a storytelling conversation. The expression of positive emotion will be interpreted as motivating when followers make sense of the story in a positive way for them personally. However, interpretation of a leader's emotional expression will depend in part on the gender of the leader. Previous research supports the idea that interpretation of emotional expression will vary based on leader gender due to gender-role expectations (Lewis, 2000) and stereotypes associated with emotion-display rules (Brody & Hall, 2000). Interpretation of leader behaviors – including emotional display – is complex and involves expectations and norms associated with the organizational role of the individual (in this case, the role of a leader) (Moskowitz, Suh, & Desaulniers, 1994). Thus, followers may interpret a leader's emotional expression with regard to consistency in respect to both leader-role expectations and gender-role expectations.

Eagly and Johannesen-Schmidt (2001) argue that a number of factors determine how followers will evaluate a leader's behavior in terms of these two role expectations. First, the leader will be evaluated based on whether that leader's role is associated with masculine characteristics. If the traditional view associated with this leader is of an authoritative and strong leader, or if men in the past have been the predominant gender in leader roles in an organization or industry, then gender-role expectations will be more salient when interpreting leader behaviors. Consistent with this, my previous research found that followers associated anger with effectiveness as a leader when expressed by men but not by women, presumably due to gender-role expectations associated with emotional expression (Lewis, 2000). These gender-role expectations are also consistent with historical leader-role expectations of a leader as an authority figure to be feared and obeyed. As noted earlier, recent research has identified the transformational leadership style as more effective in today's organizations (Bass, 1998). Followers are expected to be intrinsically motivated to take initiative in their work, creatively approaching their tasks for the goals of the organization (Bono & Judge, 2003). Transformational leaders inspire followers to adopt the organization's goals as their own by communicating how the individual follower can identify with these goals on a personal level (Kanungo & Mendonca, 1996). Followers are motivated when the goals of the organization are those that they have internalized and identified with (Shamir, House, & Arthur, 1993). Thus, in some contexts, gender-role expectations may be less salient as followers look to leaders for visionary guidance and inspiration rather than directive task assignments.

If a leader's role is less associated with masculine characteristics, then leader behaviors are more likely to be evaluated on their own merit, with less consideration of gender-role expectations (Eagly & Johannesen-Schmidt, 2001). In this case, the expression of emotion will likely be evaluated on the basis of whether the emotion is consistent with the message and story and less on whether it is consistent with gender roles. Consequently, followers see leadership and guidance as most important in that situation, and they seek this help from their leader independent of the leader's gender.

In my previous research, leaders who expressed negative emotional expression – both active (i.e., anger) and passive (i.e., sadness) – were evaluated partly based on gender-role expectations. Female leaders who expressed no emotion were evaluated as far more effective in leadership than female leaders who expressed anger or sadness. In contrast, men who expressed no emotion were evaluated to be just as effective as men who expressed anger, and men who expressed sadness were perceived as least effective (Lewis, 2000).

Transformational leadership involves positive emotional expression, both active (i.e., excitement and enthusiasm) and passive (i.e., empathy and sympathy). Eagly and her colleagues (Eagly et al., 2003) found that evaluating leader style and emotional expression was influenced by both leader behavior and leader gender. Perhaps those female leaders perceived as strongest in transformational leadership were also perceived as expressing more positive emotion, consistent with gender-role expectations. Men who express anger – consistent with transactional behaviors such as correcting mistakes and waiting for lapses in an employee's behavior before addressing the employee – may initially be perceived as effective leaders because they are expressing emotion consistent with their gender role. This is consistent with the recent findings of Simpson and Stroh (2004) that women more frequently conform to female display rules (i.e., suppression of negative emotions and simulation of positive emotions) in the workplace. Simpson and Stroh (2004) also found that men were less likely to suppress negative emotions and more likely to suppress positive emotions, consistent with masculine display rules. Because follower motivation may be negatively affected by negative emotions through emotional contagion and the cognitive processing of this experience, suppression of the negative emotions and simulation of positive emotions may have a positive impact on followers' emotions (Hamilton, Katz, & Leirer, 1980; Hatfield et al., 1994). In exploring leader storytelling, it is clear that positive emotions are seen as more inspirational, as discussed previously.

Recommendations for Leaders

Based on our understanding of how followers emotionally experience a leader's gender and emotional expression during storytelling, there are some recommendations we can make to those interested in increasing their leadership effectiveness. When expressing emotion in storytelling, leader emotional expression must be perceived as consistent with several factors to be an effective part of leader storytelling. First, it must be perceived as consistent with the story that is told. For example, when a leader is telling a story of challenge and hardship, expressing optimism, hope, and enthusiasm for the opportunity available in the challenge will seem appropriate and motivating. When experiences of hardship are frustrating for employees, expressing anger and sadness may also be perceived as appropriate. As indicated in the previous discussion, expressing empathy with those emotions as experienced by followers is key. Empathy that is authentic – both felt and expressed – is a positive passive emotion that will inspire connection and identification with others. Paired with enthusiasm and excitement for opportunities, empathy with negative emotions experienced by followers is consistent with a transformational leadership style.

Second, a leader's emotional expression must be consistent with the perceived role of the leader in the events described in the story.

Here is where the role of transformational leadership is important. Transformational-leadership behaviors include mentoring, motivating pride and identification in organizational goals, and rewarding goal achievement with thoughtful and individually appropriate rewards. If a leader is perceived as transformational, then positive emotional expression will seem appropriate and consistent with past leader behavior.

Finally, a leader's emotional expression must be consistent with gender-role expectations. This may be a challenge for some female leaders whose inclination is to communicate anger in the context of storytelling. However, because female leaders may be more comfortable with the excitement, enthusiasm, and empathy associated with effective transformational-leader storytelling, these emotional expressions may be seen as more consistent with the female gender role. The challenge for male leaders may be to avoid the use of anger and negative emotions and increase their use of positive empathy and enthusiasm when trying to inspire others, thereby increasing the ability to lead with a transformational leadership style.

When followers perceive emotional expression of a leader to be consistent with the situation, as well as leader and gender roles, they are likely to be much more open to being emotionally affected by the experience themselves. As they engage in the leader's story, they open up to the positive emotional expression and increase their commitment and motivation to the vision described in the storytelling dialogue. Followers identify with the values illustrated in the story and want to participate in positively addressing the issues described.

Conclusion

When challenging events occur in an organization, leaders have the opportunity to guide interpretation of those events. Through storytelling, a leader can motivate and inspire positive emotional experiences in followers, helping them to collectively see challenges as opportunities and to internalize this vision as a personal opportunity for positive experience. Enhancing the storytelling experience through positive emotional expression has the potential to emotionally affect the audience in a positive way. Transformational leaders express positive emotion in their leadership role, communicating that emotion to followers and "infecting" them with enthusiasm and excitement for the challenge.

Expressing empathy and calm resolve further enhances the connection made with followers, fostering strong commitment to the leader and identification with the organization's goals.

Both men and women may adopt a more transformational leadership style and use emotional expression to enhance positive emotional experience in followers as they experience challenging events. Indeed, the example of Moynihan in New York City illustrates how a man may be motivational and inspiring using positive emotional expression. Research shows, however, that women are more frequently identified as having a transformational leadership style (Eagly et al., 2003). Perhaps this is because expressing the positive emotions associated with transformational leadership is both leader-role and gender-role consistent. Female leaders can make the best of a transformational style because it involves enthusiasm and excitement, as well as mentoring and nurturing others through sympathy and empathy (Brody & Hall, 2000; Stephens, 2003). During storytelling, engaging the audience through these positive emotions is consistent with gender-role expectations for women. In current organizations, it is also an important part of the transformational leader role expectations. Because these role expectations are consistent, women leaders have the potential to be perceived as effective transformational leaders and, as such, can use storytelling effectively to motivate and inspire followers during times of crisis, challenge, and hardship.

Regardless of a leader's gender, expressing positive emotion during storytelling can positively affect followers in a number of ways. For example, followers will experience positive emotions themselves, "catching" the contagious effect of the enthusiasm and energy of the leader. In addition, followers may perceive leaders as more effective and thus feel more intrinsically motivated. This happens as their clearer and deeper understanding of the events that have taken place leads them to see their work as more meaningful to them personally. By using positive emotion to help followers see ambiguous and challenging events through an optimistic lens, leaders can enhance the possibility that followers will attempt to use creative approaches in response to the challenges. These are just a few of the benefits of using positive emotion in storytelling. As scholars and practitioners continue their quest for insight into effective leadership practices, greater understanding of the impact of emotion in leader storytelling is worthy of further inquiry.

References

Ackoff, R. L. (1999). Transformational leadership. *Strategy and Leadership.* January/February.

Avolio, B. J., Gardner, W., Walumbwa, F. O., Luthans, F., & May, D. R. (2004). Unlocking the mask: A look at the process by which authentic leaders impact follower attitudes and behaviors. *Leadership Quarterly, 15,* 801–823.

Bass, B. M. (1990). *Handbook of leadership: A survey of theory and research.* New York: Free Press.

Bass, B. M. (1998). *Transformational leadership.* Mahwah, NJ: Lawrence Erlbaum Associates.

Bass, B. M., & Avolio, B. J. (1994). *Improving organizational effectiveness through transformational leadership.* Thousand Oaks, CA: Sage Publications.

Bass, B. M., & Steidlmeier, P. (1999). Ethics, character, and authentic transformational leadership behavior. *Leadership Quarterly, 10,* 181–217.

Berger, P. L., & Luckmann, T. (1966). *The social construction of reality.* New York: Bantam Doubleday.

Boje, D. M. (1991). The storytelling organization: A study of story performance in an office supply company. *Administrative Science Quarterly, 36,* 106–126.

Boje, D. M. (1995). Stories of the storytelling organization: A postmodern analysis of Disney as "Tamaraland." *Academy of Management Journal, 38,* 4, 997–1035.

Bono, J. E., & Judge, T. A. (2003). Self-concordance at work: Toward understanding the motivational effects of transformational leaders. *Academy of Management Journal, 46,* 554–571.

Boyce, M. E. (1995). Collective centering and collective sensemaking. *Organizational Studies, 16,* 107–130.

Brief, A. P., & Weiss, H. M. (2002). Organizational behavior: Affect in the workplace. *Annual Review of Psychology, 53,* 279–307.

Brody, L. R., & Hall, J. A. (2000). Gender, emotion, and expression. In M. Lewis & J. M. Haviland (Eds.), *Handbook of emotions* (2nd ed.) (pp. 447–460). New York: Guilford Press.

Burke, M. J., Brief, A. P., George, J. M., Roberson, L., & Webster, J. (1989). Measuring affect at work: Confirmatory analyses of competing mood structures with conceptual linkage to cortical regulatory systems. *Journal of Personality and Social Psychology, 57,* 1091–1102.

Burns, J. M. (1978). *Leadership.* New York: Harper & Row.

Carless, S. (1998). Gender differences in transformational leadership: An examination of superior, leader, and subordinate perspectives. *Sex Roles, 39,* 887–897.

Conger, J., & Kanungo, R. (1994). Charismatic leadership in organizations: Perceived behavioral attributes and their measurement. *Journal of Organizational Behavior, 15,* 439–452.

Conger, J., & Kanungo, R. (1998). *Charismatic leadership in organizations.* Thousand Oaks, CA: Sage Publications.

Crawford, J., Kippax, S., Onyx, J., Gault, U., & Benton, P. (1992). *Emotion and gender, constructing meaning from memory.* London: Sage Publications.

Dess, G. G., & Picken, J. C. (2000). Changing roles, leadership in the 21st century. *Organizational Dynamics, 28,* 18–34.

Eagly, A. H., & Johnson, B. T. (1990). Gender and leadership style: A meta-analysis. *Psychological Bulletin, 108*, 233–256.

Eagly, A. H., Karau, S. J., & Makhijani, M. G. (1995). Gender and effectiveness of leaders: A meta-analysis. *Psychological Bulletin, 117*, 125–145.

Eagly, A. H., & Johannesen-Schmidt, M. C. (2001). The leadership styles of women and men. *Journal of Social Issues, 57*, 781–797.

Eagly, A. H., Johannesen-Schmidt, M. C., & van Engen, M. L. (2003). Transformational, transactional, and laissez-faire leadership styles: A meta-analysis comparing women and men. *Psychological Bulletin, 129*, 569–591.

Fineman, S. (1993). Organizations as emotional arenas. In S. Fineman (Ed.), *Emotion in organizations*. London: Sage Publications.

Fineman, S. (2003). *Understanding emotion at work*. Thousand Oaks, CA: Sage Publications.

Frederickson, B. L., & Joiner, T. (2002). Positive emotions trigger upward spirals toward emotional well-being. *Psychological Science, 13*, 172–175.

Frijda, N. H. (1986). *The emotions*. Cambridge: Cambridge University Press.

Frost, P. (2003). *Toxic emotions at work: How compassionate managers handle pain and conflict*. Cambridge, MA: Harvard Business School Publishing.

Frost, P. (2004). Handling the hurt: A critical skill for leaders. *Ivey Business Journal Online*, January/February, 1.

Fullan, M. (2001). *Leading in a culture of change*. San Francisco, CA: Jossey-Bass.

Gaddis, B., Connelly, S., & Mumford, M. D. (2004). Failure feedback as an affective event: Influences of leader affect on subordinate attitudes and performance. *Leadership Quarterly, 15*, 663–686.

George, J. M. (1989). Mood and absence. *Journal of Applied Psychology, 74*, 317–324.

George, J. M. (1995). Leader positive mood and group performance: The case of customer service. *Journal of Applied Social Psychology, 25*, 778–794.

George, J. M., & Jones, G. R. (1997). Experiencing work: values, attitudes, and moods. *Human Relations, 50*, 393–416.

Gioia, D. A., & Thomas, J. B. (1996). Identity, image, and issue interpretation: Sensemaking during strategic change in academia. *Administrative Science Quarterly, 41*, 370–393.

Goleman, D. (1998). *Working with emotional intelligence*. New York: Bantam.

Goleman, D. (2000). Leadership that gets results. *Harvard Business Review*, March/April, 78–90.

Grandey, A. A., Fisk, G. M., Matilla, A. S., Jansen, K. J., & Sideman, L. A. (2005). Is "service with a smile" enough? Authenticity of positive displays during service encounters. *Organizational Behavior and Human Decision Processes, 96*, 38–55.

Greenberg, D. N. (1995). Blue versus gray: A metaphor constraining sensemaking around a restructuring. *Group & Organizational Management, 20*, 183–209.

Groves, K. S. (2005). Linking leader skills, follower attitudes, and contextual variables via an integrated model of charismatic leadership. *Journal of Management, 31*, 255–277.

Hamilton, D. L., Katz, L. B., & Leirer, V. O. (1980). Organization processes in impression formation. In R. Hastie, T. M. Ostrom, E. B. Ebbesen, R. S. Wyer,

Jr., D. L. Hamilton, & D. E. Carlston (Eds.), *Person memory: The cognitive basis of social perception.* Hillsdale, NJ: Lawrence Erlbaum Associates.

Hatfield, E., Cacioppo, J., & Rapson, R. (1994). *Emotional contagion.* New York: Cambridge University Press.

Hill, R. C., & Levenhagen, M. (1995). Metaphors and mental models: Sensemaking and sensegiving in innovative and entrepreneurial activities. *Journal of Management, 26,* 1057–1074.

Hochschild, A. R. (1979). Emotion work, feeling rules, and social structure. *American Journal of Sociology, 85,* 551–575.

Hochschild, A. R. (1983). *The managed heart: The commercialization of human feeling.* Berkeley, CA: University of California Press.

House, R. J., Spangler, W. D., & Woycke, J. (1991). Personality and charisma in the US Presidency: A psychological theory of leader effectiveness. *Administrative Science Quarterly, 36,* 364–396.

Isen, A. M., Daubman, K. A., & Nowicki, G. P. (1987). Positive affect facilitates creative problem solving. *Journal of Personality and Social Psychology, 52,* 1122–1131.

Izard, C. E. (1977). *Human emotions.* New York: Academic Press.

Izard, C. E., Kagan, J., & Zajonc, R. B. (1984). *Emotions, cognition and behavior.* Cambridge: Cambridge University Press.

Judge, P. C. (2001). The architecture of hope. *Fast Company Web-Exclusives,* October.

Kanungo, R. N., & Mendonca, M. (1996). *Ethical dimensions of leadership.* Thousand Oaks, CA: Sage Publications.

Larsen, R. J., & Diener, E. (1992). Promises and problems with the circumplex model of emotion. In M. S. Clark (Ed). *Emotion, review of personality and social psychology, No. 13.* Newbury Park, CA: Sage Publications.

Lewis, K. M. (2000). When leaders display emotion: How followers respond to negative emotional expression of male and female leaders. *Journal of Organizational Behavior, 21,* 221–234.

Lowe, K. B., Kroeck, K. G., & Sivasubramaniam, N. (1996). Effectiveness correlates of transformational and transactional leadership: A meta-analytical review of the MLQ literature. *Leadership Quarterly, 7,* 385–425.

Madell, R. (2000). Uniting people and products: Myrtle Potter – 2000 HBA Woman of the Year. *Pharmaceutical Executive,* April, 48–60.

Mandell, B., & Pherwani, S. (2003). Relationship between emotional intelligence and transformational leadership style: A gender comparison. *Journal of Business and Psychology, 17,* 387–404.

May, D. R., Chan, A. Y. L., Hodges, T. D., & Avolio, B. J. (2003). Developing the moral component of authentic leadership. *Organizational Dynamics, 3,* 247–262.

McHugo, G. J., Lanzetta, J. T., Sullivan, D. G., Masters, R. D., & Englis, B. G. (1985). Emotional reactions to a political leader's expressive displays. *Journal of Personality and Social Psychology, 49,* 1513–1529.

Moskowitz, D. W., Suh, E. J., & Desaulniers, J. (1994). Situational influences on gender differences in agency and communion. *Journal of Personality and Social Psychology, 66,* 753–761.

Perkins, D. N. T. (2000). *Leading at the edge.* New York: AMACOM.

Pitcher, P. (1997). *The drama of leadership.* New York: Wiley Publishers.

Rafaeli, A., & Sutton, R. I. (1987). Expression of emotion as part of the work role. *Academy of Management Review, 12*, 23–37.

Rafaeli, A., & Sutton, R. I. (1989). The expression of emotion in organizational life. In B. M. Staw and L. L. Cummings (Eds.), *Research in Organizational Behavior, 11*, 1–42. Greenwich, CT: JAI.

Rafaeli, A., & Sutton, R. I. (1990). Busy stores and demanding customers: How do they affect the display of positive emotion? *Academy of Management Journal, 33*, 623–637.

Shamir, B., House, R. J., & Arthur, M. B. (1993). The motivational effects of charismatic leadership: A self-concept based theory. *Organization Science, 4*, 577–594.

Sharpe, E. K. (2005). "Going above and beyond": The emotional labor of adventure guides. *Journal of Leisure Research, 37*, 29–50.

Simpson, P. A., & Stroh, L. K. (2004). Gender differences: Emotional expression and feelings of personal inauthenticity. *Journal of Applied Psychology, 89*, 715–736.

Spicochi, R. L., & Tyran, K. L. (2002). *A tale of two leaders: Exploring the role of leader storytelling and follower sensemaking in transforming organizations.* Presented at the Academy of Management Conference, Denver, CO.

Staw, B., Sutton, R., & Pelled, L. (1994). Employee positive emotion and favorable outcomes at the workplace. *Organization Science, 5*, 51–71.

Stephens, J. (2003). The rhetoric of women's leadership: Language, memory and imagination. *Journal of Leadership and Organizational Studies, 9*, 45–60.

Sutton, R. I. (1991). Maintaining norms about expressed emotions: The case of bill collectors. *Administrative Science Quarterly, 36*, 245–268.

Sutton, R. I., & Rafaeli, A. (1988). Untangling the relationship between displayed emotions and organizational sales: The case of convenience stores. *Academy of Management Journal, 31*, 461–487.

Sy, T., Cote, S., & Saavedra, R. (2005). The contagious leader: Impact of the leader's mood on the mood of group members, group affective tone, and group processes. *Journal of Applied Psychology, 90*, 295–320.

Vecchio, R. P. (Ed.) (1997). *Leadership, understanding the dynamics of power and influence in organizations.* Notre Dame, IN: University of Notre Dame Press.

Verbeke, W. (1997). Individual differences in emotional contagion of salespersons: Its effect on performance and burnout. *Psychology & Marketing, 14*, 617–636.

Weick, K. E. (1995). *Sensemaking in organizations.* Thousand Oaks, CA: Sage Publications.

Weil, E. (1998). Every leader tells a story. *Fast Company, 15*, 38.

Welch, J. (2001). *Straight from the gut.* New York: Warner Books.

7. Apples and Oranges

Methodological Requirements for Testing a Possible Ingroup Advantage in Emotion Judgments from Facial Expressions

David Matsumoto

Author's Note

I thank Marija Drezgic, Shannon Pacaoa, Janice Cheng, Aaron Estrada, and Victoriya Tebeleva for their assistance in the general laboratory program.

Correspondence concerning this chapter should be addressed to David Matsumoto, Department of Psychology, San Francisco State University, 1600 Holloway Avenue, San Francisco, CA 94132; telephone (415) 338-1114, fax (510) 217-9608, or e-mail at dm@sfsu.edu.b.

Introduction

The ability to recognize certain facial expressions of emotion is universal. Studies reported more than thirty years ago provided the first systematic and reliable evidence of this (Ekman, 1972; Ekman & Friesen, 1971; Ekman, Sorenson, & Friesen, 1969; Izard, 1971), and those studies have been replicated time and again by different researchers using different methodologies (Elfenbein & Ambady, 2002b; Matsumoto, 2001). A recent meta-analysis including 168 data sets involving judgments of emotion in different cultures summarized this area and indicated that the core components of emotion recognition are pancultural and likely biological (Elfenbein & Ambady, 2002b).

However, there are also cultural differences in emotion judgments. One of the first studies that documented cultural differences reported correlations between Hofstede's cultural dimension data (Hofstede, 1980, 1984) with accuracy rates of judgments of universal facial expressions of emotion across cultures in an ecological analysis (Matsumoto, 1988). Subsequent studies showed that cultural differences existed between Americans and Japanese (Matsumoto, 1992), and then across a broader range of cultures (Biehl et al., 1997) and ethnic groups (Matsumoto, 1993), and in bilinguals depending on the language in which they are tested (Matsumoto & Assar, 1992).

Based on these types of differences, I previously proposed (Matsumoto, 1989a, 1992; Matsumoto et al., 2002; Matsumoto & Ekman, 1989; Matsumoto et al., 1999) the existence of cultural *decoding rules* (Buck, 1984) – that is, rules that govern modifications in how people judge the emotions of others and that are linked to the concept of cultural display rules (Ekman & Friesen, 1969). On the one hand, for instance, people from cultures that dictate the suppression of emotional expression in certain situations might infer that others may be feeling emotions more internally relative to how much they express them externally. On the other hand, people from cultures who amplify their expressions may judge others to feel emotions less, compensating for the display rule to amplify. And, in fact, the most recent studies from our laboratory have now provided the link between individual-level display rules and these types of emotion judgments, demonstrating that such linkage mediates previously documented cultural differences in judgments (Matsumoto et al., 2003).

One type of cultural difference in judgment that has recently received attention concerns the possibility of an ingroup advantage in emotion recognition (Elfenbein & Ambady, 2002b). This notion is defined as the tendency whereby individuals can more easily and accurately understand emotional expressions originating from members of their own cultural group rather than expressions originating from members of a different cultural group (Elfenbein, this volume, Chapter 3). Previous research that tested this hypothesis (e.g., Boucher & Carlson, 1980; Kilbride & Yarczower, 1983; Markham & Wang, 1996) provided mixed results. In their meta-analysis, however, Elfenbein and Ambady (2002b) reported support for it across the studies they analyzed, as well as separately for emotion, channel of communication, cross-cultural exposure, and other potential moderators. To account for the effect, they suggested the viability of an interactionist interpretation focusing on cultural learning and expressive style, differences in emotional concepts and cognitive representations, cultural specificity of emotional experiences and linguistic expressions, cultural learning of emotional behavior, and culture-specific information-processing systems (Elfenbein & Ambady, 2002b).

Elfenbein and Ambady have continued to build a case for the ingroup-advantage hypothesis. One of their latest studies, for instance, involved a meta-analysis of four studies in which observers in multiple cultures judged the expressions portrayed by one of those cultures (Elfenbein & Ambady, 2003a). Physical distance, determined by the distance between the capital cities of the countries included in the samples, and cultural distance, computed by difference scores of Hofstede cultural dimensions between the expressor and judge cultures, were both negatively correlated with emotion recognition accuracy rates, providing evidence in support of a "distance theory" of emotion recognition. In two other studies, Elfenbein and her colleagues demonstrated the existence of an ingroup effect among American, Japanese, and Indian observers and expressors (Elfenbein, Mandal, Ambady, & Harizuka, 2002) and among non-Asian American and Chinese observers who judged Caucasian and Chinese expressions (Elfenbein & Ambady, 2003b).

The ingroup-advantage hypothesis is interesting and, if true, would have important implications for theory and practice. Thus, it is important to have a good grasp of the evidentiary basis of the hypothesis. The purpose of this chapter is to discuss what I believe to be the proper methodological requirements for testing it and to review the available evidence concerning it vis-à-vis those requirements. I demonstrate that, once studies that meet the proposed standards are considered, the evidence that supports its existence is inconclusive. Moreover, when studies are considered in relation to the possible sources that could contribute to the ingroup effect, there is no evidence that demonstrates it exists because of cultural differences in emotional expressivity.

The Statistical Conditions in Which the Ingroup Effect Has Been Found

The ingroup advantage is tested only in studies employing balanced designs involving two or more judge and encoder cultures, in which decoders of all cultures judge expressions of encoders from all cultures (Elfenbein & Ambady, 2002a; Matsumoto, 2002). This design allows for a full-factorial analysis of judge and encoder effects, as well as other identifiable effects in the study. The ingroup effect is demonstrated by a significant interaction between decoder and encoder culture in accuracy scores.

Because the ingroup effect is demonstrated in an interaction, it is important to understand at least two ways in which the effect may exist. These correspond to the two ways by which interactions can be interpreted. In the first, interactions can be interpreted using cell means and tested by examining the simple effects associated with the interaction (Keppel, 1991). In this manner, interactions corresponding to the ingroup effect may directly demonstrate that judges of Culture A have a higher mean accuracy score when judging expressors from Culture A (than B), whereas judges of Culture B have a higher mean accuracy score when judging expressors from Culture B (than A). In this case, the ingroup effect would reflect a difference in direction of the cell means involved in the interaction. Let's call this the "simple effects" version of the ingroup-advantage hypothesis.

In the second way, interactions can be understood by analyzing the cross-over variance pattern of residualized means after the main effects have been removed (Rosenthal & Rosnow, 1985, 1991). Whereas the analysis of residualized means can certainly detect differences in the direction of cell means as described previously, it may also detect the case in which judges of one culture judge encoders of their own culture better than encoders of another culture – but only relative to the same difference observed for other judge cultures. This effect may exist even though the actual observed cell means do not directly demonstrate a difference in direction. In this case, the ingroup effect would reflect a difference in the degree of difference between the cell means. Let's call this the "relative difference" version of the ingroup-advantage hypothesis.

Understanding interactions associated with the ingroup advantage is more complex because of the existence of judge culture main effects, which have been amply replicated in many studies (Biehl et al., 1997; Elfenbein & Ambady, 2003b; Elfenbein et al., 2002; Matsumoto, 1992, 2002). As statistical sources of variance they are orthogonal to any interaction effects, including those associated with the ingroup advantage. Theoretically they may be orthogonal as well; people of different cultures may be differentially better at judging emotions on the whole than people of other cultures, for a variety of reasons. Thus, it is possible that cultures exert influences on the overall decoding process of emotions but make it possible for emotions to be differentially recognized according to the familiarity with whom one judges. The existence of overall judge culture decoding main effects need not argue for the non-existence of any possible ingroup effect, or vice versa.

To support the ingroup-advantage hypothesis, Elfenbein and her colleagues have reported significant encoder by decoder culture interactions in their original meta-analysis (Elfenbein & Ambady, 2002b), as well as in their subsequent studies (Elfenbein & Ambady, 2003a, 2003b;

Table 7.1. *Unbiased Hit Rate (H_u), Emotion Recognition Accuracy Mean Values, and Interaction across Nations of Expressors and Judges (from Elfenbein et al., 2002)*

Perceiver	Expressor			
	India	Japan	USA	Total
Mean Values				
India	0.738	0.378	0.885	0.667
Japan	0.556	0.397	0.730	0.561
USA	0.716	0.450	1.009	0.725
TOTAL	0.670	0.408	0.874	0.651
Interaction Effect				
India	0.052	(0.046)	(0.006)	
Japan	(0.024)	0.079	(0.055)	
USA	(0.028)	(0.032)	0.060	

Elfenbein et al., 2002). The reported interactions involved the analysis of cross-over residuals, and the cell means they reported make it clear that the ingroup-advantage effect they describe refers not to differences in direction in the cell means but rather to *relative* differences among them. For example, Table 7.1 (from Elfenbein et al., 2002), reprinted here, indicated that Indian, Japanese, and American judges all judged the American expressors most accurately, and that the Japanese judges judged the Japanese expressors the least accurately, in terms of cell means. Thus, there is no support for the simple effects version of the ingroup-advantage hypothesis. In addition, the judge culture main effect was significant, indicating that Americans were more accurate than Indians, who were more accurate than the Japanese overall. Yet, the interaction between judge and encoder culture was significant, and follow-up contrasts of *residualized* means indicated that judges were more likely to be accurate when judging encoders of their culture *relative to* the cell main effects observed. The same effect was reported in their subsequent study involving Americans of non-Asian descent, Chinese Americans, and Chinese (Elfenbein & Ambady, 2003b).

Thus, it is important to understand that the data to date offered for the ingroup-advantage hypothesis support the relative difference version of the hypothesis but not the simple effects version. Moreover, the relative difference version of the ingroup advantage co-exists with overall judge culture effects. A more refined definition of the ingroup effect that has been argued to exist to date, therefore, would be that *members of a cultural group tend to be more accurate in recognizing emotions of their own cultural group compared to encoders of other cultures, relative to strong judge and encoder culture effects.* The effect does not exist if one analyzes the judge by encoder culture interaction on the level of the simple effects of cell means; rather, the effect exists relative to those cell means.

This difference in the interpretation of the interaction has important consequences. That the ingroup effect may not exist on the level of cell means suggests that people may not really be more accurate when judging others of their own culture in an absolute sense or in terms of real-life phenomena. That the ingroup effect does exist when analyzing residualized cell means suggests that people recognize others of their own culture relatively better than encoders of a different culture. However, in an absolute sense, they may still recognize encoders of a different culture better than members of their own. Stated quite bluntly, people may be *relatively* better at decoding displays from their own group but, in terms of raw accuracies, may be actually worse at doing so. These distinctions are important to make theoretically, empirically, and pragmatically.

Methodological Requirements for Testing a Possible Ingroup Advantage in Emotion Recognition

Balanced Designs and Stimulus Equivalence

Matsumoto (2002) suggested that two methodological requirements were necessary for a study to test adequately the ingroup-advantage hypothesis. First, studies should employ balanced designs in which all judged cultures view expressions portrayed by members of all the other cultures in the study. In a two-culture design, observers of Cultures A and B should judge expressions of members of Cultures A and B. An unbalanced design occurs in two ways. In one, judges of Cultures A and B see expressions portrayed only by members of A; in the other, judges of only Culture A see expressions of A and B. Matsumoto argued that data from these studies cannot be used to test the ingroup effect (although they can provide evidence that may not be consistent with the effect). In the first type of unbalanced design, which is the way an overwhelming number of studies have been conducted, if judges of Culture B are less accurate in recognizing emotions, one cannot be sure that the same observers of B will be more accurate when they judge expressions portrayed by B, precisely because those expressions were not included in the study.

The second requirement concerned the necessity for stimulus equivalence. Because balanced studies include stimuli expressed by people of multiple cultures, it is necessary to ensure that the stimuli are equivalent across the cultural groups in terms of their physical-signaling properties related to emotion. As mentioned previously, in Ekman and Friesen's (1978) Facial Action Coding System (FACS) terminology, the same Action Units (AUs) need to be innervated at the same intensity levels. If the expressions of Culture A have different AUs or the same AUs at different intensities than those of Culture B in a balanced design, then cultural differences in the judgments are inextricably confounded with differences in the expressions being judged. One would not be sure that the differences observed truly reflected the ingroup advantage or were due to differences in the stimuli.

Consider, for example, the study conducted by Ricci-Bitti and his colleagues (Ricci-Bitti et al., 1989), in which American, Northern Italian, and Southern Italian encoders role-played situations designed to elicit contempt and were allowed to try out the expressions repeatedly to obtain ones that best corresponded to contempt (cited in Elfenbein and Ambady's original meta-analysis in support of the ingroup effect). Two independent judges from the same cultural background as the encoders then selected the best exemplars for a judgment study. The findings indicated that although there were no differences in the recognition rates of Northern Italians judging Northern or Southern Italian expressions, Southern Italians had significantly higher recognition rates for Southern Italian expressions than for Northern Italian expressions, which provides partial support for the ingroup-advantage hypothesis. FACS coding of the expressions produced, however, indicated that Southern Italians' contempt expressions included strong, bilateral upper-lip raises (AU 10), sometimes but not always in combination with weak nose wrinkles (AU 9); the Northern Italians' expressions included combinations of upper-lip raises and unilateral lip tightening (AUs 10 + 14). Thus, although an ingroup effect was produced, it is impossible to determine whether it was due to sources in the decoders or the differences in the expressions, precisely because expression differences confounded the judge cultures. And, because the judge culture decoding differences are occurring in relation to different stimuli being judged, some may interpret this effect as resulting because of a methodological artifact, much as a cultural difference that occurs when members of two cultures rate two different questionnaires that supposedly measure the same construct or different items within a questionnaire.

Given both of these methodological concerns, Matsumoto (2002) concluded that Elfenbein and Ambady's original meta-analysis could not support the ingroup-advantage hypothesis because they did not review the studies as to whether they met those requirements. (To be sure, Matsumoto did not argue against the possibility that the ingroup advantage may exist but rather against the scientific evidence for it.) Applying these requirements would also suggest that their subsequent meta-analysis (Elfenbein & Ambady, 2003a) did not support the ingroup-advantage hypothesis because those studies did not meet the requirements either. And, even though a balanced design was used in Elfenbein et al. (2002) and in Elfenbein and Ambady (2003b), they attempted to achieve stimulus equivalence in both studies by using recognition rates of the expressions by separate samples of observers. But, observer judgment cannot validate the equivalence of the physical-signaling properties of emotion in the face because it is not clear as to what signals observers use to make their judgments. Two different expressions may have the same recognition-agreement levels but not necessarily involve the same muscle innervations, and those differences inherently confound any judgments of those expressions. That the external observer agreement rates in Elfenbein et al. (2002) were 70 percent for the Indians and Japanese and 88 percent for the Americans in that study further confounded the judgments in that study (the recognition rates were equivalent in Elfenbein & Ambady, 2003b). Without measuring the physical signaling properties related to emotion (i.e., in the case of facial expression of emotion, the facial muscles innervated in the expression), one cannot be sure that judgment differences reflected differences in judgments or were due to differences in the stimuli being judged.

Elfenbein and Ambady (2002a) agreed that balanced designs "provide the strongest evidence for the ingroup advantage in emotion" (p. 244) and actually employed a balanced design in two subsequent studies (Elfenbein et al., 2002; Elfenbein & Ambady, 2003b). They disagreed, however, with the importance of stimulus equivalence across cultures, stating that stimuli "should be representative and created inside that cultural context, using posers who are members of and reside in that culture, preferably with experimenters who are members of that culture." And, "Emotion itself should be elicited from participants, rather than specific expressions determined or hand-picked by the experimenter. Expressions should be as natural as possible, and not imitations of preselected theoretical models" (pp. 243–244).

They further stated that stimulus equivalence "forcibly erased" the "possibility that natural emotional expression may not be exactly equivalent across cultures" (p. 244) and that "the forcible erasing of cultural differences as a methodological requirement prevents the possibility of learning about these differences" (p. 244). In this framework, *non*equivalence in expressions is vital because these differences are precisely what Elfenbein and colleagues suggested produce the ingroup effect. Thus, it is understandable that they defended the use of stimuli that were not equivalent in their physical signaling properties. Therefore, an alternative view of the study conducted by Ricci-Bitti and colleagues (Ricci-Bitti et al., 1989) described previously is that it shows the existence of the ingroup effect *precisely because* of the use of culture-specific expressions, corresponding to Elfenbein and Ambady's (2003a, 2003b) notion of emotion dialects.

Establishing Stimulus Equivalence with Culturally Different Expressions

I disagree. Elfenbein and Ambady (2002a) mistakenly interpreted my position as suggesting that culture-specific expressions generated by culture-specific display rules cannot be studied. On the contrary, I strongly feel that studies involving culture-specific expressions can and should be conducted. However, I feel equally strongly that they need to be conducted within the methodological guidelines as described previously: that the stimuli and study need to be balanced for ethnicity and gender and the stimuli need to be equivalent in the physical signaling characteristics of emotion.

How can this be done? To study culture-specific displays expressed by people of different cultures, researchers need to ensure that, in a two-group comparison, culture-specific expressions from Culture A are also represented in expressions by members of Culture B and vice versa and that observers of both cultures judge all expressions. Even though an expression may be specific to a culture, it is entirely possible that it exists in other cultures but to different degrees or may not be labeled as such. It may be necessary to get members of Culture B to pose those expressions that occur spontaneously in Culture A; this is acceptable as long as the physical signaling characteristics of the expressions are equivalent. This would be true regardless of whether one studies spontaneous, naturally occurring expressions; imitated; posed; partial; or any other type of expression; the key is for the expressions to be equivalent in their physical-signaling properties related to emotion and to be expressed by members of all observer cultures. Studies involving an expression from Culture A without the same expression from Culture B and an expression from Culture B without the same expression from Culture A cannot address questions about the ingroup advantage because the judgments are inherently confounded by expression type.

Consider, for instance, a hypothetical study in which members of Cultures A and B judge culture-specific, nonequivalent expressions of both A and B, and the data show that A is relatively more accurate when judging expressions of A, and B is relatively more accurate when judging expressions of B (which is the way many of the studies to date have been conducted). Although this finding has been interpreted as evidence for an ingroup advantage, it is impossible to know whether the effect occurs because people judge other people of their same culture better or they judge those particular expressions more accurately. Whereas some may conclude that cultural meaning and expression cannot be separated in this fashion, I suggest that it is an empirical question that should be addressed by data. For example, the study would also need to include local expressions of A expressed by B and local expressions of B expressed by A. In this fully balanced and equivalent design, it is possible that judges of Culture A are more accurate than judges of Culture B when judging local expressions of A expressed by B. If this were the case, then the first set of findings that suggests the existence of an ingroup advantage really are not occurring because people judge other *people of their same culture* more accurately but rather because they judge certain *expressions* more accurately – and that they will do so *regardless of the people expressing them*, thus not reflecting a cultural ingroup advantage per se. Such a finding would also empirically test the assumption that culture and expressions are inseparable. (To be sure, if people of Culture B do not actually do the culture-specific expressions of Culture A, the ecological validity of this experiment would be questionable. Data on expression usage would be needed to address this issue.)

To clarify the implication of this problem, let us suppose that we conducted a study like that of Ricci-Bitti and colleagues (1989) described earlier that included not only the previous expressions but also expressions of Southern Italians' contempt (i.e., AU 10 sometimes with AU 9) portrayed by Northern Italians, and expressions of Northern Italians' contempt (i.e., AUs 10 + 14) by Southern Italians. If Southern Italians judged expressions of AU 10 sometimes with AU 9 portrayed by Northern

Italians as well as Southern Italians, then the decoding differences are not representative of an ingroup advantage per se but rather of an advantage in judging those expressions *regardless of who displays it*. Although expression usage data may indeed show that Southern Italians actually portray this expression more than others, such a finding would lead to a somewhat different conclusion about the nature of judge culture differences, indicating that the ingroup effect does not occur because of a match between encoder and decoder cultures but because of a match between decoders and expressions with which they are more familiar.

Although this notion may not be far removed from Elfenbein and colleagues' notion of emotion dialects, I believe this distinction is a crucial one for social psychology to make because it has implications for our understanding of interpersonal processes and the development of intercultural sensitivity. If we believe that the ingroup-advantage effect occurs because of matches between people's visible cultural characteristics, this implies that there is something inherently different about people from different cultures solely because of the visible facial cues associated with their ethnicity or race (which is exactly the assumption made in all the studies to date). If, however, we believe that the ingroup-advantage effect occurs because of our familiarity with expressions – not necessarily people of other cultures per se – this understanding implies that we are different not because of our visible facial cues due to race or ethnicity but rather because of differences in learned social practices. This is an important distinction to make vis-à-vis our understanding of social interactions.

Thus, as I stated earlier (Matsumoto, 2002), the requirement of stimulus equivalence is *not* mutually exclusive to the desirability of spontaneous and/or culture-specific expressions. Stimulus equivalence can and should be established for such stimuli, and the creation of such stimuli is not a problem and, in fact, is desirable. It would still be methodologically necessary to establish that stimuli generated in this fashion *in multiple cultures* were equivalent in their physical signaling properties. Without stimulus equivalence judge culture differences are unavoidably confounded by stimulus differences.

Possible Sources of the Ingroup Effect and Additional Methodological Requirements

I believe that Elfenbein and Ambady's (2002a) suggestion that nonequivalent expressions are the only type that should be used to test the ingroup-advantage hypothesis is also limited because it ignores the possibility that the ingroup effect may occur for reasons *other* than cultural differences in expression. The ingroup-advantage hypothesis itself – *that members of a cultural group are more accurate in recognizing the emotions of members of their own culture than of other, relatively more disparate groups* – might occur because of culture-specific expressions and because they are decoded more accurately by people of the same culture. However, the effect can also exist for other reasons, including other encoder effects as well as those inside the decoder. The use of nonequivalent stimuli, however, renders it impossible to separate encoder from decoder effects in the design because judge culture differences in judgments are inherently confounded by expression differences across encoder cultures (which may also represent a methodological artifact). In considering the most appropriate methodological requirements to test the ingroup effect, therefore, it is important to identify the potential sources of the effect and to incorporate them into studies examining it, if one wants to make claims about why the effect exists. In this section, I discuss the two main theoretical sources of the effect: encoder and decoder effects.

Encoder Effects

Elfenbein and colleagues suggested that the ingroup effect exists because of cultural differences in emotional expression (which they called "emotion dialects") and that people are more accurate when judging such expressions because those expressions are differentially used in their culture (Elfenbein & Ambady, 2003a, 2003b; Elfenbein et al., 2002). Thus, for instance, raising an eyebrow could be a sign of skepticism in a culture. If people of that culture judged expressions of encoders raising an eyebrow, they are likely to respond that the expression was one of skepticism. A judge from another culture, however, may not respond with skepticism because the expression may not be used or may have a different meaning in that culture.

A major limitation to Elfenbein and colleagues' previous studies, however, is the fact that Elfenbein and colleagues never measured the emotional expressions portrayed in the stimuli used in their judgment studies, nor have they used such culturally different expressions. They simply used stimuli that were available, found evidence for differential judgments of them, and interpreted those differential judgments to occur because of *presumed* expression differences in the encoders.

But, because expressions were never measured in any study, there is, in fact, no direct linkage of expression differences in the stimuli with the decoding differences in the judges. Thus, interpretations concerning ingroup effects occurring because of "subtle expression differences" are strictly unwarranted by the data and speculative (albeit interesting) until a study directly links them.

For example, in all studies they have reported until now, the American stimuli have included Ekman and Friesen's Pictures of Facial Affect (PFA) (Ekman & Friesen, 1976). The stimuli of other encoder cultures used in their studies (i.e., India, Japan, and China) were created by posing (Elfenbein & Ambady, 2003a, 2003b; Elfenbein et al., 2002). To provide some degree of equivalence among the stimulus sets, independent samples of observers in all cultures judged the expressions of the same culture in all studies; recognition rates were high in all cases, with considerable variability. Elfenbein and colleagues never measured the actual expressions used in the stimuli, nor did they link those expressive differences with actual expression differences that occur in the cultures of the encoders. Without having done so, it is methodologically impossible to suggest that the ingroup effect they observed was due to expression differences. The use of independent judgment data in this case has little meaning because similarities or differences in agreement levels on these stimuli can occur for a variety of reasons, of which expressive difference is but one factor.

Moreover, expressive differences are only one of the ways in which encoders may be a source of the effect. Expressions are produced by innervation of the facial muscles, but the messages associated with the signaling properties of the face are not limited to the morphological changes associated with muscle innervation (Ekman, 1979). For example, there are wide individual (and, it is supposed, ethnic and cultural) differences in facial physiognomies – that is, the physical features of the face – and these may contribute differentially to emotion-related signals independent of the expressions themselves. Individuals with protruding eyebrows, for instance, may be perceived as staring more, and individuals with double eyelids may produce more *sclera* – i.e., the whites above the eyes – than individuals with single eyelids for the same degree of innervation. In fact, one study did indeed find differences in judgments of fear and anger between Americans and Japanese as a function of the degree of white above the eyes shown in these emotions (Matsumoto, 1989b). Rounder faces with larger eyes give baby-face features, whereas longer faces with thinner eyes may portray a harsher message. All of these physical features associated with the face may contribute to emotion messages, although to date there have been no systematic studies of their effects.

In addition to the physiognomy, there are other signals from the face that may affect emotion judgment, including hair style and length, type and length of facial hair, and facial pigmentation, all of which may have been operating in the studies to date. Other cues in everyday life additionally compound the picture, such as cosmetics, eyeglasses, jewelry, and the like (although these were not a factor in the stimulus sets used in research to date). All of these nonexpressive facial cues contribute to the messages perceived in the face, and these most likely accounted for Marsh et al.'s (2003) finding that individuals can judge which expressors in Matsumoto and Ekman's Japanese and Caucasian Facial Expressions of Emotion (JACFEE) were Japanese nationals and which were Japanese Americans. Although these researchers attributed their findings to subtle expression differences, it is likely that those differences occurred because of differences in nonexpressive features of the faces.

In their most recent study, Elfenbein and colleagues created hemifacial composites of Indian, Japanese, and American expressions and asked observers in those countries to judge them (Elfenbein et al., 2004). They interpreted the finding that left hemifacial composites were more recognizable to ingroup members as providing some support for the notion that the ingroup effect was linked to subtle differences in the expressions. But, in the design and discussion of the study, they failed to recognize there is a major difference between neural innervation of the right and left sides of the face based on voluntary versus involuntary/spontaneous expressions. The left side is innervated more strongly than the right when expressions are produced voluntarily; when expressions are produced spontaneously, they are symmetrical (Ekman et al., 1981; Hager & Ekman, 1985; Matsumoto & Lee, 1993; Rinn, 1984). Thus, another way to interpret Elfenbein and colleagues' most recent finding on hemifacial composites is that the ingroup effect demonstrated using those stimuli (and supposedly others like it) may be limited to voluntary expressions posed for the purposes of stimulus creation. Whether the ingroup effect exists for spontaneously occurring expressions is left as an open question (and these expressions presumably are related to cultural differences in expression or emotion dialects); more important, the degree to which other possible sources of encoder contributions is unknown.

Decoder Effects

Although the interpretations of the ingroup effect to date have focused on possible encoder sources contributing to the effect (and focusing only on possible expressive differences while ignoring other potential encoder effects), it is also possible that decoder sources contribute to the effect. For instance, judges may be more motivated to recognize the emotions of members of their own culture, or their judgments may be affected by stereotype-based biases (see Chapter 2 by Hess et al., this volume). Alternatively, observers may be more anxious when judging emotions expressed by people with facial physiognomies or morphologies with which they are not familiar, despite similarities in the expressions themselves, and this anxiety may interfere with judgments. People may experience more anxiety when judging the expressions of others from a different culture because of the uncertainty concerning the expressions or the context of judgment. Uncertainty is, in fact, a major component of intercultural interactions, and research has demonstrated that people in such interactions engage in a number of strategies to reduce it (Gudykunst & Nishida, 1984; Gudykunst et al., 1986; Gudykunst et al., 1985). A recent study (Mullins & Duke, 2004), however, indicated that social anxiety, although correlated with increased response times in judging expressions, was *not* correlated with accuracy rates, arguing against this possible explanation.

Other decoder factors may contribute to the ingroup effect and, unfortunately, these effects cannot be ruled out in Elfenbein and Ambady's studies to date because those studies employed stimuli that were not equivalent in their physical-signaling properties related to emotion (see discussions by Elfenbein and Ambady [2002a] and Matsumoto [2002]). With regard to facial expressions, equivalence in the physical-signaling properties related to emotion would require that the same facial muscles be innervated at the same intensity levels across encoder cultures. In Ekman and Friesen's (1978) FACS terminology, stimulus equivalence would require the same AUs innervated at the same intensity levels. Although the stimulus sets used in their studies of Indian, Japanese, and Chinese expressions (Elfenbein & Ambady, 2003b; Elfenbein et al., 2002; Elfenbein et al., 2004) were produced using the same procedures as Ekman and Friesen's PFA (Ekman & Friesen, 1976), there were no data reported by Elfenbein and colleagues nor by the creators of those stimulus sets (Mandal et al., 1996; Wang & Markham, 1999) to suggest that the actual expressions themselves, via FACS coding or any other facial measurement system, were the same (or different, for that matter) across encoder cultures in the stimulus sets.

Two More Methodological Requirements

Based on this discussion, let me add two more methodological features that are necessary to test the ingroup-advantage hypothesis if, as Elfenbein and colleagues believe, it occurs because of cultural differences in expression. First, studies need to document those expressive differences (i.e., emotion dialects) in the cultures being tested, preferably through actual measurement of expressive behavior when emotions are spontaneously aroused. Then, stimuli need to be created that match those culturally different expressions, and the same expressions need to be portrayed in all encoder cultures. If the ingroup effect occurs with these stimuli and then only on the stimuli expressed by encoders of the same culture as the judges, then and only then can one safely conclude that the ingroup effect occurs because of cultural differences in expressivity.

Second, because nonmorphological aspects of faces, such as facial physiognomy and cosmetics, may contribute to emotion signaling, these need to be controlled across encoder cultures. If expressions used as stimuli are different across encoder cultures and the encoders differ in nonmorphological aspects of their faces, then judgment differences across encoder cultures are inherently confounded by the nonexpressive aspects of the face. Only studies eliminating this possibility and isolating the effect to expression differences would allow for an interpretation like the one made by Elfenbein and colleagues.

None of the studies reported in support of the ingroup effect meets these criteria. As described previously, all of Elfenbein and colleagues' own research involves expressions created by directed facial action tasks. Although it is true that the experimenters who created the stimulus sets in India, Japan, and China used in their studies were of the same encoder culture, in no instance did they elicit emotions from the participants in a natural way, as suggested by Elfenbein and Ambady's previous comments. Thus, not only do the stimuli not allow for an interpretation of the observed ingroup effect to occur because of cultural differences in expression, they also are not congruent with Elfenbein and colleagues' own notions of how stimuli should be created. And nowhere has there been any mention of the possible contribution of nonmorphological features of the faces to emotion judgments.

Re-Reviewing the Previous Literature

To further examine the import of these criteria in understanding the available literature regarding the ingroup hypothesis, I reexamined the sixteen balanced studies cited in Elfenbein and Ambady's (2002b) Table 4 that were the basis for their test of the ingroup effect. Although Elfenbein and Ambady meta-analyzed the statistical findings of these studies, they did not evaluate them with regard to whether the stimuli were equivalent across expressor ethnicities in their physical signaling characteristics. I evaluated them with regard to whether the stimuli were posed or spontaneously expressed, the method of emotion elicitation, the criteria the original authors used to select the expressions, and evidence that the physical signaling properties of the expressions were equivalent across ethnicities. In conducting this examination, I dropped the two studies that were unpublished dissertations (Buchman, 1973; Kretsch, 1969), but added three studies that were published since the original meta-analysis (Elfenbein & Ambady, 2003a, 2003b, Studies 1 and 2), and one previously omitted study (Mandal et al., 1996). Analyses revealed that for ten of the eighteen studies (Table 7.2), significant interactions supported the ingroup-advantage hypothesis, whereas eight did not. But, more important, five studies actually provided some evidence (i.e., filtered speech or FACS coding) that the physical signaling properties of the expressions used as stimuli were mostly equivalent in their physical signaling properties across the expressor ethnicities (Albas, McCluskey, & Albas, 1976; Kilbride & Yarczower, 1983; McCluskey, Albas, Niemi, Cuevas, & Ferrer, 1975; McCluskey & Albas, 1981; Mehta, Ward, & Strongman, 1992). Four of these were associated with nonsignificant interactions. Two studied facial expressions (Kilbride & Yarczower, 1983; Mehta et al., 1992) and both provided FACS coding for the expressions. Both are pertinent because the FACS codes were equivalent across the expressors. Yet, the relevant interactions were not significant.

With regard to the methodological requirement of naturally occurring expressions, of the seventeen studies, only one involved spontaneous emotional expressions (Machida, 1986). (Another study – Nowicki, Glanville, & Demertzis, 1998 – did involve spontaneous expressions, but they were mixed with the posed expressions so that it was not clear to what the data referred.) This study did not reveal a significant interaction either; but, at the same time, it did not provide evidence that the expressions judged were equivalent in their physical signaling

Table 7.2. *Summary of Balanced Studies Listed in Elfenbein and Ambady's (2002b) Table 4, and Recent Studies that Test the Ingroup-Advantage Hypothesis*

Study	Groups	Interaction F-Test	Channel	Posed or Spontaneous	Method of Emotion Elicitation	Criteria for Selection of Expressions	Evidence That Physical Signaling Properties of the Expressions Equivalent across Expressor Ethnicities?
Significant Interaction Fs							
(Albas et al., 1976)	Anglo-Canadian and Canadian Cree	$F(1,76) = 71.65$, $p < 0.00001$	Speech	Posed	Adults were asked to simulate the emotional states of happiness, sadness, love, and anger in any two sentences that came to mind.	None; all speech utterances were used.	Yes; speech was content filtered.
(Bond, Omar, Mahmoud, & Bonser, 1990)	Jordan, USA	$F(1,188) = 34.92$, $p < 0.00001$	Face and Body	Posed	Expressors participated in an experiment concerning deception and were asked to describe a person they liked, disliked, liked as if disliked, and disliked as if liked, and to conceal or convey their lies. No verification of any emotion in the stimuli was presented.	None	No

(continued)

Table 7.2 (continued)

Study	Groups	Interaction F-Test	Channel	Posed or Spontaneous	Method of Emotion Elicitation	Criteria for Selection of Expressions	Evidence That Physical Signaling Properties of the Expressions Equivalent across Expressor Ethnicities?
(Nowicki et al., 1998) Study 3a	African American, European American	$F(1,125) = 5.98$, $p = 0.016$	Face	Posed and spontaneous	Individuals engaged in a discussion of events that made them happy, sad, angry, or fearful. Then they were read vignettes that involved themes of these emotions and were asked to create facial expressions consistent with those themes.	Recognition rates greater than 80% by a separate group of judges.	No
(Nowicki et al., 1998) Study 3b	African American, European American	$F(1,98) = 6.03$, $p = 0.016$	Face		Same as immediately above		
(Ricci-Bitti et al., 1989)	Northern Italy, Southern Italy	$F(1,156) = 7.85$, $p = 0.006$	Face	Posed	Encoders role-played situations designed to elicit contempt, and were allowed to try out the expression repeatedly.	Expressions were chosen by judges belonging to the same cultural group as the encoders.	No; expressions were FACS coded but the FACS codes were different for the different expressions.

(continued)

Citation	Cultures	Statistics	Modality	Type	Method	Validation	Bias
(Shimoda et al., 1978)	England, Italy, Japan	omnibus $F_{(4,483)} = 21.17$, $p < 0.00001$; Contrast $F_{(1,483)} = 81.07$, $p < 0.00001$	Face	Posed	Posers were asked to act out each of 12 expressions (surprised, sad, depressed, friendly, submissive, angry, fear, happy, anxious, disgust, superior, hostile both in English and in their native language.	Performers and "coaches" reviewed videotapes of the performances and agreed on their selection.	No
(Mandal et al., 1996)	Canadians, Indians	$F_{(5,420)} = 6.47$, $p < 0.001$	Face	Posed	For Canadians, PFA: Directed facial action. In India, posers were instructed to imagine an emotional situation and to pose an appropriate expression for each emotion.	Recognition rates greater than 70% in separate judgment data.	No
(Elfenbein et al., 2002)	Non-Asian Americans, Japanese, and Indians	$F_{(4,380)} = 11.70$, $p < 0.01$ conventional $F_{(4, 380)} = 10.60$, $p < 0.01$, unbiased	Face	Posed	PFA: Directed facial action. In India and Japan, posers were instructed to imagine an emotional situation and to pose an appropriate expression for each emotion.	Recognition rates greater than 70% in separate judgment data.	No

Table 7.2 (continued)

Study	Groups	Interaction F-Test	Channel	Posed or Spontaneous	Method of Emotion Elicitation	Criteria for Selection of Expressions	Evidence That Physical Signaling Properties of the Expressions Equivalent across Expressor Ethnicities?
(Elfenbein & Ambady, 2003b) Study 1	Non–Asian Americans, Chinese Americans, Chinese living in the US, and Chinese living in China	F(3,190) = 4.67, p < 0.004	Face	Posed	PFA: Directed facial action. Wang and Markham: Expressors imagined an experience that elicited anger, disgust, fear, happiness, sadness, and surprise. Photos were selected by four graduate students as the best representatives, then judged by at least 70% of two separate groups of raters.	Matched recognition rates of separate judgment data.	No
(Elfenbein & Ambady, 2003b) Study 2	Tibetans living in China and Africans living in the USA	F(1, 19) = 3.37, p = 0.08, r = 0.39 (unbiased hit rate) F(1, 19) = 4.40, p < 0.05, r = 0.43	Face		Same as immediately above		

Nonsignificant Interaction Fs

Study	Groups	Nonsignificant Interaction Fs	View	Posed/Spontaneous	Description	Notes	FACS coded
(Gitter, Black, & Mostofsky, 1972b)	African American, European American	$F(1,144) = 0.11$, $p = 0.739$	3/4 Full Figure	Posed	Actors were filmed while enacting anger, happiness, surprise, fear, disgust, pain, and sadness while saying "What are you, what are you doing?"	Three graduate students selected a point in each film that was "most typical of the particular emotion."	No
(Gitter, Black, & Mostofsky, 1972a)	African American, European American	$F(1,40) = 1.18$, $p = -0.285$	Same as immediately above, but only angry, happy, surprised, and pain expressions were used.				
(Gitter, Mostofsky, & Quincy, 1971)	African American, European American	$F(1,72) = 0.15$, $p = -0.703$	Same as (Gitter et al., 1972a)				
(Kilbride & Yarczower, 1983)	USA, Zambia	$F(1,202) = 0.83$, $p = 0.364$	Face	Posed	Students were photographed while they imitated happiness, anger, fear, and sadness depicted in photos from Izard (1971) either with or without an experimenter present.	There were no differences in the number of AUs between American and Zambian faces relative to the Izard faces.	Yes. All expressions were FACS coded.
(Machida, 1986)	European American, Mexican American	$F(1,28) = 0.18$, $p = 0.671$	Face and Body	Spontaneous	European- and Mexican-American children were videotaped while they were given a lesson on animal habitats.	None; a two-minute version of each child's tape was used.	No

(continued)

Table 7.2 (continued)

Study	Groups	Interaction F-Test	Channel	Posed or Spontaneous	Method of Emotion Elicitation	Criteria for Selection of Expressions	Evidence That Physical Signaling Properties of the Expressions Equivalent across Expressor Ethnicities?
(McCluskey & Albas, 1981)	Canada, Mexico	$F(1,196) = 0.03$, $p = 0.868$	Speech	Posed	Adults were asked to simulate the emotional states of happiness, sadness, love, and anger in any two sentences that came to mind.	Separate raters judged that the speakers communicated the emotion intended.	Yes; speech was content filtered.
(McCluskey et al., 1975)	Canada, Mexico	$F(1,276) = 0.48$, $p = -0.490$	Speech	Posed	Adults were asked to simulate the emotional states of happiness, sadness, love, and anger in any two sentences that came to mind.	Separate raters judged that the speakers communicated the emotion intended.	Yes; speech was content filtered.
(Mehta et al., 1992)	European New Zealanders, New Zealand Maori	$F(1,50) = 0.57$, $p = 0.454$	Face	Posed	Maori and Pakeha individuals were asked to pose anger, contempt, disgust, fear, happiness, sadness, surprise, and neutral.	Two: Expressors had to match their expression with the correct emotions, and a 66% match of FACS AUs between the two expressor groups.	Yes. All expressions were FACS coded.

162

properties. Thus, of the seventeen studies, none involved spontaneous expressions by individuals of two different cultures that were equivalent in their physical signaling properties.

There is one lone exception, however, that was omitted from Elfenbein and Ambady's (2002b) meta-analysis. Ekman's classic report with Japanese and American participants included two studies that involved the judgment of spontaneous expressions across the two cultures (Ekman, 1972). In the expression condition of their experiment, American and Japanese students viewed neutral and stressful stimuli. Their spontaneous expressions of disgust, anger, fear, sadness, and happiness were comparable to each other (the correlation between the coded facial behaviors of Americans and Japanese = 0.88); however, they were not perfectly matched (77.44 percent overlap; 22.56 percent nonoverlap), thereby providing some evidence of culture-specific responding. One-minute clips of the participants' spontaneous behaviors from both the neutral and stress film conditions were shown to different samples of both American and Japanese observers, who judged which film the participants were watching. Simple effects comparisons of observer and expressor culture that corresponded exactly to the target interactions predicted by the ingroup-advantage hypothesis were all nonsignificant. Also, correlations between the Japanese and American observer responses separately for each expressor were high for both expressor cultures in both studies (ranging from 0.77 to 0.86), arguing against the ingroup-advantage hypothesis. These are the only studies to date that involve spontaneous emotional expressions by two different cultures and judged by both cultures and did not support the ingroup-advantage hypothesis.

Summary

This review makes clear that although the ingroup-advantage hypothesis is interesting, provocative, and certainly worthy of further exploration, the evidence presented to date does not support it. The studies conducted by Elfenbein and her colleagues do not meet the requirements of stimulus equivalence or spontaneously elicited emotion, and the meta-analyses and literature reviews conducted to date have not reviewed the studies in terms of whether they utilized stimuli that were equivalent in their physical signaling properties. Moreover, none of the studies have controlled for the possible influence of nonmorphological aspects of the faces on judgments. Although Elfenbein and

Ambady (2003a) concluded that "the effect replicates across a range of experimental methods and nonverbal channels of communication" (p. 95), I suggest that no definitive conclusions about it can be made based on that evidence.

Studies Testing the Ingroup-Advantage Hypothesis Using the Japanese and Caucasian Facial Expressions of Emotion (JACFEE)

In addition to the studies described previously, cross-cultural research from our laboratory involving judgments of Matsumoto and Ekman's JACFEE (Matsumoto & Ekman, 1988) by American, Japanese, and Asian American observers (Biehl et al., 1997; Matsumoto, 1992, 1993) also speak to the ingroup-advantage hypothesis. The JACFEE consists of fifty-six expressions – that is, eight examples of seven emotions – portrayed by different individuals: half by Caucasians, the other half by Japanese (half male, half female). All faces were reliably coded using the FACS (Ekman & Friesen, 1978) to ensure that the muscles innervated in the expressions corresponded to the universal, prototypical signals of emotion (as depicted by Ekman & Friesen, 1975). Within emotion, the expressions include exactly the same facial muscles innervated at exactly the same intensity levels according to FACS coding, not a group of observers. Thus, balanced studies involving the JACFEE provide a valid test of the ingroup-advantage hypothesis.

Elfenbein and Ambady (2002a) questioned the use of the JACFEE on two grounds. First, they argued that because some of the posers were Japanese Americans and others were Japanese nationals living in the United States, the Japanese expressions of the JACFEE were not really Japanese; instead, they labeled these expressors as "Americans" (Elfenbein & Ambady, 2002a, p. 245) and suggested that this characteristic limited the ability of the JACFEE to test the ingroup-advantage hypothesis. Second, Elfenbein and Ambady argued that the JACFEE expressions used "imitation facial musculature patterns" because "posers of Japanese ethnicity were essentially asked to pose American faces – expressions that met American norms regarding emotional expression" (Elfenbein & Ambady, 2002a, pp. 245–246) and that the faces did not portray Japanese expressions. Elfenbein and Ambady concluded that the previous JACFEE studies essentially included "American faces and imitations of expressions empirically derived from American faces" (p. 246) and, for that reason, one would expect no ingroup-advantage effects.

Because Elfenbein and Ambady (2002a) made these claims about the JACFEE, it is important to discuss the validity base of the JACFEE to portray emotion prior to presenting findings from the studies using it relevant to the ingroup-advantage hypothesis.

The Validity of the JACFEE

Elfenbein and Ambady's (2002a) characterization of the expressions portrayed in the JACFEE is incorrect. Multiple studies examining spontaneous facial behaviors in various types of emotion-eliciting situations have amply demonstrated that the facial-muscle configurations in the JACFEE expressions represent emotional expressions that actually occur spontaneously in real life situations (Berenbaum & Oltmanns, 1992; Bonanno & Keltner, 2004; Camras et al., 1992; Chesney et al., 1990; Ekman et al., 1990; Ekman et al., 1980; Ekman et al., 1988; Ekman et al., 1997; Ellgring, 1986; Frank et al., 1993; Gosselin et al., 1995; Heller & Haynal, 1994; Keltner et al., 1995; Rosenberg & Ekman, 1994; Ruch, 1993, 1995). All of these studies reported facial muscle configurations arising from spontaneously elicited emotion corresponding to those in the JACFEE. It is important that the studies involved not only American participants but also participants from other countries.

Data from Ekman's (1972) study of the spontaneous facial behaviors of Americans and Japanese viewing stress films also indicated clearly that the expressions of the JACFEE correspond to spontaneously occurring emotional expressions produced by Japanese individuals. In that study, participants in both cultures viewed a neutral and highly stressful film (comprised of four separate clips). Unbeknownst to them, their facial behaviors were recorded throughout the entire experiment. Ekman coded the last three minutes of facial behavior videotaped during the neutral films and the entire three minutes of the last stress film clip using the Facial Affect Scoring Technique (FAST), a precursor to and ultimately a subset of FACS. FAST coding identified facial-muscle configurations associated with six emotions: anger, disgust, fear, happiness, sadness, and surprise. All corresponded to the facial expressions portrayed in the stimuli used in their judgment studies (Ekman, 1972; Ekman, Friesen, & Ellsworth, 1972; Ekman et al., 1969) in the descriptions of the universal emotions in their book, *Unmasking the Face* (Ekman & Friesen, 1975); in their stimulus set, *Pictures of Facial Affect* (Ekman & Friesen, 1976); and in the JACFEE (see Ekman, 1972, Chart 1, pp. 251–252). These configurations identified by FAST also corresponded to those currently in use in Ekman and Friesen's Emotion FACS (EMFACS) coding system (Gottman, 1993; Matsumoto, Ekman, & Fridlund, 1991). Two sets of analyses were performed on the FAST codes, one involving separate facial areas and one involving the whole face, combining codes from all facial areas; data on the second analysis are especially pertinent to the JACFEE. Analysis of the frequency of the types of emotions portrayed in the whole face indicated that disgust, sadness, anger, and surprise were the most frequently displayed emotions, but fear and happiness were also displayed (see Table 2, Ekman, 1972, p. 256). The correlation between the Americans and the Japanese on the frequencies of these whole face emotions expressed spontaneously was 0.88, indicating a high degree of consistency in the spontaneous production of whole face expression configurations by both Americans and Japanese corresponding to those portrayed in the JACFEE.

Furthermore, the spontaneous emotional displays of Japanese and American infants were more recently examined in a study by Camras and her colleagues (Camras, Oster, Campos, Miyake, & Bradshaw, 1992), who videotaped babies' reactions to an experimental procedure known as arm restraint. In this procedure, experimenters hold a baby's hands folded across the stomach until the baby shows distress or for a maximum of three minutes. Videotapes of the babies' facial reactions were coded using a modified version of FACS. FACS coding indicated facial muscle configurations corresponding to the JACFEE configurations of anger, sadness, fear, and happiness. Examination of differences in these expressions produced a nonsignificant culture effect, indicating that there were no differences in the spontaneous expressions of Japanese and American infants. A progress report by the same team of researchers on a new project involving American, Japanese, and Chinese eleven-month-old infants also produced the same nonsignificant culture effects on facial displays (Campos et al., 2004).

A final source of data supporting the contention that the expressions portrayed in the JACFEE are not of "American norms" is the wealth of judgment data involving not only Japanese observers but also observers from many cultures of the world, including preliterate cultures that reliably judge the expressions portrayed in the JACFEE (and of Ekman and Friesen's PFA) as the emotions intended (Biehl et al., 1997; Ekman & Friesen, 1971; Ekman et al., 1969; Ekman, 1972; Ekman, Friesen, O'Sullivan, Chan, et al., 1987; Elfenbein & Ambady, 2002b; Izard, 1971; Matsumoto, 2001). Many of these studies were conducted independently by multiple scientists (see a review of twenty-seven studies compiled in Matsumoto, 2001). If the expressions were imitations of American norms, it would be highly unlikely that such data would be obtained so consistently.

Elfenbein and Ambady's (2002a) claim is also somewhat mitigated by their own subsequent work in which they demonstrated that Americans could reliably guess that the expressors who were Japanese nationals were indeed born and raised in Japan (Marsh, Elfenbein, & Ambady, 2003). If participants can make such deductions, then the claim that the JACFEE's Japanese expressions are of Americans is questionable. Moreover, the more valid question is whether Japanese observers would reasonably assume that the Japanese expressions are portrayed by Japanese and that the Caucasian expressions are not. We believe that this assumption is reasonable. Furthermore, in one of the studies we conducted (described herein), American and Japanese observers were instructed that the Caucasian expressors are U.S.–born and raised as Americans and the Japanese expressors are Japan–born and raised Japanese, and there was still no evidence of the ingroup-advantage effect.

Based on the evidence available, therefore, I conclude that the JACFEE portrays expressions that are spontaneously produced not only by Americans and Japanese but also panculturally.

Why Use the JACFEE If the Ingroup Advantage Occurs Because of Culture-Specific Expressions?

Elfenbein and colleagues used the term "emotion dialects" to label cultural variations in emotional displays or expressive styles and to explain why the ingroup advantage exists (Elfenbein & Ambady, 2002a, 2003a, 2003b). (The degree to which this concept is different than Ekman's notion of display rules is not clear.) They propose that members of a culture can better recognize the emotions of others in the same culture because the cultural variations are more recognizable to them. If this is the case, then one question that arises is whether the JACFEE can be used to test the ingroup-advantage hypothesis at all because the expressions in the JACFEE are clearly *not* expressions of such culturally prescribed emotion dialects.

I suggest that the JACFEE should be used to test the ingroup-advantage hypothesis (along with other types of stimuli, of course). Elfenbein and Ambady included multiple studies involving universal prototypical facial emotions like those in the JACFEE (Ekman & Friesen, 1971; Ekman et al., 1987; Ekman et al., 1969; Haidt & Keltner, 1999; Izard, 1971) in their original meta-analysis in which they reported evidence in support of an ingroup effect (Elfenbein & Ambady, 2002b). Some, in fact, included the JACFEE (Biehl et al., 1997; Matsumoto & Assar, 1992; Matsumoto & Ekman, 1988). Additionally, two of their latest studies involved Ekman and Friesen's PFA, which portray the same expressions as in the JACFEE, and expressions produced in other cultures based on the PFA (Elfenbein, Mandal, Ambady, & Harizuka, 2002; Elfenbein & Ambady, 2003b). The inclusion of these studies gives the impression that the ingroup advantage existed *despite* the lack of differences in the expressions used to test recognition – that is, that there might have been something inherent in the visual cues related to culture or ethnicity that made it easier for people of a culture to recognize the expressions of members of their own culture. Elfenbein and colleagues call these "non-verbal accents" (Marsh et al., 2003).

Moreover, studies involving the JACFEE allow us to isolate possible sources of the effect if found. That is, because the stimuli portrayed in the JACFEE are exactly equivalent, if the ingroup effect is found with such stimuli, it would indicate that the effect exists *despite* the fact that the expressions were the same; thus, the effect would have to exist because of decoder effects. If the effect did not occur, however, we would be fairly confident in ruling out decoder effects in contributing to it.

For these reasons, studies of the ingroup-advantage hypothesis using universal prototypical facial emotions are just as important as studies involving culturally varied expressions. We contend that the expressions portrayed in the JACFEE reflect prototypical, full face expressions of emotions that occur panculturally; that the facial muscle configurations portrayed in the JACFEE correspond to emotional expressions that spontaneously occur with people of different cultures, including Japanese; and that they constitute a valid set of stimuli with which to test the ingroup-advantage hypothesis. Neither the Japanese nor the Caucasian expressions in the JACFEE represent Japanese or American norms in expression; they were never designed to represent such norms, nor has it ever been claimed to do so. We do not agree with the suggestion that it cannot test the ingroup-advantage hypothesis because it does not represent such norms; rather, it tests the ingroup-advantage hypothesis with expressions that occur across cultures (but, clearly, they cannot be used to test the emotion dialect hypothesis of Elfenbein and others). Studies using the JACFEE were included in Elfenbein and Ambady's original meta-analysis, so it met their criteria for inclusion to examine the effect as well. Our reliance on the JACFEE in previous studies is not to imply that other types of expressions are not worthy of study. Certainly, there are other expressions that need to be studied, including culture-specific ones, provided those studies meet the methodological requirements of balanced designs and stimulus equivalence.

Research Testing the Ingroup-Advantage Hypothesis Using the JACFEE

Of the studies reported until now that showed the JACFEE to American and Japanese judges, none found any support for the ingroup-advantage hypothesis (Matsumoto, 2002). When cultural differences were reported, they showed that Americans judge the expressions more accurately than the Japanese regardless of the ethnicity of the expressor (Matsumoto, 1992), supporting the notion of cultural decoding rules introduced earlier. A study comparing judgments of Asian versus European Americans also found no evidence for the hypothesis (Matsumoto, 1993).

Different Versions of the Ingroup-Advantage Hypothesis

In Elfenbein and Ambady's (2002b) meta-analysis, the cultural congruence between observer and expressor was operationalized by the congruence of the origins of the expressors and perceivers. But, in all studies when observers judged stimuli, they had no information whatsoever about the cultural background of the expressors other than whatever physical characteristics they could see or hear. If cultural congruence influenced judgments, it must have done so through the similarity or discrepancy of the physical characteristics of the expressors portrayed to the observers in an *implicit* comparison because this was the only source of information about the expressor given to the observers.

If this is so, then different forms of the ingroup-advantage hypothesis can be derived (although we suggest herein that this may not be the most fruitful way to conceptualize the hypothesis). Elfenbein and Ambady's (2002b) original meta-analysis and their subsequent studies (Elfenbein & Ambady, 2003a; Elfenbein et al., 2002) focused on the ethnic/racial/cultural congruence between expressor and perceiver, stating that people were more accurate in judging emotions of others who were of the same cultural group than of those who were from different cultural groups. We call this the *cultural* ingroup-advantage hypothesis.

If there are differences in emotional expression between men and women, and if gender can be construed as a product of culture, then another version of the ingroup-advantage hypothesis would suggest that men more accurately perceive the emotions of other men and women more accurately those of other women. In fact, there are ample studies documenting expression and judgment differences between men and women (Hall, 1978, 1984). There are also a number of works suggesting that gender is a cultural product and that gender differences are a type of cultural difference (Bem, 1981). Elfenbein and Ambady themselves stated that "depending on the definition of culture one uses, gender might also be appropriate to include as a cultural group" (Elfenbein & Ambady, 2002b, p. 207). If this is the case, a logical extension of the ingroup-advantage hypothesis is that it occurs for gender as well. We call this the *gender* ingroup-advantage hypothesis.

In actuality, the question of possible gender ingroup advantage in decoding accuracy was addressed well in the previous literature. Hall's (1978) meta-analysis published more than twenty-five years ago, for instance, examined that question both between and within studies and reported no evidence for it; no study since has reported such evidence either. But, because it is unclear as to whether the physical-signal characteristics associated with the stimuli used in previous studies testing the effect were equivalent across gender, our recent studies using the JACFEE have tested for this version of the ingroup-advantage hypothesis as well.

Recent Research

Recently, we conducted three studies using the JACFEE to test the cultural and gender ingroup-advantage hypothesis (Matsumoto & Choi, 2004). In Study 1, we aggregated judgment data from seven previous studies in which both American and Japanese judges saw the JACFEE at different intensity levels and judged the emotions they saw in the stimuli. This allowed us to test the culture and gender ingroup-advantage hypotheses for both high- and low-intensity expressions. The total sample included 1,020 U.S.–born and raised Americans and 382 Japan–born and raised Japanese. The stimuli included the fifty-six full-face expressions of the JACFEE; in some studies, judges saw low-intensity versions of sixteen of the JACFEE expressions produced by computer morphing techniques. In all studies participants were asked to judge the emotion in the face using a fixed choice judgment task involving either emotion labels or stories. We recoded the categorical judgment data into hit/miss scores, averaged across examples of each expressor type, and computed full factorial Analyses of Variance (ANOVAs). (Because these data are averaged across expressions, they are not binary; in actuality, they are counts of the number of accurate recognitions within the various subject factors. For the target interaction being tested, the score ranges from 0 to 56.) The culture and gender ingroup-advantage hypotheses were tested by examining judge culture by expressor ethnicity and judge gender by expressor gender interactions, respectively. The ingroup-advantage hypothesis would predict that these interactions are significant and in a specific direction. Both interactions, however, were not significant, indicating no support for either version of the ingroup-advantage hypothesis.

In Study 2, we tried to optimize the degree to which observers thought that the Caucasian expressors of the JACFEE were Americans while the Asian expressors were Japanese. In this study, we blocked the Caucasian expressions into one set and the Japanese expressions into another to maximize the differences between them and explicitly told American and Japanese observers that the Caucasians were U.S.–born and raised as Americans and that the Japanese were Japan–born and raised as Japanese. We also included a control group of American observers who did not receive the nationality instructions. The judgment task was the same fixed-choice task as used in Study 1. The findings produced non-significant interactions for the culture and gender ingroup-advantage hypotheses, once again indicating no support for them.

In Study 3, we aggregated data from two previous studies (Matsumoto, LeRoux, Bernhard, & Gray, 2004; Matsumoto et al., 2000) involving American judges that utilized the Japanese and Caucasian Brief Affect Recognition Test (JACBART), which is a high-speed presentation of the JACFEE expressions that produces reliable individual differences in emotion recognition accuracy (Matsumoto et al., 2000) to test the gender ingroup-advantage hypothesis. The JACBART randomly presents each of the fifty-six JACFEE expressions for 1/5 s embedded within a 1s neutral presentation of the same expressor's neutral expression. There is a 3s inter-stimulus interval and an orienting tone 1s prior to each presentation. Accuracy rates on the JACBART are much lower than for either high- or low-intensity expressions presented at long exposures such as those used in Studies 1 and 2. The JACBART also provides good item discrimination and reliable individual differences (Matsumoto et al., 2000). Because the only difference between the JACFEE and JACBART is the speed of presentation, not the nature of the expressions themselves, they allow for a direct comparison of results that can isolate the cause of judgment differences, if any. The judgment task was the same fixed choice task used in Studies 1 and 2. The analyses produced a nonsignificant interaction between judge gender and expressor gender, once again indicating no support for this version of the hypothesis.

In all studies, we also examined the judge culture and gender main effects. These effects are orthogonal to the interactions, and previous research consistently reported moderate judge culture effects (Biehl et al., 1997; Matsumoto, 1992; Matsumoto et al., 2002; Matsumoto, Kasri, & Kooken, 1999) and weak-moderate judge sex effects (Hall, 1978; Hall & Matsumoto, 2004). In the past, the interactions reflecting the ingroup-advantage hypothesis were used to argue against overall judge culture decoding effects (see Elfenbein et al., 2002). But, given that they represent two orthogonal effects, the presence of one does not speak to the presence or absence of the other. Certainly, an ingroup-advantage effect theoretically may coexist simultaneously with overall judge culture decoding effects. In Study 1, the judge culture main effect was significant for both high- and low-intensity expressions, indicating that Americans were more accurate at recognizing the emotions than were the Japanese. The same results were obtained in Study 2. These findings lent further support for the notion of cultural decoding rules affecting judgments. Likewise, judge sex main effects were significant in most analyses, replicating the well-established finding that women are more accurate in recognizing emotions than men.

Thus, across all studies, neither the culture nor the gender ingroup-advantage hypothesis was supported regardless of whether observers judged full-face, high- or low-intensity expressions (Study 1); even when observers were explicitly told that Caucasian expressors were U.S.–born and raised as Americans and that the Asian expressors were Japan–born and raised as Japanese (Study 2); and when the stimuli were presented at high speeds to reduce ceiling effects and produce individual differences (Study 3). We believe that these studies are the most appropriate to test both versions of the hypothesis because of the balanced design and the equivalence in the physical-signaling properties of the stimuli across ethnicities and genders, and because the expressions are valid analogs of expressions that occur in real life. Furthermore, I reviewed the findings of the three studies reported previously with regard to whether they differed according to whether the Asian expressors were Japanese or Japanese American; they did not. The same argument cannot be made about the male and female expressors, and the gender version of the ingroup-advantage hypothesis was not supported either. Finally, a recent study conducted by another laboratory using stimuli that were equivalent in their physical-signaling properties comparing judgments and expressions of various Canadian ethnic groups found no evidence of the ingroup effect either (Beaupré & Hess, 2005).

Conclusion

The absence of the ingroup effect using the JACFEE – that is, when the stimuli were equivalent in their physical signaling properties related to emotion – rules out the possibility that superficial differences in physical appearance across encoder cultures comprise the basis for the ingroup advantage observed in other studies. As mentioned earlier, the ingroup advantage that was observed previously may have occurred because of factors associated with either the encoder or the decoder. The non-findings strongly suggest that the ingroup advantage, therefore, may be occurring because of encoder effects.

Although on the surface this interpretation would appear to provide support for Elfenbein and colleagues' position that the ingroup effect occurs because of cultural differences in emotional expressions, as I discussed earlier, a number of nonexpressive (i.e., nonmorphological) characteristics of the encoders may also have produced previous effects. These characteristics include facial physiognomy, facial hair and hairstyles, and the like. These factors may contribute to emotion signals above and beyond or even instead of expression, and future studies will need to systematically tease out these factors to isolate the cause of the ingroup effect.

One way to examine whether the ingroup effect exists because of cultural differences in emotional expression, as Elfenbein and colleagues contend, and not because of nonmorphological characteristics of the encoders used in the studies would be to test for the effect using culturally different expressions while keeping constant the nonmorphological characteristics of the faces being judged. That is, individual and ethnic differences in facial physiognomies, hair style and length, facial hair, skin pigmentation, and other variables will need to be kept constant while varying only the differences in the expressions. If the ingroup advantage exists under such circumstances, it would be safe to conclude that it exists because of cultural differences in expression. In the absence of such data, however, it is difficult to reach that conclusion and to rule out the possibility that the effect is due to methodological artifacts. Measurement systems to assess nonmorphological aspects of faces that may contribute to emotion signaling – that is, craniofacial anthropometry – exist in other disciplines (e.g., dentistry, facial surgery, and physical anthropology), and I encourage researchers interested in isolating such effects to develop them.

To some degree, however, some facial characteristics, such as skin pigmentation, may be inherently associated with differences in ethnicity and thus inseparable from encoder expressions. In these cases, future studies can examine their effects by systematically controlling for the effects of different nonmorphological characteristics to determine which, if any, contribute to emotion signaling and thus to the ingroup effect.

Elfenbein and colleagues' study (2003b) involving Chinese, Chinese American, and non–Asian American judgments of American and Chinese faces is relevant to this point. In that study, the accuracy advantage for American over Chinese emotional expressions was largest for non–Asian Americans, next largest for Chinese Americans, followed by Chinese living in the United States, and smallest for Chinese in China. They interpreted that the ingroup effect was preserved even when judges were of the same ethnicity (Chinese in China versus Chinese Americans) and that this finding was likely due to different expressions to communicate emotions. However, this interpretation of the data ignores the fact that across the three Chinese groups, the expressions were held constant; thus, differences in relative accuracy across them could not possibly be attributed to differences in expressions because the expressions being judged were all the same. Instead, those differences must have been linked to other nonexpressive aspects of the judgment task or stimuli, such as familiarity with judging Caucasians or with such judgment tasks in general.

In future tests of the ingroup-advantage hypothesis, it will be necessary to isolate differences in expressions across encoder cultures while holding constant nonmorphological features of the face that may contribute to emotion signaling. In conducting such tests, I reaffirm that the expressions must be equivalent in their physical-signaling properties across encoder cultures to isolate that the effect occurs because of encoder, not decoder, influences. Furthermore, the ingroup-advantage hypothesis as stated by Elfenbein and Ambady, which is based on the match between a judge-culture group and the physical characteristics of expressors supposedly from their own culture and how I have tested it myself in the past, is probably not the most fruitful way to examine possible ingroup-advantage effects. Ingroups are defined not so much by the physical similarities between people based on their ethnic, racial, or gender compositions as by social psychological characteristics (Tajfel, 1982). Ingroup members share familiarity, intimacy, trust, and commitment to future relationships. There is no such sharing between a participant in our research studies or in any of those that Elfenbein and Ambady used in their meta-analyses or conducted studies. A better examination of any possible ingroup effects would be studies that manipulated these social-psychological parameters between judge and expressor all the while ensuring that stimuli and study are balanced and that the stimuli are equivalent. Such studies will be difficult to conduct properly but I encourage the conduct of them.

Although I have found no support for either the culture or gender ingroup-advantage hypothesis in any of the studies I conducted or in my re-review of the literature, other researchers and I consistently found judge culture differences regardless of expressor ethnicity. These differences suggest the existence of cultural decoding rules that affect judgments. In fact, Elfenbein and colleagues' most recent studies also found evidence for judge-culture main effects among Americans, Indians, and Japanese (Elfenbein et al., 2002) and between Chinese and non–Asian Americans (Elfenbein & Ambady, 2003b), which supports this notion.

If judge culture effects in judging emotions exist, it is easy to see how they can contribute to the *appearance* of possible ingroup effects in unbalanced studies. In a two-culture comparison in which judges of Cultures A and B view expressions only of Culture A, and in which a judge-culture effect exists such that members of Culture A have higher recognition-accuracy rates, judges of Culture B will have lower recognition rates when judging expressions of Culture A that are suggestive of the existence of possible ingroup effects. We believe that this is what most of the studies reviewed by Elfenbein and Ambady obtained (Elfenbein & Ambady, 2002b). In this light, it is significant that there was no support for the ingroup-advantage hypothesis in our study described previously for low-intensity expressions, even though both Americans and Japanese were more accurate in judging Japanese expressions.

The ingroup-advantage effect, if it exists, need not be mutually exclusive of overall judge-culture decoding effects. As Elfenbein and colleagues themselves demonstrated (Elfenbein et al., 2002; Elfenbein & Ambady, 2003b), both effects may exist within the same data set. It makes sense that both effects are possible empirically and theoretically. Using an ANOVA analogy, judge-culture overall effects are represented in judge-culture main effects, whereas the ingroup effect is represented by the interaction of judge-culture and expressor ethnicity. In ANOVA, these effects are orthogonal to each other. Theoretically, it may be possible that cultures exert influences on the overall decoding process of emotions but make it possible for emotions to be differentially recognized according to the familiarity with whom one judges. The existence of one need not argue for the nonexistence of the other.

In summary, I welcome the ingroup-advantage hypothesis and its related distance theory; they are worthy hypotheses to be pursued in future research. I also believe that these hypotheses may be true under certain circumstances. At the same time, however, I strongly believe that the available evidence, when carefully scrutinized, does not support the hypotheses. To date, there has been no study that has employed a balanced design involving stimuli portrayed by people of different cultures that were equivalent in their physical-signaling properties related to emotion. Moreover, no study to date has involved stimuli that have been empirically related to culturally different expressions or dialects, nor has any study attempted to control for the possible contribution of nonmorphological features of the faces to emotion judgments. Thus, whereas the hypothesis is truly a worthy one to pursue, the evidence brought to bear on it to date simply does not support its existence at this time. Researchers interested in promoting such claims should give consideration to those methodological requirements to test for it.

References

Albas, D. C., McCluskey, K. W., & Albas, C. A. (1976). Perception of the emotional content of speech: A comparison of two Canadian groups. *Journal of Cross-Cultural Psychology, 7*, 481–490.

Beaupré, M., & Hess, U. (2005). Cross-cultural emotion recognition among Canadian ethnic groups. *Journal of Cross-Cultural Psychology, 36*, 355–370.

Bem, S. L. (1981). The BSRI and gender schema theory: A reply to Spence and Helmreich. *Psychological Review, 88*, 369–371.

Berenbaum, H., & Oltmanns, T. (1992). Emotional experience and expression in schizophrenia and depression. *Journal of Abnormal Psychology, 101*, 37–44.

Biehl, M., Matsumoto, D., Ekman, P., Hearn, V., Heider, K., Kudoh, T., & Ton, V. (1997). Matsumoto and Ekman's Japanese and Caucasian Facial Expressions of Emotion (JACFEE): Reliability data and cross-national differences. *Journal of Nonverbal Behavior, 21*, 3–21.

Bonanno, G. A., & Keltner, D. (2004). The coherence of emotion systems: Comparing "on-line" measures of appraisal and facial expressions, and self-report. *Cognition and Emotion, 18*, 431–444.

Bond, C., Omar, A., Mahmoud, A., Bonser, R. N. (1990). Lie detection across cultures. *Journal of Nonverbal Behavior, 14*, 189–204.

Boucher, J. D., & Carlson, G. E. (1980). Recognition of facial expression in three cultures. *Journal of Cross-Cultural Psychology, 11*, 263–280.

Buchman, J. S. (1973). Nonverbal communication of emotions among New York City cultural groups. *Dissertation Abstracts International, 34*, 406–407.

Buck, R. W. (1984). *The communication of emotion.* New York: Guilford Press.

Campos, J., Oster, H., Camras, L. A., Miyake, K., Ujiiee, T., Meng, Z. L., et al. (2004). *Emotional expression in American, Japanese, and Chinese infants.* Paper presented at the 2004 Annual Convention of the American Psychological Association, Honolulu, HI.

Camras, L. A., Oster, H., Campos, J., Miyake, K., & Bradshaw, D. (1992). Japanese and American infants' responses to arm restraint. *Developmental Psychology, 28*, 578–583.

Chesney, M. A., Ekman, P., Friesen, W. V., Black, G. W., & Hecker, M. H. L. (1990). Type A behavior pattern: Facial behavior and speech components. *Psychosomatic Medicine, 52*, 307–319.

Ekman, P. (1972). Universal and cultural differences in facial expression of emotion. In J. R. Cole (Ed.), *Nebraska Symposium on Motivation, 1971* (pp. 207–283). Lincoln, NE: University of Nebraska Press.

Ekman, P. (1979). Facial signs: Facts, fantasies, and possibilities. In T. Sebeok (Ed.), *Sight, sound, and sense* (pp. 124–156). Bloomington, IN: Indiana University Press.

Ekman, P., Davidson, R. J., & Friesen, W. V. (1990). The Duchenne smile: Emotional expression and brain physiology: II. *Journal of Personality & Social Psychology, 58*, 342–353.

Ekman, P., & Friesen, W. (1969). The repertoire of nonverbal behavior: Categories, origins, usage, and coding. *Semiotica, 1*, 49–98.

Ekman, P., & Friesen, W. (1971). Constants across culture in the face and emotion. *Journal of Personality and Social Psychology, 17*, 124–129.

Ekman, P., & Friesen, W. V. (1975). *Unmasking the face; a guide to recognizing emotions from facial clues.* Englewood Cliffs, NJ: Prentice-Hall.

Ekman, P., & Friesen, W. V. (1976). *Pictures of facial affect.* Palo Alto, CA: Consulting Psychologists Press.

Ekman, P., & Friesen, W. V. (1978). *Facial action coding system: Investigator's guide.* Palo Alto, CA: Consulting Psychologists Press.

Ekman, P., Friesen, W., & Ancoli, S. (1980). Facial signs of emotional experience. *Journal of Personality and Social Psychology, 39*, 1125–1134.

Ekman, P., Friesen, W. V., & Ellsworth, P. (1972). *Emotion in the human face: Guide-lines for research and an integration of findings.* New York: Pergamon Press.

Ekman, P., Friesen, W. V., & O'Sullivan, M. (1988). Smiles when lying. *Journal of Personality & Social Psychology, 54*, 414–420.

Ekman, P., Friesen, W. V., O'Sullivan, M., Chan, A., Diacoyanni-Tarlatzis, I., Heider, K., et al. (1987). Universals and cultural differences in the judgments of facial expressions of emotion. *Journal of Personality & Social Psychology, 53*, 712–717.

Ekman, P., Hager, J., & Friesen, W. (1981). The symmetry of emotional and deliberate facial actions. *Psychophysiology, 18*, 101–106.

Ekman, P., Matsumoto, D., & Friesen, W. (1997). Facial expression in affective disorders. In P. Ekman & E. L. Rosenberg (Eds.), *What the face reveals: Basic and applied studies of spontaneous expression using the Facial Action Coding System (FACS)* (pp. 331–341). New York: Oxford University Press.

Ekman, P., Sorenson, E. R., & Friesen, W. V. (1969). Pancultural elements in facial displays of emotion. *Science, 164,* 86–88.

Elfenbein, H. A., & Ambady, N. (2002a). Is there an ingroup advantage in emotion recognition? *Psychological Bulletin, 128,* 243–249.

Elfenbein, H. A., & Ambady, N. (2002b). On the universality and cultural specificity of emotion recognition: A meta-analysis. *Psychological Bulletin, 128,* 205–235.

Elfenbein, H. A., & Ambady, N. (2003a). Cultural similarity's consequences: A distance perspective on cross-cultural differences in emotion recognition. *Journal of Cross-Cultural Psychology, 34,* 92–110.

Elfenbein, H. A., & Ambady, N. (2003b). When familiarity breeds accuracy: Cultural exposure and facial emotion recognition. *Journal of Personality and Social Psychology, 85,* 276–290.

Elfenbein, H. A., Mandal, M. K., Ambady, N., & Harizuka, S. (2002). Cross-cultural patterns in emotion recognition: Highlighting design and analytic techniques. *Emotion, 2,* 75–84.

Elfenbein, H. A., Mandal, M. K., Ambady, N., Harizuka, S., & Kumar, S. (2004). Hemifacial differences in the ingroup advantage in emotion recognition. *Cognition & Emotion, 18,* 613–629.

Ellgring, H. (1986). Nonverbal expression of psychological states in psychiatric patients. *European Archives of Psychiatry and Neurological Sciences, 236,* 31–34.

Frank, M. G., Ekman, P., & Friesen, W. V. (1993). Behavioral markers and recognizability of the smile of enjoyment. *Journal of Personality & Social Psychology, 64,* 83–93.

Gitter, A. G., Black, H., & Mostofsky, D. (1971a). Race and sex in the communication of emotion. *Journal of Social Psychology, 88,* 273–276.

Gitter, A. G., Black, H., Mostofsky, D. (1971b). Race and sex in the perception of emotion. *Journal of Social Issues, 28,* 63–78.

Gitter, A G., Mostofsky, D. I., & Quincy, A. J. (1971). Race and sex differences in the child's perception of emotion. *Child Development, 42,* 2071–2075.

Gosselin, P., Kirouac, G., & Dore, F. (1995). Components and recognition of facial expression in the communication of emotion by actors. *Journal of Personality and Social Psychology, 68,* 83–96.

Gottman, J. M. (1993). Studying emotion in social interaction. In M. Lewis & J. M. Haviland (Eds.), *Handbook of emotions* (pp. 475–487). New York: Guilford Press.

Gudykunst, W. B., & Nishida, T. (1984). Individual and cultural influences on uncertainty reduction. *Communication Monographs, 51,* 23–36.

Gudykunst, W. B., Nishida, T., & Chua, E. (1986). Uncertainty reduction in Japanese–North American dyads. *Communication Research Reports, 3,* 39–46.

Gudykunst, W. B., Yang, S.-M., & Nishida, T. (1985). A cross-cultural test of uncertainty reduction theory: Comparisons of acquaintances, friends, and dating relationships in Japan, Korea, and the United States. *Human Communication Research, 11*, 407–455.

Hager, J. C., & Ekman, P. (1985). The asymmetry of facial actions is inconsistent with models of hemispheric specialization. *Psychophysiology, 22*, 307–318.

Haidt, J., & Keltner, D. (1999). Culture and facial expression: Open-ended methods find more expressions and a gradient of recognition. *Cognition & Emotion, 13*, 225–266.

Hall, J. A. (1978). Gender effects in decoding nonverbal cues. *Psychological Bulletin, 85*, 845–857.

Hall, J. A. (1984). *Nonverbal sex differences: Accuracy of communication and expressive style*. Baltimore: Johns Hopkins University Press.

Hall, J. A., & Matsumoto, D. (2004). Sex differences in judgments of multiple emotions from facial expressions. *Emotion, 4*, 201–206.

Heller, M., & Haynal, V. (1994). Depression and suicide faces. *Cahiers Psychiatriques Genevois, 16*, 107–117.

Hofstede, G. H. (1980). *Culture's consequences: International differences in work-related values*. Beverly Hills: Sage Publications.

Hofstede, G. H. (1984). *Culture's consequences: International differences in work-related values* (Abridged ed.). Beverly Hills: Sage Publications.

Izard, C. E. (1971). *The face of emotion*. East Norwalk, CT: Appleton-Century-Crofts.

Keltner, D., Moffitt, T., & Stouthamer-Loeber, M. (1995). Facial expressions of emotion and psychopathology in adolescent boys. *Journal of Abnormal Psychology, 104*, 644–652.

Keppel, G. (1991). *Design and analysis: A researcher's handbook* (3rd ed.). Englewood Cliffs, NJ: Prentice Hall.

Kilbride, J. E., & Yarczower, M. (1980). Recognition and imitation of facial expressions: A cross-cultural comparison between Zambia and the United States. *Journal of Cross-Cultural Psychology, 11*, 281–296.

Kretsch, R. A. (1969). Communication of emotional meaning across national groups. *Dissertation Abstracts International, 29*, 3914.

Machida, S. K. (1986). Teacher accuracy in decoding nonverbal indicants of comprehension and noncomprehension in Anglo- and Mexican-American children. *Journal of Educational Psychology, 78*, 454–464.

Mandal, M. K., Bryden, M. P., & Bulman-Fleming, M. B. (1996). Similarities and variations in facial expressions of emotion: Cross-cultural evidence. *International Journal of Psychology, 31*, 49–58.

Markham, R., & Wang, L. (1996). Recognition of emotion by Chinese and Australian children. *Journal of Cross-Cultural Psychology, 27*, 616–643.

Marsh, A. A., Elfenbein, H. A., & Ambady, N. (2003). Nonverbal "accents": Cultural differences in facial expressions of emotion. *Psychological Science, 14*, 373–378.

Matsumoto, D. (1993). Ethnic differences in affect intensity, emotion judgments, display rule attitudes, and self-reported emotional expression in an American sample. *Motivation & Emotion, 17*, 107–123.

Matsumoto, D. (1989a). Cultural influences on the perception of emotion. *Journal of Cross-Cultural Psychology, 20*, 92–105.

Matsumoto, D. (1989b). Face, culture, and judgments of anger and fear: Do the eyes have it? *Journal of Nonverbal Behavior, 13*, 171–188.

Matsumoto, D. (1992). American–Japanese cultural differences in the recognition of universal facial expressions. *Journal of Cross-Cultural Psychology, 23*, 72–84.

Matsumoto, D. (1993). Ethnic differences in affect intensity, emotion judgments, display rule attitudes, and self-reported emotional expression in an American sample. *Motivation & Emotion, 17*, 107–123.

Matsumoto, D. (2001). Culture and emotion. In D. Matsumoto (Ed.), *The handbook of culture and psychology* (pp. 171–194). New York: Oxford University Press.

Matsumoto, D. (2002). Methodological requirements to test a possible ingroup advantage in judging emotions across cultures: Comments on Elfenbein and Ambady and evidence. *Psychological Bulletin, 128*, 236–242.

Matsumoto, D., & Assar, M. (1992). The effects of language on judgments of universal facial expressions of emotion. *Journal of Nonverbal Behavior, 16*, 85–99.

Matsumoto, D., & Choi, J. W. (2004). *Exploring decoder sources of the ingroup advantage effect in recognizing facial expressions of emotions.* Unpublished manuscript.

Matsumoto, D., Choi, J. W., Hirayama, S., Domae, A., & Yamaguchi, S. (2003). Culture, display rules, emotion regulation, and emotion judgments. *Manuscript currently submitted for publication.*

Matsumoto, D., Consolacion, T., Yamada, H., Suzuki, R., Franklin, B., Paul, S., Ray, R., & Uchida, H. (2002). American–Japanese cultural differences in judgments of emotional expressions of different intensities. *Cognition & Emotion, 16*, 721–747.

Matsumoto, D., & Ekman, P. (1988). American–Japanese cultural differences in intensity ratings of facial expressions of emotion. *Motivation & Emotion, 13*, 143–157.

Matsumoto, D., Ekman, P., & Fridlund, A. (1991). Analyzing nonverbal behavior. In P. W. Dowrick (Ed.), *Practical guide to using video in the behavioral sciences* (pp. 153–165). New York: John Wiley & Sons.

Matsumoto, D., Kasri, F., & Kooken, K. (1999). American–Japanese cultural differences in judgments of expression intensity and subjective experience. *Cognition & Emotion, 13*, 201–218.

Matsumoto, D., & Lee, M. (1993). Consciousness, volition, and the neuropsychology of facial expressions of emotion. *Consciousness & Cognition: An International Journal, 2*, 237–254.

Matsumoto, D., LeRoux, J. A., Bernhard, R., & Gray, H. (2004). Personality and behavioral correlates of intercultural adjustment potential. *International Journal of Intercultural Relations, 28*, 281–309.

Matsumoto, D., LeRoux, J. A., Wilson-Cohn, C., Raroque, J., Kooken, K., Ekman, P., Yrizavvy, N., Loewinjer, S., Uchida, H., Yee, A., Amo, L., & Goh, A. (2000). A new test to measure emotion recognition ability: Matsumoto and Ekman's Japanese and Caucasian Brief Affect Recognition Test (JACBART). *Journal of Nonverbal Behavior, 24*, 179–209.

McCluskey, K., Albas, D., Niemi, R., Cuevas, C., & Ferrer, C. (1975). Cultural differences in the perception of the emotional content of speech: A study of the development of sensitivity in Canadian and Mexican children. *Developmental Psychology, 11*, 551–555.

Mehta, S. D., Ward, C., & Strongman, K. (1992). Cross-cultural recognition of posed facial expressions of emotion. *New Zealand Journal of Psychology, 21*, 74–77.

Mullins, D. T., & Duke, M. P. (2004). Effects of social anxiety on nonverbal accuracy and response time, I: Facial expressions. *Journal of Nonverbal Behavior, 28*, 3–33.

Nowicki, S., Jr., Glanville, D., & Demertzis, A. (1998). A test of the ability to recognize emotion in the facial expression of African American adults. *Journal of Black Psychology, 24*, 333–348.

Ricci-Bitti, P. E., Brighetti, G., Garotti, P. L., & Boggi-Cavallo, P. (1989). Is contempt expressed by pancultural facial movements? In J. P. Forgas & J. M. Innes (Eds.), *Recent advances in social psychology: An international perspective* (pp. 329–339). Amsterdam, NL: Elsevier.

Rinn, W. E. (1984). The neuropsychology of facial expression: A review of the neurological and psychological mechanisms for producing facial expressions. *Psychological Bulletin, 95*, 52–77.

Rosenberg, E. L., & Ekman, P. (1994). Coherence between expressive and experiential systems in emotion. *Cognition & Emotion, 8*, 201–229.

Rosenthal, R., & Rosnow, R. L. (1985). *Contrast analysis: Focused comparisons in the analysis of variance.* Cambridge and New York: Cambridge University Press.

Rosenthal, R., & Rosnow, R. L. (1991). *Essentials of behavioral research: Methods and data analysis* (2nd ed.). New York: McGraw-Hill.

Ruch, W. (1993). Extraversion, alcohol, and enjoyment. *Personality & Individual Differences, 16*, 89–102.

Ruch, W. (1995). Will the real relationship between facial expression and affective experience stand up: The case of exhilaration. *Cognition & Emotion, 9*, 33–58.

Shimoda, K., Argyle, M., & Ricci Bitti, P. (1978). The intercultural recognition of emotional expressions by three national racial groups: English, Italian and Japanese. *European Journal of Social Psychology, 8*, 169–179.

Tajfel, H. (1982). Social psychology of intergroup relations. *Annual Review of Psychology, 33*, 1–39.

Wang, L., & Markham, R. (1999). The development of a series of photographs of Chinese facial expressions of emotion. *Journal of Cross-Cultural Psychology, 30*, 397–410.

8. Others' Faces' Tales

An Integration

Ursula Hess and Pierre Philippot

Authors' Note

The writing of this chapter was facilitated by grants from the "Fonds National de la Recherche Scientifique de Belgique" 8.4510.99 and 8.4510.03, and by a grant ARC 96/01-198 from the University of Louvain to the second author and by a grant from the "Fond Québecois de la Recherche sur la société et la culture" to the first author. Correspondence regarding this chapter should be addressed to Ursula Hess at Hess.Ursula@UQAM.ca.

The aim of this book was to present recent thinking and research on the *interaction* between encoding and decoding processes from a social context perspective. In this context, we wanted to emphasize the influence that norms and beliefs, as well as the social characteristics of both the encoder and the decoder, have on the perception of emotion. That the interpretation of emotion displays should be informed by the social context is an important corollary of not only social-constructivist approaches which place emotions entirely in the service of social coordination but also by evolutionist approaches. Thus, Turner (1997) asserts that emotions evolved in part to provide the means for effective sanctioning and the enforcement of moral codes within groups of hominids. His basic argument is that the communication of emotions in humans was a necessary prerequisite for social bonding among hominids. In a similar vein, Preuschoft and Van Hooff (1997) presented evidence that the degree to which situational determinants of the primate silent bared-teeth display (i.e., the presumed precursor of the human smile) and the relaxed open-mouth display (i.e., the presumed precursor of human laughter) overlap can be traced to the social relationships within primate groups – specifically, to the level of hierarchical structure within the group. These notions have in common that "emotion norms" in groups of early hominids depended on the specific structure of the group – that is, differed between groups.

As mentioned in the preface, the literature on the decoding of emotional expression focuses mainly on the ability of the decoder. One aspect that is taken for granted in this research is that the decoders are motivated to exert themselves to the extent of their ability and that they use the encoders' expressive behavior as the *only* source of information for decoding rather than to rely on (real or stereotype) knowledge about the situation or the social group of which the interaction partner is a member (Kirouac & Hess, 1999).

In fact, there are two means of decoding an emotion expression: first, the sender's facial, vocal, postural, etc. expressions can be used to draw inferences regarding the presumed emotional state of the sender using a pattern-matching approach (e.g., Buck, 1984). Thus, the presence of upturned corners of the mouth and wrinkles around the eyes can be interpreted as signaling happiness. The second source of information is the knowledge that the receiver possesses regarding both the sender and the social situation in which the interaction takes place and that permits the receiver to take the perspective of the sender, thereby helping deduce the emotional state that the sender most likely experiences in a given situation.

Social-group characteristics such as the gender or ethnic group of both the encoder and decoder can bias both processes. Thus, decoders may interpret facial-expressive movements differently depending on the facial morphology of the sender. Facial-morphological differences between men and women, as well as between members of different racial groups, may enhance or obscure expressive elements and, hence, bias pattern-matching, as was found by Hess et al. (see Chapter 2, this volume). Furthermore, Richeson et al. (see Chapter 1, this volume) show how the goals, concerns, motivations and emotions that interaction partners bring into the interaction may attract attention away from pertinent facial cues.

In turn, stereotypical expectations regarding the emotionality of members of a certain social group are susceptible to influencing perspective-taking. In case of doubt, the expected emotion may be the one that is perceived as the more likely shown. Similarly, the study by Warner and Shields (see Chapter 5, this volume) suggests that the interpretation of described emotional behavior may vary as a function of the beliefs we have about the sender's emotional style. When decoding motivation is lacking, then these influences should be stronger, but even highly motivated decoders may be influenced.

Richeson et al. present a model that outlines the different social factors that can be expected to influence decoding. These include not only stereotypes, social norms, and display rules but also familiarity with the encoder's social group, as well as intergroup relations with emphasis on the relative status of encoder and decoder. These latter factors are important specifically because of the motivational consequences they may entrain. In fact, given that many expressive episodes in everyday life are fleeting and ambiguous, a potential decoder's motivation to understand what just happened is of importance. The expressions of individuals who are close to us (Thibault, Bourgeois, & Hess, 2006) and of those who have power over us may invite more motivational investment than expressions by individuals whose emotions have less impact on ours. Richeson et al. also make the important observation that motivation to decode well is not the only motivational factor at hand. Specifically, the individuals' previous experiences, goals, concerns, and attitudes are likely to influence the ways in which they express and interpret facial displays of emotion during intergroup interactions. In short, in some situations, decoders may be motivated to see certain emotions rather than others. In an ambiguous social interaction, a person may see a sign of positive affect where another sees the lack thereof based on their own social concerns and expectancies.

Yet, in a social context, the decoder's task consists not only of labeling the expressor's emotion expression; rather, the social-signal value of the expression has to be understood. In this context, it is important to assess whether the expression reflects genuine emotion and is meant to be manipulative and to know what it says about the other person. Thus, a person who cries may be perceived either as genuinely distressed, albeit weak, or as manipulative. Similarly, emotions expressed in difficult circumstances may be perceived to be either encouraging and motivating or fake.

Warner and Shields (see Chapter 5) for the case of crying, and Tyran (see Chapter 6) for the case of positive emotion expression focus specifically on the influence that expressive gender norms have on the signal value of an expression. Specifically, as a consequence of the difference in expressive norms for men and women, the same expression may be perceived quite differently depending on the gender of the expressor.

In particular, Warner and Shields describe a form of socially endorsed emotional expressive style that they call "manly emotions" – construed as controlled expression that conveys deep and authentically felt emotion, which reflects the rationality and self-control ideals of white heterosexual masculinity. In the context of crying, a moist eye in a sad context would correspond to the ideal of manly emotion expressions, whereas copious tears would not. In a vignette study, Warner and Shields showed that when responding to a sad event, men who were described as "tearing up" were perceived more positively than were women or men who were described as crying. Also, women's tears were described as more intense, regardless of the actual vignette description. Angry tears were generally perceived negatively. Warner and Shields note that the tears are perceived as more appropriate when the person actually had no power to redress the situation (sad tears) than when tears signaled helplessness (angry tears). Thus, the ideal to appear competent and in control can be fulfilled by a moist eye but not by copious crying. Hence, restrained tears are perceived more positively. In turn, men are perceived as more competent and in emotional control; therefore, their tears are perceived as more restrained. In sum, social-role expectations bias not only the interpretation of the behavior but also the actual perception of the behavior.

In turn, Tyran (see Chapter 6) points to the very real stakes for leaders in this context. Specifically, she points out that leaders' emotional expressions are evaluated with regard to both leadership norms (i.e., authoritative versus transactional) and gender norms. Hence, men's and women's emotion expression in a leadership context may not lead to the same attributions. For example, whereas showing anger may serve to make a male leader appear more competent, the same is not the case for a female leader. Thus, it is not only important that a leader's emotions are situation-congruent, they must also be congruent with prevailing social and organizational norms to be effective in a leadership context.

In sum, the signal value of an expression may be greatly impacted by the degree to which the expression is perceived as gender norm congruent or, in a larger sense, role congruent. Thus, the same emotion may be perceived as signaling rather different states when shown by a man or a woman. Expressions that violate social roles are perceived as inappropriate, their genuineness may be doubted or they may seem impolite. In turn, a person's social role can bias the actual perception of the expression in line with the stereotypical expectations, further augmenting this effect. Thus, as a consequence, the same expression may make one person appear in a positive light, potentially entraining better future relationships or soliciting support in the present, whereas on a different face, this expression may have quite the opposite effect. This is also a conclusion drawn by Hess et al. (see Chapter 2), who focus on the impact of the morphological differences between men's and women's faces and how these difference may, in turn, interact with stereotypes or social-role expectations to bias emotion judgments.

Specifically, Hess et al. (see Chapter 2) for the case of gender and Philippot et al. (see Chapter 4) for the case of ethnic-group membership showed that the physical characteristics of the expressive stimulus may serve to activate stereotypes or to imply social roles. In this context, Hess et al. observed effects of social role expectations, which interacted with physical appearance cues, for both neutral and explicitly emotional faces. They found that the interaction between the level of dominance and affiliation communicated by facial morphology cues and the gender of the sender biased both judgments of the perceived emotionality of the sender, and judgments of the type and intensity of emotional facial expressions shown by the sender. That is, the physical characteristics of the face were found to influence both the pattern-matching process by accentuating or obscuring expressive features of anger and happiness differentially in men and women, and the perspective-taking process by activating different social-role expectations as a function of perceived dominance and affiliation. It is important that they showed that the perceived emotionality of a person is derived preferentially from appearance cues and social role information with only very little variance explained by gender per se. This line of research suggests that the emotional stereotypes that we hold about men and women are essentially derived from expectations about their behavior in terms of nurturance and dominance.

In turn, Philippot et al. (see Chapter 4) found that physiognomic markers of racial group – in a way, similar to gender markers – activate existing stereotypes regarding the emotionality of members of different racial groups. Specifically, the stereotypes that Belgians hold with regard to North Africans bias the attribution of emotions and action tendencies to individuals from these two groups based on facial stimuli. Furthermore, a corresponding bias was found for the decoding of identical facial stimuli that were labeled to represent either Flemish or Walloon Belgians. This bias was more evident and associated with faster response times for high-prejudiced compared to low-prejudiced individuals. However, different than the gender markers studied by

Hess et al., which actually interfered with emotion perception when prototypical emotions were shown, this bias was only found when the facial displays were emotionally ambiguous – specifically, when neutral rather than explicitly emotional faces were shown. That is, the racial markers did not seem to interfere with the pattern-matching process, but rather observers treat these physical characteristics as ancillary emotion information that is helpful in the decoding of ambiguous stimuli. Thus, when stimuli are unambiguous – that is, show well-recognizable emotion expressions – this latter information renders the stereotypical information superfluous because the observer can easily derive an emotion judgment from the expressive stimulus alone.

These findings suggest that a face, even in the absence of discernable facial-expressive movements, is never emotionally neutral. Observers discern emotions, emotional dispositions and behavioral intentions from neutral faces. These judgments, in turn, are biased by stereotypes and social role expectancies. Thus, perceived dominance and affiliation interact with gender to influence the perceived emotionality of the sender (Hess et al., see Chapter 2), and racial group membership influences perceptions of emotions and behavioral intentions in line with group stereotypes (Philippot et al., see Chapter 4). In fact, as Philippot et al. point out, neutral faces are particularly apt to be interpreted in line with stereotypical notions.

This has a number of important implications for social interactions between members of different groups. Specifically, inhibiting emotion expressions may have unintended consequences. Rather than avoiding the sending of an emotional message, one may actually send a stereotype-congruent message that reinforces the interaction partner's preconceived notions. In fact, the observation that husbands tend to interpret the simple absence of smiling during a marital dispute as a sign of hostility on the part of their wives, whereas wives tend to interpret the simple absence of hostility displays by their husbands in such a dispute as a sign of love (Gaelick, Bodenhausen, & Wyer, 1985) might be understood in this sense.

The complexity of the interaction between encoder and decoder group is especially central to the discussion of the ingroup-advantage hypothesis by Elfenbein (see Chapter 3) and Matsumoto (see Chapter 7). The ingroup advantage, defined as the tendency to more easily and accurately understand emotional expressions originating from members of one's own cultural group rather than expressions originating from members of a different cultural group, is a phenomenon that cannot be explained only by an encoder–decoder interaction effect but, in fact, is defined as such. Thus, with regard to the ingroup advantage, Elfenbein emphasizes "that it matters not only who is doing the judging, but also their match or mismatch with who is being judged." And, as Matsumoto points out, the ingroup advantage is rarely found when looking at raw cell means but rather describes the relative contribution of the statistical interaction.

Elfenbein presents evidence for the dialect account of the ingroup advantage – specifically, that ingroup members are better at decoding each other's expressions because there are subtle differences in the local "nonverbal dialects" of emotion expressions. Ingroup members are more familiar with these dialects, whereas outgroup members may be more easily confused. Additionally, ingroup members may be more motivated to decode each other's expressions and, hence, are more likely to attend to subtle information (Thibault, Bourgeois, & Hess, 2006).

In contrast, the decoding-rule account favored by Matsumoto (see Chapter 7) stresses the importance of social rules and norms that guide expressions and that differ between cultures. In this view, ingroup members would be better decoders because they can apply their accurate normative knowledge to the situation. However, decoding rules are more often invoked when it comes to explaining why members of certain cultures show overall reductions in decoding ability for certain emotions – regardless of who expresses them. Also, most described expressive norms, such as the one that members of collectivist cultures should avoid to both acknowledge negative emotions in others and show themselves to preserve group harmony, would lead one to predict an outgroup rather than an ingroup advantage.

Matsumoto (see Chapter 7) stresses that there are a number of particular challenges for research that emphasize encoder–decoder interactions. He outlines a number of specific concerns that become relevant in this context. Not only is it preferable for studies be balanced (i.e., members of both groups should decode expressions from both groups), but also it is important to assure that the decoder actually is presented with identical expressions from different encoder groups. Thus, Philippot et al. (see Chapter 4) used the same faces but labeled them as Flemish or Walloon. Similarly, Hess et al. (see Chapter 2) used the same faces but changed hair style, a potent marker of gender. If this is not done, then group differences are confounded with stimulus differences.

In sum, this book shows the rich interaction between encoding and decoding processes. Specifically, it becomes clear that to consider these processes in isolation may be a fallacy. Rather, encoding and decoding processes have to be seen as embedded in dyadic and intergroup processes and, therefore, fundamentally subject to social influences. Thus, the seemingly better or worse decoding skills of an observer may well be due to the prevalent motivations, emotions or goals of the observer, which impact on the deployment of attentional resources – but could just as well be due to the prevalent motivations, emotions or goals of the expressor, which impact on the ability to clearly express a given emotion in a given situation, as suggested by Richeson et al. Also, the seemingly better or worse decoding skills may well be due to stereotype influences that help or hinder the decoder in labeling the emotion, as was found by Hess et al. for expressions of anger and happiness shown by men and women. As well, the meaning of expressive behavior is not independent of who shows it. Rather, such factors as relative status and gender of the interaction partners will impact on meaning. Thus, the same tear may be seen as a sign of honest emotion in one person and a means of manipulation in another, as shown by Wagner and Shields (see Chapter 5). In short, the meaning of emotional facial expressions depends fundamentally on who shows what to whom – and in which context.

To conclude, for a long time, the study of nonverbal communication has mostly focused on the nonverbal signal itself, as well as on decoder and encoder characteristics, with little emphasis on the nature of the social forces operating in their ongoing interactions. Such an approach does not give justice to the fact that nonverbal behavior is mostly a means of social communication and regulation. Failure to recognize this aspect of the very nature of nonverbal behavior prevents the understanding of significant aspects of its meaning and determinants.

In this book, we hope we demonstrated that, in the understanding of nonverbal communication, important dividends are to be taken from the consideration of the social forces constraining the nonverbal interplay between interaction partners. On the one hand, this book presented both integrative and domain-specific models that provide sound theoretical bases for the study of group dynamics in nonverbal communication. On the other hand, these theoretical models were applied to a diversity of research domains, generating an already impressive amount of empirical data. Still, this is just the beginning of a new journey, and we are aware that much work still needs to be done. We hope that this book contributed to the building of this new scientific avenue.

References

Buck, R. (1984). *The communication of emotion*. New York: Guilford Press.

Gaelick, L., Bodenhausen, G. V., & Wyer, R. S. (1985). Emotional communication in close relationships. *Journal of Personality and Social Psychology, 49*, 1246–1265.

Kirouac, G., & Hess, U. (1999). Group membership and the decoding of nonverbal behavior. In P. Philippot, R. Feldman, & E. Coats (Eds.), *The social context of nonverbal behavior* (pp. 182–210). Cambridge, UK: Cambridge University Press.

Preuschoft, S., & van Hooff, J. A. R. A. M (1997). The social function of "smile" and "laughter": Variations across primate species and societies. In U. Segerståle & P. Molnár (Eds.), *Nonverbal communication: Where nature meets culture* (pp. 171–190). Mahwah, NJ: Lawrence Erlbaum Associates.

Thibault, P., Bourgeois, P., & Hess, U. (2006). The effect of group-identification on emotion recognition: The case of cats and basketball players. *Journal of Experimental Social Psychology, 42*, 676–683.

Turner, J. H. (1997). The evolution of emotions: The nonverbal basis of human social organisation. In U. Segerståle & P. Molnár (Eds.), *Nonverbal communication: Where nature meets culture* (pp. 211–223). Mahwah, NJ: Lawrence Erlbaum Associates.

Index